AMERICAN INDIAN ENGLISH

AMERICAN INDIAN ENGLISH

WILLIAM L. LEAP

UNIVERSITY OF UTAH PRESS   SALT LAKE CITY

LIBRARY OF CONGRESS CATALOGING-IN-PUBLICATION DATA

Leap, William.
    American Indian English / William L. Leap.
        p.   cm.
    Includes bibliographical references (p.) and index.
    ISBN 0-87480-416-7
    1. Indians of North America—Languages. 2. English language—
United States—Foreign elements—Indian. 3. Indian languages—
Influence on English. 4. Languages in contact—United States.
5. Americanisms. I. Title.
PE3102.I55L4   1993
427'.9'08997—dc20   93-26946

CONTENTS

PREFACE

I am writing this preface in April 1993—some six years after I began drafting the text of this book. Many friends and colleagues have supported my work with American Indian English throughout this period, particularly Dan McLaughlin, Forrest Cuch, Venita Taveapont, Ina Lou Chapoose, Evan Norris, Pat Locke, Gina Harvey, Dick Heiser, Bates Hoffer, Betty Lou Dubois, M. Estellie Smith, Brett Williams, Laszlo Kurti, Donna Donaldson, Judy Lewis, Ellen Berner, Steve Stout, and Signithia Fordham. Along with naming Forrest, Venita, and Ina Lou, I want to acknowledge the many individuals from the Northern Ute reservation who encouraged my studies of language and educational needs at that site and actively participated in the research process.

Jeff Grathwohl, my editor and sponsor at the University of Utah Press, provided even-handed guidance as I polished and refined the chapters. Nancy Hornberger and an unidentified reader prepared useful comments on the second draft of the text. Doug Bruce helped greatly with text clarity and with the bibliography. Kathy Lewis and Alan Hersker deserve accolades for careful copy editing and proofreading.

Angui Madera has endured this project with patience and understanding, even when my writing made unwarranted intrusion into our private life.

Finally, I dedicate this volume to the memory of George L. Trager—my major professor in graduate school, my dissertation advisor, and a strong supporter of my work with Indian English when others were more skeptical and less enthusiastic about these themes.

INTRODUCTION

This is a book about the English of American Indians —the English they use at home, on the job, in the classroom, at the grocery store, in church, and in other areas of daily experience.[1] There are many varieties of *Indian English* (my cover term for these codes in this book); in some cases, their linguistic details are quite similar to those found in the English of their non-Indian neighbors, coworkers, and classmates. More commonly, Indian English shows extensive influence from the speaker's ancestral (or "native") language tradition(s) or from other language sources and differs accordingly from non-Indian notions of "standard" grammar and "appropriate" speech. Here are some examples (Examples in the text without citation of source come from my field notes):

○ A pueblo Indian third grader runs up to the (non-Indian) teacher supervising school recess and loudly calls for the teacher to come to the swing set. A fellow student lost his balance while hanging from the cross-pole and fell to the ground. "Did he hurt his arm?" the teacher asks. *No*, the student replies, trying to urge her to move quickly and tend to the injured child, *he didn't hurt no arm*.

○ A young Miccosukee man explains to his laughing buddies why the front of his trousers was wet and sticky: *My Coke spilled and got my pants wet*.

○ A middle-aged Tewa pueblo woman, describing the activities during her visit to a feast day at a neighboring pueblo, introduces one segment of her narrative by saying, *That night when they were at we could see it*; later in the narrative, she describes young people's eagerness to learn about the pueblo's traditional foods by saying: *They ask questions how it's prepared*.

○ During coffee break at an Indian education conference, I compliment a Haida woman on the silver and turquoise necklace she is wearing. She smiles and replies: "An Apache student made this at the Art School and his teacher put it in the window on display. *I visited that necklace for eighteen months*, and then I bought it."

o A middle-aged Choctaw man, giving an address at an Indian mission in Los Angeles, explains the importance of retaining Choctaw language and culture by noting:

> A lot of us are aware of the fact that we have had a Choctaw class going in the process of teaching the Choctaw language, the culture, to keep the interest in our younger generation. . . . So I'd like to express my feelings about—I know that we have a tight schedule in life in order to keep our nose above the water today; I know we all have got our movement in our everyday pattern of living—but I hope that we might keep in our minds that somewhere along the way that we might allow ourselves not to forget our culture. (Weibel-Orlando 1991: 166; ellipsis mine)

o An older pueblo Indian man, who has been drawing pictures of life in his community for an East Coast anthropologist, begins a letter to that anthropologist as follows (I retain the writer's original spelling):

> Dear friend:
> I have recived your letter at last and recived $20.00 which you had send me. And I was very glad to hear from you, and I am enclosing another 4 drawing I hope you are sadesfied for getting real stuff that you never thought of getting it because no one knows about secret even if thirs some Indian never saw this, someday they will surprise. . . . (Goldfrank 1967: 67)

o When her teacher asked her to make up a story about the old days, a fourth grade Rosebud Sioux student turned in the following essay:

> One day there was hundred
> of Indian And they had
> a big war with the cowboy
> And they were all still alive
> And the dead cowboy and
> The Indians were happy
> and they live in hill.
> The End

I will be discussing some of the differences between Indian English and "standard" English throughout this volume, because these differences have implications for school success, employability, and other domains of Indian opportunity. I will also be discussing differences between *particular* Indian English codes. As other examples will suggest, sounds and sound sequences, word structures, sentence forms, reference contrasts, and approaches of metaphor and imagery are not the same for all Indian English codes—so much so that many American Indians claim to be able to identify people's tribal background simply by listening to their English.

The community-specific ties between Indian English and ancestral language grammar help account for these conditions. Given that there are at least 200 different Indian languages still spoken in the United States (Leap 1981c: 129), it is likely that there are at least 200 different Indian Englishes as well. Probably there are more than 200, given the contrasts in Indian English usage associated with age and generational position, gender differences, schooling, occupational and residential experiences, or other conditions associated with the social, cultural, and historical experiences of each community.

Community-level language pluralism is another factor affecting Indian English diversity. At some sites, American Indians and Alaska Natives use their ancestral language(s) as well as Indian English in daily conversation. When this happens, speakers develop criteria to help them determine which language option is more appropriate for a given topic, discourse setting, or conversation with a particular individual. In part, these criteria reflect speaker assumptions about ease of expression or other functional concerns, but questions of speaker identity and presentation of "self" are also influential in this regard.

At other sites, Indian English is the only *Indian*-related language tradition that community members have maintained or the only such tradition that older community members have been willing to transmit to the younger generation. When this is the case, Indian English fluency becomes a highly valued social skill, and the nonstandard features of the Indian English conversation have an even greater cultural significance for their speakers.

The same conditions apply in instances when Indian English is the only form of *English* that community members regularly acquire. Under these circumstances, speakers may refrain from talking English when context or topic favor a more standardized usage and reward usage accordingly, or speakers may go ahead and participate actively, in Indian English terms, in what is otherwise a standard English conversation. There may be linguistic reasons why speakers do not acquire a more standardized usage, even when exposed to it in face-to-face discussions, but questions of power, politics, and inequality are much more likely sources of barriers and resistance—there is nothing in the grammar of Indian English that prevents its speakers from becoming proficient in standard English.

In fact, some speakers of Indian English are also speakers of standard English or something that closely approximates "American standard." Again, whether they use the standard code, Indian English, or some other language variety inside or outside of home and community settings depends on political, not grammatical, factors. Among other things, this makes a good case for using Indian English fluency as a foundation for the development of standard English skills and for restoring or strengthening speaker fluency in the ancestral language of the tribe. Some schools serving American Indian and Alaska Native students have restructured their language arts curricula in these terms; see Renker and Arnold (1988), Rosier and Farella (1976), Watahomigie and Yamamoto (1987) for examples. Most schools serving American Indian and Alaska Native students have not made such changes, and the absence of revision in this area of classroom instruction contributes greatly, in my opinion, to the dismal statistics on Indian student school-leaving reviewed, for example, in Swisher and Hoisch (1992).

PURPOSE AND GOALS OF THIS BOOK

I began studying Indian English when I was in graduate school at Southern Methodist University (1967–1970), and I have published regularly on these themes throughout my professional career. When I started my work, there were very few linguists and anthropologists interested in Indian English. Some scholars (see Leechman and Hall 1955 and other citations in Dreschel 1977) had documented the existence of American Indian/European language "pidgins," but they had not tried to connect the emergence of those codes during the colonial period with the Indian English usage found in contemporary tribal settings. Other scholars had noticed the presence of nonstandard English usage in reservation communities and Indian schools (Wax et al. 1964, esp. pp. 80–82) or had begun to tabulate the "errors" and "problems" presented by such usage in school settings (Cook and Sharp 1966). But the number of these studies was quite small; in the main, as of 1970, American Indian English was an unexplored terrain.

Conditions have changed greatly since that time. Indian self-determination and tribal empowerment, the popularity of Indian bilingual education and other programs aimed at ancestral language renewal, and the entrance of American Indians into linguistics, anthropology, and education have shifted the goals of Indian language research and broadened the interests of the scholars—Indian and non-Indian—who are now at work in this field (Leap 1988). In addition to increased efforts at curriculum building, literacy development, and language planning, this refocusing of Indian language research interests has led to a range of site-specific studies of Indian English codes as well as assessments of their significance for different domains of contemporary Indian life.[2]

The information presented in studies of Indian English that have appeared in print since 1970, supplemented by unpublished findings from my work with Indian English in reservation, rural, and urban Indian settings since that time, constitutes the database for this book. I will use information from this database to answer questions such as the following:

o What *linguistic features* (sound patterns, word structures, sentence constructions, reference conventions, principles of rhetoric and metaphor, etc.) are *characteristic of American Indian English*?

o What *similarities in grammar and discourse* are shared by specific Indian English codes? What *points of difference* distinguish them from each other? To what extent do these details resemble the characteristics of grammar and discourse found in Black English vernaculars or in other varieties of nonstandard American English?

o Who are the *speakers* of American Indian English? Why have some Indian people become proficient speakers (and writers—see below) of these codes, while others actively resist any type of discourse in these terms? What criteria determine whether non-Indians will become proficient in these codes?

o *How do people learn* American Indian English? What mechanisms within Indian speech communities promote fluency? Do these mechanisms coincide with, or conflict with, mechanisms promoting fluency in ancestral languages at these sites? How can there be Indian English fluency in a tribal community if the ancestral language of that community is no longer spoken?

o What historical events led to *the emergence of Indian varieties of English*? Did the other European languages that came to be spoken in Native North America also contribute to the construction of these codes? And what about the influence of Indian language–based *trade languages* and other *linguae francae*?

o *What functions* does Indian English serve in contemporary Indian speech communities? If Indian English fluency poses no barriers to standard English skill, what factors *do* create obstacles to fluency in this regard?

o What effects does speaking Indian English have on the *school experiences of American Indian students*? And in what ways can schools and classrooms be restructured, in order to address these students' language needs more effectively?

So it is my purpose in this volume to address the following goals:

o to document the linguistic and cultural diversity associated with the English of American Indian and Alaska Natives;
o to demonstrate the significance of Indian English for today's American Indian and Alaska Native communities;
o to describe the social, historical, and other factors that have contributed to the construction, maintenance, and persistence of these codes.

ASSUMPTIONS ABOUT LANGUAGE

Before going any further with this discussion, I need to review the points of method and theory that have guided my Indian English research and have influenced the synthesis of research findings I plan to present in the following chapters.

I start with the assumptions about language and linguistic description that are relevant to this enterprise.

Language, for purposes of this discussion, is a rule-governed system of human communication, a culturally based mechanism for constructing and exchanging meaning that figures significantly in every domain of social life. Language is a *socially acquired* phenomenon; people are born with the ability to use language, but information from social experience provides the details that enable them to put that potential into practice. Language is also *socially constructed*; innate knowledge gives a certain uniformity to all linguistic systems, but features like the complex of "plural markers" used on nouns in English, the nonbiological gender distinctions of nouns in Spanish and French, and the classification of nouns according to shape and other physical properties in Navajo and Apache suggest that context-specific factors can be just as influential in shaping linguistic detail.

Many people consider language, in some fundamental sense, to be a spoken or verbal phenomenon. However, there are written languages and languages that depend on hand shapes or on other visual clues for the presentation of meaning. Some of these languages may have been derived from spoken language traditions at particular times, but all of them are fully developed linguistic systems in their own right, whose rules of grammar and discourse may or may not be similar to the grammars and discourses of the spoken languages with which they may be associated.

Hence, references to specific languages such as "the" English language spoken by "the" people of the United States, are really references to aggregates of *language varieties* or *codes* (I use these terms interchangeably throughout this book), each of which constitutes a distinct approach to context-specific communication on the part of a certain group of language users (speakers, writers, signers, etc.). Individual language varieties can also be linked to discussion of particular topics, regardless of situation or co-participants, or linked to other social and cultural elements relevant to particular instances of message-exchange.

My concern in this book is with a specific set of language varieties—Indian English. As the examples cited at the opening of this chapter have already suggested, there are written as well as spoken varieties of Indian English, and I will explore Indian English-based communication in both of those formats throughout this volume. (There may also be signed varieties of Indian English, tribe/community-based manual codes that differ from the "signed English" or American Sign Language [ASL] taught by speech therapists or through other means. But I have not addressed this question in my own work, and I am not aware of studies that have explored this question in any detail.)

To meet these goals, I need to examine the *grammar* of Indian English, the *knowledge of language* that people have to acquire, in order to be able to communicate fluently and proficiently in one or more of these codes. Knowledge of language in this sense includes *syntax* (information pertaining to form and organization of sentences and other sequences), *semantics* (information pertaining to language-related meaning and reference), and *pragmatics* (information pertaining to expected relationships between language form and context or situational detail).

Information within each of these areas is stored in the form of *rules*, some of which help people establish basic structures (or "kernels") underlying phrases, sentences, and other, more inclusive linguistic sequences; others provide people with ways of combining and rearranging those basic structures so they can produce the range of linguistics constructions and link their statements to the particular concerns of the speaking task.

Studies of grammar reveal what people *can* do with the knowledge of language they have acquired. To find out what people *actually do* with their knowledge of Indian English when faced with specific communication tasks, the focus of the analysis shifts from grammar to *discourse*—ongoing, language-related, meaningful social interaction. Accordingly, the analysis itself shifts from the study of language-general properties to the study of context-specific features of language use—the process I will refer to here as *text analysis*.

Texts, under this framework, are *bounded segments of discourse*; that is, they begin and end at particular points in space and time. Their boundaries define

---

the linguistic context within which particular features of message and meaning relevant to that segment of the discourse then become displayed.

The information contained within text-boundaries may be presented in a variety of ways, some of which may be more understandable to the co-participants in the discourse setting than are others. But whatever their format, texts are always *purposeful* constructions. That is, speakers (writers, signers, etc.) intend texts to communicate, and they draw connections between text form and text meaning to make certain that the intended message will be conveyed. For example, in the instance of spoken or written texts, people use repetition of words and phrases, noun-pronoun cross-reference, sequencing of verb tenses, and other details of syntax, semantics, and pragmatics to keep listener/reader attention focused on their intended theme. In the case of visual texts or texts in other media, *text coherence* is expressed in additional ways.

Central to understanding the process of text construction is the idea of language-related *choice-making*. This is not a new idea in linguistic theory, although previous work with this theme—notions of language pluralism, register shifting, and code-switching—did not always make clear that the language users are the active participants (or *actors*) in the discourse process. For me, studying text construction as a by-product of choice-making keeps speaker (writer, signer, etc.) agency in the forefront of the analysis—which is very important if, as is the case in Indian English research, the results of linguistic analysis will have implications for social policy.

LIMITATIONS OF THIS VOLUME

I tried, in the preceding section, to describe the points of method and theory that have oriented the preparation of this volume. I am aware, however, that what I am going to say about Indian English grammar and discourse will not always measure up to these standards.

The analysis of text in Indian English research is particularly problematic in this regard. Where it has been possible for researchers to record the whole text as speakers constructed it in the original speech setting, some researchers have focused on the whole text as an uninterrupted data set, amplified by their familiarity with the context of text construction, the backgrounds of the actors, and so on. For their analysis, they work through the text, describing characteristics found in individual segments, then tracing the content-themes and other mechanisms that bind the segments into a larger and inclusive whole. In instances where verbatim recordings of whole texts were not possible—as is usually the case when working in homes or public areas inside an Indian speech community—researchers have had to focus on individual text segments, or on particular constructions within segments, and then use their findings to identify characteristics likely to be present within the remainder of the text and (perhaps) within the larger discourse of which it is a part.

Because much of the available database is skewed in the direction of individual constructions, not text-wholes, my discussion of current research has been focused in similar terms. Fortunately, most researchers provide some sense of context when they focus on individual constructions—for example, they outline the purpose of the speech event in which the text-making occurred, they comment on the social and linguistic background of the speakers, they identify assumptions about discourse relevant to the construction but not necessarily evident from it. And to the extent they are available, I will summarize those comments, as well.

Let me acknowledge some other limitations of my database. I say very little here about Native English issues in Alaska, Hawaii, or Canada. I do not mean to imply, by taking this position or by using the cover-term *Indian English* throughout the volume, that the issues raised in these chapters are irrelevant to the Native peoples outside of the forty-eight contiguous states. I am certain that the issues *are* relevant. But I have not been able to observe Indian English usage in those settings, and I have found only a limited number of source materials on these codes. I have incorporated these into this volume, but without more data I am unwilling to offer generalizations that extend outside of the "lower 48."

Finally, I am embarrassed to admit that my discussion of Indian English overlooks gender issues, and gender differences, in all but a handful of examples. This is a serious omission, but it is unavoidable, given the uniform avoidance of gender themes in the Indian English literature. No one, to my knowledge, has examined female/male differences in Indian English grammar and discourse or looked at how differences in English usage indicate different constructions of female genders or male genders in particular tribal settings. Given the significance of gender marking in many Indian languages, and the range of gender constructions in contemporary tribal societies, studies of this area of Indian English discourse should prove to be rewarding indeed.

PART I

SPEAKERS AND STRUCTURES

My first task in this book is to identify people who speak Indian English and to describe the speech communities to which they belong. I do this in chapter 1 by combining statistical profiles on the American Indian population of the United States with findings from national and tribal surveys of language skills and language needs. To situate this information, I then present brief descriptions of several American Indian speech communities, examining some of the relationships between context and opportunity for speaking that will continue to be of interest throughout this volume.

Next I turn to the varieties of English spoken by members of these communities. In chapter 2, I present an inventory of the characteristics of Indian English grammars and discourse as described in published reports and other studies of these English varieties. This inventory suggests the range of linguistic issues relevant to the interests of this volume and offers a foundation for the more tightly focused analysis of linguistic, historical, and social themes to be presented in the following chapters.

SPEAKERS AND
SPEECH COMMUNITIES

I begin this discussion of American Indian English with some comments about the people who speak American Indian English as their language-of-choice in daily life.[1] As might be expected, at the core of this group, regardless of the context in question, are persons of American Indian and Alaska Native background. However, not everyone who claims affiliation with a particular tribe, Indian community, or Alaska Native village is automatically a speaker of Indian English. Some Indians and Alaska Natives are fluent only in their tribes' ancestral languages, do not speak English in public or private settings, and, if they are able to understand English, do not usually make such knowledge known to outsiders. Other Indians and Alaska Natives are fluent only in standard English and resist opportunities to speak in any other code. For some, Indian English is their only (or primary) means of daily communication; others are comfortable using Indian English, standard English, and—as often happens—ancestral language varieties as well.

There are also non-Indian speakers of Indian English; this includes persons living or working on or near reservation lands or adjacent to Indian neighborhoods in cities, some of whom may be speakers of the local Indian language. Again, there are other non-Indians, equally familiar with the local social terrain, who are unable to understand Indian English (or claim they are unable to do so) when they hear other people talking English in these terms.

Identifying the speakers of Indian English becomes a complex task in social description. The boundaries separating speakers from nonspeakers in this case are not always self-evident, and differing degrees of linguistic proficiency among persons who claim to be speakers make it even more difficult to construct fine-line designations here.

One way to resolve these problems is to focus quite closely on conditions surrounding Indian English fluency within specific American Indian and Alaska Native community settings. This is the approach I will follow when presenting profiles of several American Indian speech communities in the second half of this chapter. Community history, tribal language diversity, proximity to non-Indian settlements, and frequency of relationships with outsiders are some of the variables determining the significance of Indian English fluency at these sites, yet their effect on Indian English discourse differs considerably, site by site, as the information presented in each profile will suggest.

To set the stage for that discussion, I want to make some general comments about Indian English fluency and its place within Indian country as a whole. And I begin those comments by discussing the meaning of the terms *American Indian* and *Alaska Native*, since these categories anchor the questions about English fluency that are of interest in this book.

DEFINING THE POPULATION

Viewed in terms of historical/political perspectives, the categories *American Indian* and *Alaska Native* blend together at least three different groups of persons, each of which has its own historical background and political status within Indian and non-Indian society.[2]

First, there are the members of the federally recognized tribes, groups whose status as Indians has been affirmed through treaty-making, trust agreements, or other forms of federal/tribal action. This category includes members of the Alaska Native villages assigned the status of tribes under the terms of the Alaska Native Land Claims Settlement Act of 1971. Importantly, under the terms of this legislation, children born to those villagers before 1980 are also eligible for village membership, although children born after 1980 are not.

According to the Bureau of Indian Affairs (BIA, the "lead agency" responsible for services to American Indians and Alaska Natives within the federal government), there are 263 federally recognized tribes, bands, pueblos, and other organized Indian entities in the forty-eight contiguous states and in Alaska and more than 200 federally recognized Alaska Native villages. The BIA estimates the total Indian population living "on or near" federally protected lands at 1 million. This figure does not include members of federally recognized tribes who have moved away from their reservations or native communities and into the cities.

Then there are the members of the state-recognized tribes, groups whose status as Indians has been affirmed by the action of one or more state governments, but has not been acknowledged as such by federal-level action. U.S. Department of Commerce statistics identify 56 Indian entities. There are no accurate estimates of the total membership in this category.

Finally there are members of self-identified Indian entities, groups who affirm their own status as Indians even if federal and state agencies have yet to do so, as well as the individuals who self-identify as Indians but do not need to affiliate with any larger Native group when they do so. There are no estimates of the number of Indian groups, or individuals, within this category.

Persons fall in the first two categories if they meet the requirements for tribal membership (often termed enrollment criteria) specified within tribal constitutions, corporation charters, or other public documents. In some instances, these criteria merely formalize what have been traditional practices regarding membership within the tribal community; in others, the criteria define membership in more rigorous ways.

The terms of the criteria themselves vary considerably, from one tribe to the next. Some tribes require that both parents already be tribal members before children can be enrolled; others allow enrollment if one parent is already a member and the other parent is enrolled in another tribe; still others place no restrictions on the second parent's enrollment status. Some tribes enroll potentially eligible children only if they were born on the reservation. Others pay no attention to birthplace, if specified blood quantum requirements (that is, minimum percentage of "Indian blood") have been met. Tribes do not necessarily use the same minimum percentage to define blood quantum; some follow the federal government's policy and expect 25% "Indian blood," while others impose a 50% or higher requirement.

So it can happen that children included in categories 1 or 2, or other close relatives of those persons, will not meet the criteria for tribal enrollment: for example, one parent is non-Indian, parents may be enrolled in different tribes, or (as is the case for some of the Native villages in Alaska) additional stipulations may prevent children from being enrolled. In such instances, even though the children's "place" within the family's kin-network is secure, their relationship to tribal governing structure and their status within tribal political process is less clearly defined.

Conflicts between federal and state definitions of *Indian* frequently produce similar conditions and similar conflicts. According to the Bureau of Indian Affairs, any member of a federally recognized tribe (including Alaska Native villages) is eligible to receive Indian-related services provided through BIA administration. However, some of its programs have their own eligibility criteria, and they are less stringent than enrollment criteria adopted by some of the tribes. This means that persons who are affiliated with a tribe by birth or blood tie, but are not officially enrolled in that tribe, can receive BIA services—and have the status Indian—under certain circumstances, but not under others. Understandably, the number of Indians or Alaska Natives reported for any site by any two BIA programs will not necessarily be the same.

Other federal agencies providing services to Indians and Alaska Natives also have their own definitions of *Indian*, which increases the complications I am describing here. A few agencies require membership in a federally recognized tribe, in the sense defined by BIA policy, to establish an individual's eligibility for Indian-related services. Some are satisfied if the applicant simply self-identifies as Indian; the U.S. Bureau of the Census is one of these agencies, and its estimates of the national Indian population are unavoidably affected by this policy.

Other agencies have expanded on the idea of self-identification by replacing American Indian and Alaska Native with an entirely new designation—*Native American*. Persons fall within this category if they can claim descent or other association with any population indigenous to the Americas. This definition groups together:

o American Indians (regardless of eligibility for tribal membership or the "status" of the tribe with which a person claims association);
o Alaska Natives (regardless of a person's village membership or birthdate);
o Native Hawaiians;
o Native Samoans;
o Native persons of the (former) Pacific Trust territories;
o Native Puerto Ricans (that is, citizens of the Commonwealth who trace descent from the original inhabitants of the island, instead of from the Spanish colonists or the African slaves); and
o Descendants of any other peoples indigenous to the contiguous states, Alaska, Hawaii, or its possessions.

The boundaries established by this term are far-reaching, and they unite many categories of persons whose interests have not been connected with "Indian affairs" in previous years. Certainly there can be political advantages and other benefits to research or policy statements developed in these terms. But framing discussion in terms of an all-inclusive *Native American* population becomes problematic for persons interested specifically in the experiences of American Indians in the "lower 48" or the Indian, Inuit, Inupiaq, and Aleut peoples in Alaska. Certainly, whatever the issues under discussion, it is not appropriate to assume that *Indian* and *Native American* are equivalent, interchangeable terms.

This is why, when defining the purposes and goals of this volume, I used the terms *American Indian* and *Alaska Native*. The details of grammar and discourse that I am going to describe here may be applicable to Native Hawaiian, Native Samoan, or other Native American speech communities; however, I do not have the database to explore those possibilities in this volume. I am concerned only with the emergence of a set of English codes that have close ties to American Indian/Alaska Native languages and cultural traditions and that differ from other varieties of American English as a result of those ties.

Most of the studies of Indian English known to me have examined the varieties of English spoken by members of federally recognized tribes; what I have to say about Indian English grammar and discourse in the following chapters draws heavily on examples from those settings, and my references to *American Indians* and *Alaska Native* peoples need to be interpreted accordingly. At the same time, there is good evidence that Indian English varieties emerged among some state-recognized tribes and among some groups whose "status as Indians" has not been affirmed by outside agencies and that some of these varieties continue to be maintained among speakers within those settings. I cannot deny these people their rights to "voice" in this volume, and I include references to their language and culture history in the discussion in each chapter, whenever relevant source materials are available.

WHO SPEAKS INDIAN ENGLISH?

The *National Adult Indian Education Needs Survey* determined, on the basis of home interviews with 4,000 randomly selected American Indian adults, that 75% of all American Indian adults speak English in some form, and that "most have at least some difficulty" when they speak it (Brod and McQuiston 1983: 11). All of the persons in the research sample were either members of federally and state-recognized tribes or directly affiliated with those tribes in some way. Some of these persons were speakers of their tribe's ancestral languages; others spoke no language besides English. Survey findings do not indicate how many respondents fall into each category or whether ancestral language fluency affects the speakers' English skill in any way. Nor do survey findings indicate the levels of fluency found among the monolingual English speakers.

However, the survey findings do suggest that 25% of all American Indian adults do not speak English at all and that 44% spoke only their ancestral language at home when they were children and learned English as a second language in some outside setting. I conclude from these statistics that 31% of the national adult Indian population have been speakers of (some form of) English exclusively throughout their lives. If "most" of the adult Indian speakers of English "have at least some difficulty" with English, as Brod and McQuiston suggest, I can also conclude that a large portion of the 31% who speak English exclusively are likely to have "difficulty" speaking that language, as well.

These statistics will shift, of course, when examined in terms of conditions within specific Indian/Alaska Native speech communities. Only 10% of the adults on the Northern Ute reservation (Utah), for example, have been monolingual English speakers throughout their lives, compared to 64% percent at Makah reservation (Neah Bay, Washington), and 23% in Chippewa communities of northern Wisconsin (Leap 1981b). Even so, site-specific data confirm the inference that Indian adults who do not speak their ancestral languages may still have difficulties with English. Community-specific inquiry is necessary to understand the significance of this finding.

There has been no systematic national assessment of the language skills of adult American Indians and Alaska Natives since the completion of Brod and McQuiston's survey. The most detailed analysis, to date, of the language skills of American Indian and Alaska Native young people comes from the *Comprehensive Indian Bilingual-Bicultural Education Needs Assessment* (Roberts et al. 1981), conducted under a contract from the Bureau of Indian Affairs. The target population for this project included American Indian and Alaska Native elementary and secondary school students who were attending (1) BIA-administered day schools and off-reservation dormitory programs; (2) BIA-funded contract schools, operated by tribal governments or recognized tribes or tribally sanctioned educational organizations; or (3) public schools located "on or near" reservation lands that receive funding from the Department of Interior's Johnson-O'Malley program to assist in the education of Indian students.[3] Researchers sampled Indian student language skills at 100 of these sites, stratified according to type of school (in the sense just described) and the school's geographic location. Of the 100 schools contacted by the research team, 72% contributed data to this project. Overall, the language skills of 32,000 students were represented in the project's research sample, as measured by teacher assessments, parental commentaries, home/community language surveys, and other indirect means.

According to survey findings, 57.9% of the students in the sample live in communities where English is the predominantly spoken language, and 51.4% of these students are themselves monolingual English speakers or, while familiar to some degree with their ancestral language, are highly dominant in English. At the same time, 66% of these students come from homes where at least one member of the family speaks the ancestral language, and 48.6% of them are speakers of that ancestral language themselves.

Apparently, even when English has become the predominant language of an Indian community, Indian language fluency may remain strong within individual households. But home-based ancestral language fluency does not prevent English from becoming the students' primary language or from being the only language that they acquire.

These findings made it worthwhile to determine how many of the students who are speakers of their ancestral languages (48.6% of the sample as a whole) also are speakers of English, and how proficient they are in their respective use of those languages. Survey findings in this area are as follows:

- o 2% of the students in the sample are monolingual speakers of their ancestral languages;
- o 15% are highly dominant in their ancestral languages and have only nominal familiarity with English;
- o 15% of these students have comparable proficiency in their ancestral language and English;
- o 16% of these students are English dominant and speak their ancestral language at some level of proficiency; and, as noted above,
- o 51% of these students are monolingual English speakers or are highly dominant in English with only a nominal familiarity with their ancestral language.

Given that 98% of the students receiving BIA educational services are speakers of English (only 2% are speakers of their ancestral languages exclusively) and 48.6% of these students are speakers of their ancestral languages, I conclude that 49.4% of these students are monolingual speakers of English and that 1.6% of these students are (to use the wording just cited) "highly dominant in English and have only a minimal familiarity with their ancestral language."

Table 1.1 compares findings from Roberts et al. (1981) and Brod and McQuiston (1983), to see how difference in generation may be affecting patterns of English fluency in Indian country. The larger percentage for students who speak English in each group (75% adults vs. 98% students) reflects the larger number of students (49.4%) vs. adults (31%) who did not learn their ancestral language at home and are speakers of English exclusively.[4] Importantly, the percentage of students vs. adults who learned their ancestral language at home and learned English as a second language remains consistent across generations. This suggests (contrary to popular assumption—cf. Gundlach and Busch 1981)

TABLE 1.1   AMERICAN INDIAN/ALASKA NATIVE ADULT AND
STUDENT LANGUAGE SKILLS, COMPARED

	Adult respondents N=4,000	Student respondents N=32,000
% who speak English	75%	98%
% who do not speak English	25%	2%
% who spoke ancestral language at home and learned English as second language	44%	48.6%
% who did not learn ancestral language and are monolingual in English	31%	49.4%
% who speak English "with difficulty"	"most" of 75%	15%

Sources: Roberts, et al. (1981); Brod and McQuiston (1983).

that generational position alone does not automatically predict presence/absence of ancestral language background among American Indians and Alaska Natives and that fluency in English need not occur at the expense of ancestral language skills.

As is the case among adult speakers, statistics on English vs. ancestral language fluency skills show somewhat different patterning when the analysis shifts from a general American Indian/Alaska Native student profile to conditions within particular speech communities. As the data in table 1.2 show,[5] the percentage of students speaking English at three of these sites (Fairbanks and Lower Kuskokwim, Alaska, and Cherokee, Oklahoma) closely parallels the percentages reported in the Roberts et al. survey (98%), while the percentage of English-speaking students at two of the sites (Pryor, Montana, and Tularosa, New Mexico) is considerably lower. Lower Kuskokwim, Cherokee, Pryor, and Tularosa are all rural sites, sociologically speaking; the data in table 1.2 caution us against making assumptions about community-based patterns of language fluency strictly in terms of urban/rural contrasts.

Totaling the values in the AL/E, al/E and E categories in each column identifies the percentage of "usual" speakers of English among students at each site. The percentages are not consistent site by site. The percentage of "usual" English speakers that Roberts et al. project for all BIA-eligible students—67 to 82% (depending on how their categories are to be interpreted)—is close to the center of this site-specific variation; however, those data do not anticipate the extent of the variation that site-specific comparisons reveal.

TABLE 1.2 ENGLISH AND ANCESTRAL LANGUAGE FLUENCIES
FOR ELEMENTARY AND SECONDARY SCHOOL AI/AN
STUDENTS IN SEVEN COMMUNITIES

	Fairbanks	Lower Kuskokwim	Chinle	Indian Oasis	Pryor	Tularosa	Cherokee
AL	0.3%	2.0%	9.4%	6.0%	55.0%	21.0%	0.0%
[E]	99.7%	98.0%	90.6%	94.0%	44.0%	79.0%	100.0%
AL/e	16.1%	76.0%	16.5%	1.0%	14.0%	38.0%	13.0%
AL/E	35.2%	18.0%	66.9%	1.0%	14.0%	27.0%	15.0%
al/E	35.2%	1.0%	3.9%	59.0% ⎫		13.0%	20.0%
				⎬ 17.0%			
E	12.8%	1.0%	1.6%	33.0% ⎭		1.0%	53.0%
"U"E	83.2%	20.0%	72.4%	93.0%	31.0%	41.0%	88.0%

Sources: Berdan et al. (1982); Leap (1985).
Language fluency designations
  AL: speak ancestral language exclusively
  AL/e: speak ancestral language as their primary language, with some English
  AL/E: speak ancestral language and English
  al/E: speak some ancestral language, with English as their primary language
  [E]:   speak English at some level of proficiency
  E: speak English exclusively.
  "U"E: "usual" English speakers
Sites
  Fairbanks   urban center, central Alaska
  Lower Kuskokwim rural Yup'ik villages, southwestern Alaska
  Chinle   rural community, Navajo reservation, north-central Arizona
  Indian Oasis   rural community, Tohono O'odham (Papago)
                     reservation, southern Arizona
  Pryor   rural community, Crow reservation, central Montana
  Tularosa   rural community, New Mexico
  Cherokee   rural communities, Cherokee Indian reservation, eastern
                     Oklahoma

The Children's Educational Services Study (summarized in O'Malley 1981) found that 67% of all U.S. students from language minority backgrounds "usually" speak English, regardless of any other languages also spoken in their homes. Assuming that data from these two studies can be meaningfully compared, the incidence of "usual" English fluency among American Indian and Alaska Native students as a whole, as shown in the Roberts et al. data (67 to 82%), is as high, or higher, than for all U.S. language minority students. This suggests that, within this population at least, English is in no sense an unfamiliar language. The data in table 1.2 suggest that at some sites (Lower Kuskokwim, Pryor, Tularosa) the percentage of "usual" English speakers can be much lower than the CESS average, which raises interesting questions about the limited penetration of English language fluency within these settings.

LEVELS OF STUDENT ENGLISH FLUENCY

Knowing the number of American Indians and Alaska Natives who speak English at a given site or throughout Indian country reveals very little about the effectiveness of these speakers' English skills. Most attempts to explore this question use the notion of *limited English proficiency* (LEP) as the basis for their commentary (some sources simply provide subjective judgments on this theme: for example, Brod and McQuiston's statement that, "most" adults who speak English "have difficulty" speaking the language).

The "official" definition of LEP is found in section 703 a(1) of the *Bilingual Education Act*. Title VII considers LEP a necessary prerequisite for receiving bilingual instruction under any of its programs. In such instances, LEP indicates a specific relationship between a student's home language background, proficiency in English, and level of academic performance in the classroom. That is, if a student's academic growth falls substantially below that of his or her classmates, and oral and written English are found to be contributing to the less-than-satisfactory achievement, then this student may be considered to be LEP for the purposes defined in the Title VII regulations.

Nationally, according to the CESS findings (cf. O'Malley 1981), some 63% of all language minority background students—or roughly 90% of all such students who "usually" speak English—are limited English proficient in Title VII's sense of that term. According to the analysis of data in Roberts et al. (1981), the incidence of LEP among American Indian and Alaska Native students eligible to receive BIA educational services could range from 17% (students who are monolingual or strongly dominant in their ancestral language) to as high as 48% (including the 17% just identified and some unspecified portion of the 15% equally proficient in English and their ancestral language and some portion of those who are dominant in English but still proficient at some level in their ancestral language).

In other words, according to the Roberts et al. data, while the percentage of American Indian and Alaska Native students who speak English may be as high or higher (67 to 82%) than for students from other language minority backgrounds (67%), the percentage of LEP among American Indian and Alaska Native students appears to be considerably lower (17 to 48%) than for language minority background students as a whole (63%).

The analysis in Roberts et al. assumes that anyone who speaks an American Indian or Alaska Native language will automatically have limited proficiency in English. Data already reviewed in this chapter suggest that ancestral language fluency does not always have such negative effects on English skill, and this observation is strongly supported by language proficiency data

TABLE 1.3   Ancestral Language Backgrounds and LEP in Eight AI/AN Native Communities

Site	Students who are ancestral language speakers	Students who come from ancestral language homes	LEP students
Chinle	96%	91%	72%
Red Lake	—	75%	82%
Hayes/Lodge Pole	60%	—	60%
Pryor	85%	80%	94%
Lake Valley	99%	100%	99%
Eagle Butte	—	45%	30%
Rapid City	90%	—	72%
Shannon County	—	60%	50%

Source: Leap (1985).
Sites:
Chinle	rural community, Navajo reservation, north-central Arizona
Red Lake	multiple rural communities, Red Lake Chippewa reservation, northern Minnesota
Hayes/Lodge Pole	rural communities, Fort Belknap reservation, northern Montana
Pryor	rural community, Crow reservation, southern Montana
Lake Valley	rural community, Navajo reservation, western New Mexico
Eagle Butte	rural community, Cheyenne River reservation, South Dakota
Rapid City	urban community, Sioux and other tribes, western South Dakota
Shannon County	rural county school system, Pine Ridge reservation, southern South Dakota

from individual American Indian and Alaska Native speech communities. As the data in table 1.3 suggest, the percentage of students who speak their ancestral language and/or come from homes where that language is regularly used in daily conversation can be greater than the percent of LEP students reported at a site, as reported for Chinle, Eagle Butte, Rapid City, and Shannon County; equal to the percent of LEP students at the site, as reported for Hayes/Lodge Pole and Lake Valley; or smaller than the LEP percentage, as reported for Red Lake and Pryor.

Rather than relying on student ancestral language skills to draw inferences regarding their English proficiency, most researchers prefer using direct measures of student English skill. Commonly used measures for this purpose include direct rating of student English skills within a specific speaking domain; informal assessment of language skills across a range of language settings; analysis of performance on standardized language arts tests; teacher evaluation of student English skills; parental evaluations; and student self-evaluation.

Table 1.4, for example, shows the extent of LEP found among elementary and secondary school American Indian/Alaska Native students enrolled at

TABLE 1.4 PERCENTAGE OF LEP STUDENTS IN SIXTEEN AI/AN COMMUNITIES
AND SCHOOLS

Site	Tribal background	AI/AN LEP students at the site
Chinle	Navajo	72%
Puerco	Navajo	73%
Tuba City	Navajo	80%
Cortez	Navajo, Ute	45.2%
Red Lake	Chippewa	82%
Hayes/Lodge Pole	Gros Ventres, Assiniboine	60%
Heart Butte	Blackfeet	77%
Lodge Grass	Crow	89.9%
Pryor	Crow	44%
Rocky Boy's	Chippewa-Cree	85%
Lake Valley	Navajo	100%
Navajo Academy	Navajo	62.5%
Eagle Butte	Lakota	30%
Rapid City	Lakota, other	72%
Shannon County	Lakota	50%
St. Francis	Lakota	59.4%

Source: Leap (1985).

Sites:

Chinle	rural community, Navajo reservation, north-central Arizona
Puerco	rural community, Navajo reservation, central Arizona
Tuba City	rural community, Navajo reservation, northwestern Arizona
Cortez	rural community, southeastern Colorado
Red Lake	multiple rural communities, Red Lake Chippewa reservation, northern Minnesota
Hays/Lodge Pole	rural communities, Fort Belknap reservation, northern Montana
Heart Butte	rural community, Blackfeet reservation, western Montana
Lodge Grass	rural community, Crow reservation, southern Montana
Pryor	rural community, Crow reservation, southern Montana
Rocky Boy's	multiple rural communities, Rocky Boy's reservation, northern Montana
Lake Valley	rural community, Navajo reservation, western New Mexico
Navajo Academy	school site, near Farmington, northwestern New Mexico
Eagle Butte	rural community, Cheyenne River reservation, South Dakota
Shannon County	rural county school system, Pine Ridge reservation, South Dakota
St. Francis	rural community, Rosebud Sioux reservation, southern South Dakota

sixteen school sites when standardized test score performance is used to assess students' English proficiency. In all of the cases listed here, students were designated LEP if they scored below the 50th percentile, for their age/grade level, on the reading and language arts tests. Unlike the case suggested by the data in Roberts et al., the average rate for student LEP calculated for these sites—67%—corresponds quite closely with the CESS estimate (63%) for U.S.

students from all non-English language backgrounds. 67% may be lower than the LEP rate estimated by Brod and McQuiston for American Indians and Alaska Native adults. Even so, these statistics suggest that as many as two-thirds of these students fall within the LEP category. This makes English language development a priority for curriculum planning for all American Indian/Alaska Native schools.

Curriculum planning in these cases has to be carried out in site-specific terms, however. According to the data in table 1.4, LEP rates for students from individual tribes and communities can be considerably higher (e.g., Tuba City, Lodge Grass, Rocky Boy's, Lake Valley) or lower (e.g., Cortez, Pryor, Eagle Butte, Shannon, St. Francis) than the rate estimated for American Indian and Alaska Native students (Roberts et al.'s 17 to 48%) or for Indian and non-Indian students as a whole (O'Malley's 63%).

SPEECH COMMUNITIES

In the remainder of this chapter, I present profiles of language use within several types of American Indian speech communities. I intend these profiles to show the range of opportunities for using English open to American Indians and Alaska Natives today and how fluency in Indian English coincides with ancestral language fluency and with standard English skills in these speech settings.

The Definition of *Speech Community*

The key concept in this discussion is *speech community*: according to Joshua Fishman's classic definition (1970: 28), this is a community, "all of whose members share at least a single speech variety and the norms for its appropriate use"; that is, members of a speech community have acquired the *grammar* (or *knowledge of language*) of that language variety and regularly use that knowledge to participate in the same, code-specific *discourse.*

A speech community is not a static phenomenon, by any means. Community boundaries are not predetermined by demographic, geographic, ethnic, racial, or political factors. Instead, they are an index of the frequency of the members' social interaction and their joint construction of speaking styles appropriate to that interaction. When some feature within a social context prompts changes in interaction patterns or in the linguistic variables associated with them, community boundaries and community membership will also be affected accordingly.

Under this definition, persons can be considered members of a speech community—by others in that community, by their own assessment, or by researchers—even when they have social or cultural backgrounds quite different from the other members. Some non-Indian trading post operators and missionaries in the eighteenth and nineteenth centuries often ended up in such a position, as do some non-Indian schoolteachers, government officials, and researchers working in community locales today.

A Typology of Community Settings

Indian English–based speech communities can be found in any number of locales. Three of these locales—*on-reservation, off-reservation/rural*, and *urban*—have played important roles in American Indian/Alaska Native social history and I will use them as the starting point for the site-specific descriptions presented in the remainder of this section.

On-reservation designates a location within an area of land held "in trust" by the federal government on behalf of one or more of the federally recognized tribes. The Indian *colonies* of Nevada, composed of Indians from different tribal backgrounds who moved into areas adjacent to the state's non-Indian settlements during the latter half of the nineteenth century, and the small segments of federally protected Indian lands termed *rancherias* (California) fall into this category, along with the *Native communities* of Alaska, designated as such under the Alaska Native Land Claims Settlement Act. Federal agencies often provide essential services to the American Indian/Alaska Native residents and businesses located on reservation lands, but tribal governments nonetheless retain their sovereignty in these settings. Also relevant to this category are the areas of state-administered land maintained on behalf of the state-recognized tribes.

Off-reservation, rural designates residence in an area adjacent to, rather than inside, one of these "trust" areas. Included here are many federally recognized tribes in Oklahoma (whose reservations—except for that of the Osage—ceased to exist when Oklahoma became a state in 1906), tribes whose "status as Indians" is no longer acknowledged by the federal government, as well as Indian groups whose Indian status has never been acknowledged by non-Indian authorities.

Urban designates residence in a metropolitan area (including a city or one of its suburbs) or in some other large, non-Indian-dominated community setting. In the recent past, urban residence involved relocation, sometimes voluntarily and other times under duress, but almost always entailing a shift in residence to a setting at some distance from family and friends. Today's urban American Indians/Alaska Natives include adults recently relocated from on-reservation or rural settings, as well as the children and grandchildren of persons who made that move at an earlier point in time. For them, the reservation or rural community is an unfamiliar domain: the urban setting is the only "Indian environment" they know.

Speech Communities in Urban Settings

There have been few studies of urban-based American Indians and Alaska Native communities.[6] Most have let poverty, chemical dependency, and despair overshadow other elements within their description. This point of view may coincide with the image of "the urban Indian" maintained in the popular media, but it does not accurately reflect life experiences for many urban Indians and Alaska Natives. A longtime Sioux resident of Chicago comments on this point (cited in Garborino 1971: 170):

> Do they ever talk about Indians in the city who keep jobs for years and years, or who go to college, or send their kids to college, or who never get into trouble? No, it's always how Indians can't adjust to city life, how they only want to get back to the reservation, how much they drink. No one ever talks about all of the different kinds of Indians here and all the different ways they behave.

Given the limitations of the available data, I have decided to draw on information from several sources (including my own work with Indian education programs in Albuquerque, Chicago, the San Francisco area, Los Angeles, Seattle, and Spokane) and talk about the opportunities for language use relevant to urban Indian life as a whole. This allows me to draw contrasts between urban and reservation/rural speech community settings and to identify the issues that sociolinguists working in urban Indian settings will someday want to explore.

The 1980 U.S. Census identified 750,000 American Indians and Alaska Natives living in urban areas. The 1990 Census identified just over 1.0 million Indians and Alaska Natives living in urban areas, a 25% increase over the 1980 findings. There has been evidence of this growth of the urban Indian/Alaska Native population for some time. Job-hunting during the Depression, returning veterans' dissatisfaction with on-reservation living after World War II, and the federal government's Indian-oriented employment assistance program (which, since the 1950s, has arranged for hundreds of American Indian and Alaska Native high school graduates to find employment in Los Angeles, Dallas, Seattle, Chicago, Minneapolis, New York City, and other urban areas) have each contributed to this trend.

Moving to the city has not necessarily produced a complete separation from tribe and community. Communication by telephone or letter, gift exchange, short-term visiting, longer cycles of "migration" as structured by school calendars, employment opportunities, ceremonial obligations, and other factors, as well as the ubiquitous flow of information through the "moccasin telegraph" (an informal network of message-exchange all across Indian country) all work together to minimize the urban dwellers' geographic and cultural distances from home.

When people are unable (or unwilling) to maintain ties with family, friends, and tribe through these means, life as an urban Indian/Native person takes on an entirely different set of meanings. Whereas on-reservation and off-reservation/rural life often centers around the cultural traditions of a single tribe, urban life encourages the formation of intertribal cultural bonds. Indian community/social centers, clinics and child-care centers, Indian-oriented churches and other religious fellowships, and Indian studies/outreach programs at urban universities and in elementary and secondary schools are influential institutions in this regard. Urban Indian powwows frequently sponsored by one or more of these institutions (see the description in Weibel-Orlando 1991: 132–52) are especially important occasions.

Urban areas are not usually thought of as environments that would support ancestral language retention, but ample efforts toward this end can be found in such domains. Navajo families living in Oakland and families from Laguna pueblo living in Los Angeles meet on a regular basis to discuss the news from home, evaluate actions taken by their tribal governments, and address concerns that they share as "nonresident" members of their tribes. Such meetings give fluent speakers a chance to demonstrate ancestral language skills and help younger people and others to strengthen their competencies in this area. Inter-family visiting and chance encounters at the grocery store, laundry, or elsewhere in a neighborhood provide additional opportunities in that regard.

Indian-oriented religious organizations may use one or more Indian languages in their liturgies, when appropriate for their congregations. Indian centers sponsor potluck dinners and other informal get-togethers where discussions in ancestral languages are encouraged. They also may sponsor Indian language classes for adults and for young people or work with Indian Studies programs at urban universities to do the same.

Regardless of the success of urban Indians and Alaska Natives in retaining ancestral language skills or acquiring those skills from other parties, urban residence always involves communication with persons who do not speak their ancestral language. These encounters may involve persons from other tribes and other Indian/Alaska Native language traditions as well as non-Indians of various cultural and linguistic backgrounds.

This is particularly the case because Indians and Alaska Natives rarely live in tightly defined, centralized, and bounded city neighborhoods, in the sense often associated with other urban-based ethnic groups. Individuals may cluster around certain service areas or in districts where housing is particularly accessible, but tribally specific residence areas, or even pan-tribal "Indian ghettos" are rare phenomena, found primarily in cities adjacent to reservation lands. Even in those cases (e.g., Navajos in Albuquerque, Ojibwa and Chippewa in Minneapolis, Lakota Sioux in Rapid City) tribal members view residence in an "Indian neighborhood" as an interim arrangement, suitable only until housing elsewhere in the city can be found. Even when neighborhoods form, there are always those who have personal reasons for choosing to live on their own.

How frequently such encounters lead people to acquire fluencies in Indian/Alaska Native languages other than their own is difficult to assess. It is clear, however, that day-to-day encounters with English are an unavoidable part of city life and familiarity with English (at some level) is an important language skill for urban Indians. Personal identity and prestige factors, particularly when they contribute to the frequency of interaction with non-Indians, also encourage English fluency—or at least an appearance thereof. William Hodge (1969: 45), writing about Navajo residents in Albuquerque, reports:

> Ninety-five percent of the Navajos speak fair to excellent English. Five percent speak Navajo only. It is expected that at least forty percent of the residents had difficulty speaking Navajo. I was cautioned by one of my Navajo interpreters not to try to speak to permanent residents in Navajo "because they'll think that you think they are stupid and don't know much English."

It is difficult to determine from Hodge's comments how much English the Navajo residents in Albuquerque actually know. National estimates of adult Indian English proficiency (e.g., Brod and McQuiston 1983) are no help here, since the statistics presented in those studies blend data on urban Indian English needs with data from other locales. Adult-oriented Indian education programs, in my experience, do acknowledge that written English skills are important to urban Indian life and treat English literacy as a central concern in their instructional programs. Yet efforts to address the spoken English needs of urban Indians tend to be based in elementary and (though less frequently) secondary schools, not in adult-oriented educational settings. This suggests that adult Indians come to the city already speaking English at some level; find ways to acquire spoken English skills on-the-job, in partnership with relatives and friends, or through other informal means; or develop strategies for coping with urban life that require only a superficial fluency in English.

Some urban Indians and Alaska Natives must be finding ways to acquire the English skills they need for city life. Weibel-Orlando (1991: 22) notes that, as of 1983, 50% of the urban Indians who lived in Los Angeles returned to their reservation/rural home communities "to live out their retirement years." By 1989, she found that only 18% of the retirement-aged Los Angeles Indians "intended to return to their places of origin in the future." She continues: "Ties to friends and children, involvement in ethnic activities, and the attainment of satisfying community statuses and roles in their urban ethnic community have fostered the growth of a small but stable core of older Indians in Los Angeles." Given the multitribal nature of urban Indian experience, as I have described here and as Weibel-Orlando's research suggests, none of these ties, involvements, or attainments could occur without these older Indians having attained some level of English language proficiency.

Speech Communities in On-Reservation and Off-Reservation, Rural Settings

Outside of urban environments, it becomes somewhat easier to construct site-specific profiles of American Indian and Alaska Native speech communities. For one thing, the database is more extensive. While published descriptions of daily life in these communities do not always contain accurate statements (Bea Medicine [1987: 291] notes that one of her Indian friends refers to these studies as "Indian joke books"), there is enough reliable information in those sources to suggest the basic characteristics of language and community life.

Second, there is much greater homogeneity in ancestral language and cultural background in reservation/rural settings, compared to urban domains. To be sure, intertribal marriage, long-term visiting patterns, adoption, employment/career opportunities (especially within the Bureau of Indian Affairs, the Indian Health Service, or other agencies providing on-site services in individual community settings), and similar factors have diversified the key actors at these sites. But these conditions rarely resemble the complex of intertribal and Indian/non-Indian interaction found in urban settings. Moreover, the linguistic and cultural traditions relevant to on-reservation and off-reservation, rural settings are always more tightly focused, if only because of the particular historical and social factors that established the American Indian/Alaska Native resident population at these sites.

On-reservation and rural residence has long been associated with a high incidence of ancestral language fluency. While in some instances (see comments on Navajo, for example, in McLaughlin 1989) local language patterns no longer support this claim, ancestral language fluencies still remain higher in these settings than in urban domains.

Equally important to language profiles in reservation/rural communities has been the rise of fluency in (some variety of) English in recent years. There continue to be cases where isolated Indian families or clusters of families, living at a distance from neighbors, sources of social services, or non-Indian settlements and institutions, are fluent only in their ancestral languages. But it is much more common for on-reservation and off-reservation rural residents to have close interaction with non-Indian institutions and individuals as well as with institutions and individuals from their own tribes. The details of that interaction may vary from one speech community to the next, but certain features are consistent across these sites—particularly the functions served by ancestral language and English language fluencies within these settings.

The four case studies that follow illustrate these similarities and contrasts.

CASE STUDY 1: THE PONCA (NORTH CENTRAL OKLAHOMA)

The Ponca of Oklahoma (or southern Ponca, to distinguish them from northern relatives who live in northeastern Nebraska) have been residents of the area south of Ponca City (a non-Indian community) since 1880.[7] Prior to that time, as Howard (1965: 7) describes it:

> ... the Ponca ... hunted and ranged over most of the area now known as the Central Great Plains. The Black Hills of South Dakota they knew well and sometimes even reached the Rockies in their search for game, scalps [*sic*] and the adventure of seeing new territory. Their main seat, the area where most of their permanent villages and forts were built, was what is now Knox County, in northeastern Nebraska. This was the heart of the Ponca domain in former times and is still the home of most of the Northern Ponca.

The Ponca people were moved to Oklahoma (called, at that time, the Indian Territory) in 1880, after a series of events awarded most of the Ponca homeland to the Teton Dakota, and Teton raids on Ponca settlements made life there unbearable. Most of that group remained in Oklahoma and are referred to today as the southern Ponca, to distinguish them from the northern Ponca, descendants of those who chose to return to Niobrara shortly after their arrival in Oklahoma.

Today's southern Ponca live on the land originally provided to the tribe shortly after relocation. This is not, however, reservation land, since (with the exception of the Osage), the federal trust status of tribal lands in the Indian Territory was terminated in 1906 when Oklahoma became a state. As of 1980, the tribe retained control over 930 acres of the original trust land, with an additional 16,500 acres allotted for use by individual Ponca families.

The administrative center for the tribe lies in the community of White Eagle, which is also home for a large portion of the tribal membership. Remaining tribal members live in smaller towns surrounding White Eagle or on individual homesites. The offices of tribal government and many of its affiliated agencies are based in White Eagle, as are several Protestant Christian congregations as well as one of the area's meeting places for the Native American Church.

While there are gas station/convenience store facilities within White Eagle, tribal members carry out shopping and business-related transactions in Ponca City, located just north of this settlement.

Despite the name, Ponca City is very much a non-Indian settlement. Business people there have done much to encourage long-term commercial ties with Ponca customers, and Ponca City schools have provided educational services for children from the tribe.[8] Still, Ponca families have never been encouraged to become permanent residents of this community. For most of the families I got to know, their desire to participate in the social, political, and religious activities in the White Eagle area made residence there much more worthwhile.

Ponca people have been fluent speakers of English for several generations, and obligatory schooling, proximity to Ponca City, and other factors ensure that fluency in English is an important element in the socialization of all Ponca children. Howard (1965: 7) reports: "As a result of their years in Oklahoma, [Southern Ponca] now speak English with a slight Southern accent, and this has affected their pronunciation of *Degiha* [the linguists' label for the Ponca ancestral language] as well. This fact their Northern kinsmen find quite amusing." To my hearing, this "slight Southern accent" is characteristic of the English of many people from north-central Oklahoma, whether Indian or non-Indian in background. It is not, however, uniformly characteristic of the English of all members of the tribe. When I worked with a tribally sponsored language program in the late 1970s, I found the English of persons over age 60 (and not everyone in this age group spoke English, I should add) to be heavily influenced by the sound pattern of their ancestral language; particularly evident in this regard was the presence of voiceless (or whispered) vowels, vowel nasalization, and the deletion of one or more segments from consonant contrasts in word-final and other positions. Spoken English syntax conformed closely to standard English patterns, though tense/aspect features and some subordinate clause structures differed quite strikingly from those models.

Howard's "Southern accent" was much more likely to show up in the English of persons in the 30–60 age range. However, the diminished presence of Ponca language influence in these persons' English did not indicate an absence of Ponca language proficiency. One of the most articulate English speakers in tribal government in the mid-1970s could shift quite easily between English and his ancestral language, particularly when his listeners were persons from various age-levels. His English could range from classroom-acceptable to quite "down home," depending on the issues under discussion and his own sense of "appropriate speech" within the given setting. Features from Ponca grammar that were so evident in the English of older persons were also present in his English and the English of others in his age grouping. However, proficiency in a more standardized English frequently masked the presence of these details in surface structures; when they did emerge, I soon discovered, their presence indicated a shift in the climate of conversation from formal to more congenial grounds.

Howard found that, as of 1961, very few young people under age 25 could speak Degiha, and they would reply in English when someone spoke to them in their ancestral language. In 1976 decline of ancestral language skills prompted the tribe to seek assistance in language renewal from the Oklahoma Indian Affairs Commission (the project that first brought me to White Eagle). The English I heard younger Ponca people using during my visits had all of the characteristics found in the English of the 30- to 60-year-olds. However, the Ponca-related features occurred with much lower frequency in the English of young people and did not always signal a change in the formality of the discourse.

CASE STUDY 2: NORTHERN UTE (NORTHEASTERN UTAH)

My next example—Northern Ute (officially, the Uintah and Ouray Tribe of Ute Indians, Inc.)—suggests a speech community constructed quite differently from that at Ponca.[9] The on-reservation context of this speech community has much to do with these contrasts, as my comments will show.

The Northern Ute reservation is located in two of Utah's northeastern counties—Uintah and Duchesne. The reservation includes 1.0 million acres of federally protected lands, reduced from the original 2.0 million acreage because of the creation of the High Uintah Wilderness area and the opening of the reservation to non-Indian settlement during a brief period at the beginning of this century (see comments below).

This area was originally the homeland for one of the fifteen bands that were part of *Noochew* (the Northern Ute term usually translated "the Ute people") in earlier times. It was placed under federal control by executive order in 1861, and over the next fifteen years ten other Ute bands were relocated there. (The remaining Ute bands were settled on the two Ute reservations in southern Colorado.)

Over time, reservation life prompted band memberships to merge and boundaries to be redrawn. Today, the Northern Ute tribal constitution recognizes three Northern Ute bands, with membership corresponding roughly to place of residence on the reservation: the White River band in the northern area, Uintah in the center, and Uncompahgre in the south. As at Ponca, while some families live by themselves on individual farms or homesteads, most live in or adjacent to one of the eight on-reservation residential communities.

Several of these communities have a much more established place within tribal history. White Rocks, for example, was the site of the first trading post in Ute country (established in 1832), and many members of the White River band were settled in this area when the U.S. government moved them out of Colorado in 1881. Similarly, the town of Ouray, in the southern end of the reservation, became the central area of settlement for the Uncompahgre, after they were moved to the reservation in 1881.

Fort Duchesne and Myton were originally army posts for the federal soldiers who monitored interaction among Utes, other Indian tribes, and non-Indian settlers during the earliest years of the reservation. Today Fort Duchesne is the location for the offices of the Tribal Business Committee (the governing body of the tribe), the offices of tribal government (e.g., Education, Health, Natural Resources) that carry out Business Committee directives, and other agencies and programs providing services to the tribe.

Other settlements have appeared over the past ten years, primarily as a result of federally funded construction of housing during the 1970s and 1980s. These communities tend to be uniformly Indian in their composition, given the regulations governing occupancy of units built under these programs. Elsewhere on the reservation, conditions have not been ethnically homogeneous for quite some time. In 1905 Congressional action opened reservation lands not otherwise claimed by the tribe or by individual families to non-Indian purchase and settlement, and by 1912 some 30,000 acres of Northern Ute reservation land had been transferred to non-Indian ownership. These transfers created a "checkerboard" pattern of on-reservation land ownership. Non-Indian families live next door to Indian families all across the reservation, and the majority of the on-reservation settlements (Roosevelt, Duchesne, Neola, Lapointe) have a predominantly non-Indian population.[10]

Hunting, gathering, and trading were traditional subsistence practices for Northern Ute people. Horse-herding became an important activity for many households after European explorers and traders brought these animals to Indian country. Government agents and missionaries introduced the Northern Ute to farming after the bands were settled on the reservation; but, except for those who grow alfalfa to feed their horses, very few tribal members have ever made long-term investments in agriculture.

The primary source of income on this reservation is wage-labor—largely under the sponsorship of one or more tribally based programs. The number of such jobs is limited, however, and unemployment rates are high.

The tribe operates a tourist facility (motel, restaurant, gas station, campgrounds, and lake for recreational boating and fishing) on U.S. Highway 40 (the major east-west roadway on the reservation). The tribe also operates a bowling alley (east of the motel) and a coin-operated laundromat in Fort Duchesne. Other gas station/grocery stores and service-oriented businesses can be found along U.S. 40, in some of the Indian settlements, and at other key locations on the reservation. Most of these are non-Indian enterprises, but tribal members regularly do business there. For substantial shopping or other services, if they have transportation, Northern Ute turn to the supermarkets and stores in the larger (non-Indian) towns on the reservation, travel to Vernal (an off-reservation, non-Indian settlement located 30 miles east of Fort Duchesne), or take a day or weekend trip to Salt Lake City (150 miles west of the reservation) or Denver (350 miles to the east).

Non-Indian towns are also sources for recreation and entertainment. Here are the reservation's movie theaters, restaurants, and several of the "Indian bars." Utes and non-Indians share access to these facilities; while one-on-one conflicts occasionally occur, conditions rarely remain openly hostile for an extended period.

Frequent interaction with non-Indians on this reservation also carries over into religious life. With very few exceptions, Christian worship at Northern Ute reservation is conducted by non-Indian religious leaders, and there are non-Indians as well as Indians in almost every congregation. Not surprisingly, English is the language of worship here.

However, churches are not located exclusively in non-Indian towns. There is a Roman Catholic church in Roosevelt, and the parish operates missions in Duchesne and Fort Duchesne. There are Episcopal missions in White Rocks and Randelette, an Assembly of God church in Roosevelt, an Indian Baptist church on the White Rocks road, and a Pentecostal church one mile north of the Baptist facility. And there are Mormon churches in all of the non-Indian settlements and in some of the Indian ones.

This means that Northern Ute people may travel considerable distances on Sundays and during the week, according to their religious preferences. For example, persons living in White Rocks who are members of the Assembly of God church in Roosevelt will make two thirty-mile trips, from home to church and back, if they attend morning and evening worship services each Sunday. Bible study classes, adult fellowship, children's activities, church committees, and private meetings with the pastor require additional travel and may not be coordinated with trips to the grocery store or to other commercial activities in town.

Importantly, practicing Christians on this reservation (including some Mormons) may also be practicing members of the Native American Church, attend sweat lodge ceremonies, and/or pledge themselves (or support others who have pledged) for the annual Sun Dance. Tribal members describe these as "traditional" religious ceremonies and Northern Ute (and other Indian languages) as well as English are used in these events. Tribal members are always in charge of them, yet it is not uncommon for non-Indians to be observers or even participants.

Indian education is another component of life on this reservation involving frequent Indian and non-Indian interaction. The first schools at Northern Ute were boarding school facilities operated by the federal government. The BIA transferred responsibility for on-reservation schooling to the Uintah and Duchesne County school districts in 1952. Since then, Ute students attend elementary and junior high school classes with non-Indian neighbors and join Utes and non-Indians from across the reservation to complete their high school education at a single site—Union High School, which straddles the Uintah-Duchesne county line.

The curriculum at these schools is almost entirely non-Indian in orientation. The six-year (1980–1986) bilingual education program at two of the on-reservation elementary schools in Uintah County has been the significant exception to this pattern in recent years, though several federally funded supplemental programs (Johnson-O'Malley, Indian Education Act, Chapter I) have provided Indian-oriented instruction on some occasions. The Tribal Division of Education, reacting to the limited effectiveness of the county vocational education and adult education programs to address tribal needs, provides adult basic education and high school completion services and job-oriented skills development in carpentry, machine-shop, and other technical areas. Tribally based teacher-training programs, operated in cooperation with Weber State University, have made several Northern Utes eligible to be certified as teachers in the state's elementary or secondary schools; few of these trainees have found employment in the on-reservation schools, however.

The bilingual education program came about, in large part, because of growing evidence that fluency in Ute was on the decline and that improving Ute language skills would have positive effects on these students' overall levels of classroom achievement. Tribal Division of Education reservation-wide language surveys estimated that 56% of all elementary and secondary school Ute students could speak their ancestral language at some level of proficiency; however, only 15% of all students could be considered fluent speakers of the language. As expected, speaker profiles among adult Utes showed higher rates of familiarity with the Ute language (90%) and fluency (44%). Importantly, the survey found that 33% of the school-aged Utes could understand when adults spoke Ute in their presence, leaving only 11% of these students without productive or receptive Ute language skills. That is quite close to the percentage reported for that category among Ute adults.

An equally interesting discovery about the status of the ancestral language on this reservation was the variability and contrast characterizing the use of Ute language skills in different speech settings. Granted, some degree of situationally based language variation can be expected among speakers of any language tradition. But at Northern Ute, many factors in addition to situational details influence such outcomes, including:

o enrollment status—whether the speaker is an enrolled member of the Northern Ute Tribe, related to an enrolled member, or considered through some other type of association;
o band membership—each of the three bands has its own ways of pronouncing Ute words, forming syntactic constructions, and designating references in certain areas of vocabulary;
o residence pattern—including amount of time spent living on and/or off the reservation, on-reservation location of the household, and site(s) of off-reservation residence;
o presence/absence of grandparents or other older speakers of Ute within the home;
o frequency of association with elders outside of the home;
·o participation in traditional religious activities;
o association with Christian religious practice—particularly the Mormon church;
o choice of marriage partner—Indian vs. non-Indian, tribal member vs. Indian from another tribe.

Certain features of Ute language structure are also relevant here, such as:

o "older" vs. "more modernized" Ute language words and phrases in conversations and narratives;
o retention/deletion of rules for vowel devoicing and for word-initial alternations between stop and spirant consonants;
o use of topicalization markers, embedding, and other mechanisms to establish connections between sentence sequences.

Particularly important are several rules of Ute language discourse, including the assumption that speakers will *personalize* their use of Ute language in any conversation to make certain that they leave their "signature" on every conversation in which they are involved.

These conditions have direct consequences for the distribution of Ute language skills in on-reservation households, and for the maintenance of Ute language fluency within the tribe as a whole. In some cases, only the elders in the household are speakers of Ute. In others, persons at all generations are Ute language proficient, with or without the presence of elders in the home. And in others, no one of any age speaks Ute.

Because I have a lot to say about Northern Ute varieties of English in the following chapters, I will make only brief comments on this topic here. There are many Ute varieties of English, and their distribution, speaker by speaker, follows the patterns found for the ancestral language. Ute English as a whole contrasts with the cluster of (non-Indian) English varieties unique to north-eastern Utah—what the locals term "Basin English"—and with the more standardized forms of English found throughout the region. Similarities between Ute English and ancestral language grammar account for many of the differences between Ute English and varieties of Indian English found in other reservation settings. Some of these similarities, particularly those having to do with features of pragmatics and discourse, influence English language use even for speakers whose syntax and semantic structures otherwise approximate standard English models.

CASE STUDY 3: ISLETA (CENTRAL NEW MEXICO)

Isleta, New Mexico, offers an entirely different picture of an on-reservation speech community.[11] There has not been an non-Indian population in residence within the reservation boundaries for some time, and other institutions and practices at this pueblo strengthen the boundaries between Isleta and outsiders that residential restrictions maintain.

Isleta pueblo (and the Isleta Indian reservation) is located in central New Mexico, fifteen miles south of the city-center of Albuquerque. This 210,000-acre reservation extends from the crest of the Manzanos mountain range across the Rio Grande to the border shared with the Laguna Indian reservation, some fifty miles to the west of the river. As at Northern Ute, there are several Indian settlements on this reservation. But there are no non-Indian settlements there, and non-Indian individuals are permitted to live at Isleta only if married to a member of the tribe.

One of the Indian settlements, called *the village* in Isleta English, is considered by Isleta tradition to be the oldest settlement on the reservation; it was established long before the Spanish first entered the Rio Grande valley in the late sixteenth century. The village is the setting for major ceremonies and other traditional activities throughout the year. The (one) kiva and the (two) dance houses, important locations in the pueblo's spiritual and political life, are located in the village, as is the plaza, the space reserved for public ceremonies and the reservation's Roman Catholic church.

A second settlement, located to the southwest of the village, is the home for descendants of a group of families from Laguna pueblo who moved to Isleta in 1882. They came to Isleta to find a place where they could practice their own religion, free from Protestant Christian interference. Harvey (1963) reports that Kachina dances and other Keres ceremonials were still being carried out in Isleta's "Laguna village" some ninety years after that migration.

The three remaining on-reservation settlements serve primarily as living areas for different Isleta families, some of whom also maintain homes in the village that they use during ceremonial periods or on other occasions. Two of these communities are located on the banks of the Rio Grande, and the third is located five miles to the east of the river. Tribal accounts differ as to the age of these settlements.

Unlike the case at other communities along the Rio Grande, the term *pueblo* at Isleta does not refer to a settlement, but to the type of political unity at this site. A pueblo, in Isleta tradition, is a group of Indians who elect a common set of administrative officials (the governor, assistants, the tribal council) and agree to comply with decisions made by those officials. Common residence is one element in defining the group here, but is not the essential feature of group membership. Isleta people may live in any one of the five on-reservation settlements, in a outlying homestead, in nearby Albuquerque, or in Los Angeles or elsewhere and still be members of the pueblo in good standing—provided they meet all of the political and religious responsibilities assigned to them by pueblo leadership.

Isleta's economy is, by tradition, agriculturally based. A complex system of irrigation canals and ditches brings water from the Rio Grande to irrigate fields of alfalfa and other grains and the gardens of corn, beans, chilis, and other vegetable crops. Tribal landholding practices guarantee that every Isleta household will have access to farmland, though households whose members do not make use of their assigned lands may find the lands assigned to some other household by action of the tribal council.

Agriculture is more than a subsistence practice at Isleta; it is an expected mode of behavior for all who belong to this pueblo. A full-time commitment to agriculture is not required. In the mid-1970s pueblo members could identify no more than 5 to 8% of Isleta households where farming was the primary economic activity, and a follow-up review of conditions in 1988 found virtually no change in that estimate. "Side farming" is the primary mode of agricultural activity at Isleta today, supplementing the income earned through on-reservation employment in one of the tribally administered service programs; at the BIA-operated day school or in some other federally funded project; in one of the grocery, arts and crafts, or other Indian-owned stores and businesses; or in one of the Hispanic towns that surround the reservation or in Albuquerque.

Interstate 25 runs north and south across the reservation land and provides Isleta people with easy access to all of Albuquerque's commercial and social resources. In fact, since the opening of this highway in the early 1970s, Isleta has begun to resemble the other "bedroom communities" adjacent to the metropolitan area. Some Isleta people have shifted residence from the reservation into the city, though they continue to maintain a home at Isleta and return there on weekends or when pueblo responsibilities require it.

Before the construction of the interstate highway, several two-lane highways connected Isleta to the city. These highways are still used; however, travel on them is difficult because of the number of small settlements through which the traffic must pass. Many of the inhabitants of these settlements are Hispanic, descendants of the Spanish settlers who occupied this area in the early sixteenth century. Some families from these settlements and some families from Isleta have enjoyed long-term, mutually beneficial personal relationships; on occasions, individual Hispanics have been invited to participate in the pueblo's ceremonial activities, which are usually closed to outsiders.

Isleta people and local Hispanics may also be linked through commercial ties, since Isleta people regularly patronize the grocery stores and other businesses in these towns. In earlier days, Hispanic Roman Catholics attended services at the on-reservation parish church. When conflicts with tribal government led to the closing of that church in the 1960s, the diocese built a new facility off the reservation, and some Isleta families began attending Sunday services there. Protestant-operated Indian "missions" are open to Hispanics as well as Isleta people. And once Isleta students complete their elementary schooling at the on-reservation day school, they attend junior and senior high school at off-reservation, county-operated facilities where neighboring Hispanics and other non-Indian age-mates are also enrolled.

The presence of English and Spanish on this reservation notwithstanding, a significant portion of the pueblo's on-reservation residents still speak Isletan Tiwa (the ancestral language of this community). This is the language of tribal government (even when speaking in the presence of outsiders) and the language of the pueblo's ceremonial life. Language retention has been strong enough here to encourage the Bureau of Indian Affairs to propose adding a bilingual component to the day school's kindergarten program, so that entering students could receive academic instruction in Tiwa as well as English. Isleta's tribal council is not enthusiastic about this proposal, arguing that ancestral language instruction is the responsibility of the pueblo and not of outside agencies like the school.

When I ask Isleta parents for their thoughts on this issue, they point out that the young people at Isleta do not speak their ancestral language as well as they should, but add that once the young people complete their schooling and settle into the day-to-day responsibilities of adult members of the pueblo community, fluency in the ancestral language will improve. Importantly, when asked, parents do not report that young people have difficulties with English or that the school needs to make improvements in its English language arts instructions; teachers, however, note that the students' "Indian language is fine, but we need to work on their English."

Inter-speaker variation, evident in so many ways among speakers of Northern Ute, is much less noticeable at Isleta. Individual speakers may differ in their use of pronominal prefixes, sentence-negating markers, and other features of Tiwa syntax, but word order and other features of sentence constructions are much more consistent across speakers than they are at Northern Ute. One important contrast involves differences in the Tiwa spoken by persons from highly traditional families, compared to the Tiwa of those aligned with fundamentalist Protestant sects.

Language variation at Isleta is more evident where non-Indian discourse is concerned. Older members of the pueblo are more likely to speak Spanish as a second language and to speak English in only limited ways; younger Isletas, in contrast, speak English (in Isleta and/or standard varieties) much more frequently than they do Spanish. Similarly, older members of the area's Hispanic communities are more likely to speak Isletan Tiwa than are younger Hispanics. Common proficiency in English (though not necessarily the same English varieties) becomes the basis for communication between younger Isletas and Hispanics; whether this use of English as a nonpartisan, "neutral" code, instead of acquisition of some level of skill in each other's languages, has affected Isletan-Hispanic relations merits closer attention.

CASE STUDY 4: COLORADO RIVER TRIBES
(SOUTHWESTERN ARIZONA, SOUTHEASTERN CALIFORNIA)

I conclude these profiles of on-reservation/rural Indian speech communities by describing conditions on the Colorado River reservation, located on the border between Arizona and California.[12] This reservation is of interest because the resident population contains persons from four distinct and traditionally unrelated tribal groups—Mohave, Chemehuevi, Hopi, and Navajo. The U.S. government established the reservation for the Mohave and Chemehuevi in

1865; Navajo and Hopi families moved there after World War II, under an incentive program for veterans operated by the Bureau of Indian Affairs.

Each of these groups recognizes the distinctiveness of its cultural and political backgrounds; in the case of some Navajo and Hopi households, people maintain close contacts with relatives on those reservations as well. However, because of mutual residence, these Navajo and Hopi join their Mohave and Chemehuevi neighbors in identifying with the more inclusive, recently created political aggregate—the Colorado River Tribes. It is common to hear individuals give both affiliations—"I'm a Mohave from the CRT"—when asked about their tribal membership.

Strictly speaking, then, the CRT is not a tribe in the sense in which the term applies to Ponca, Northern Ute, or Isleta; however, the CRT does have the status of a "tribal government" under BIA administrative policy. Governing officials are elected from all four groups and supervise programs that provide a range of educational and social services for the on-reservation Indian population as a whole.

On-reservation residence in this case centers around individual households and homesteads, not around settlements. The only town of any size on this reservation is Parker, Arizona, located in the northern area of the reservation ("up river," in the reservation's English usage.) Strictly speaking, Parker lies "on a small island of state-owned land" (Penfield-Jasper 1980: 2), so it is not legally a part of the reservation at all. It is, however, home for persons from each of the four resident tribes, for other Indians and non-Indian employees who work for tribal government, the BIA, or the Indian Health Service, and for Anglo and Mexican-American farmers who have moved into this part of the Colorado River valley in recent years. Some of these farmers lease land from the tribe or work for families who have negotiated those leases; in this sense, the checkerboard pattern of land usage found at Northern Ute is also present here. Other non-Indian families participate in Parker's commercial economy, either as owners of local businesses or as workers, as do the African Americans and East Asians who have also moved into this settlement in recent years.

Parker is also the location of the schools (three elementary and two secondary) for Indian and non-Indian children on this reservation. These are public schools, operated under state auspices by the county school board. As at Northern Ute, the federal government provides funds to support some Indian-oriented programs; but instruction is generally oriented toward the educational needs of the non-Indian mainstream. Non-Indian students outnumber Indian students in these schools by a ratio of seven to three; at the high school level, the ratio is even more unbalanced, given the high drop-out rate among Indian students, regardless of tribal background. Even so, in Penfield-Jasper's (1980:

3) assessment, these schools provide "the greatest arena for interaction between the various [segments of the] local population."

North of Parker lies a retirement community, a marina, and resort area. These are, in the main, non-Indian-oriented facilities, though they provide some revenue to the CRT; for example, the marina is a tribally operated enterprise. In recent years, the CRT officials have negotiated contracts with outside businesses to allow them to pursue manufacturing and mining on reservation lands. Here again, the activities themselves are non-Indian controlled, and the possibility of Indian employment is limited.

Levels of ancestral language fluencies vary greatly across this reservation, depending on the speaker's tribal background, age, and other factors. Speaker familiarity with different varieties of English meshes closely with ancestral language variation. Penfield-Jasper (1982: 25) reports for the Mohave: "90% of the youth under the age of 20 no longer speak the Native language. . . . [That makes it] important for many of these young people to speak English in a Mohave way." Chemehuevi, Navajo, and Hopi students also speak in their own varieties of English. As a result, Penfield-Jasper (1977: 25) found that "one can easily tell the Tribal identity of an individual by the way in which [he or she] spoke English." Importantly, these students retain these tribe-specific contrasts in English throughout their grade school careers and, apparently, into adulthood. Classroom-based instruction leads to improvements in some areas of English skill, but does not alter areas through which the speaker's tribal background can be displayed.

CHAPTER 2

SOUND PATTERNS, SENTENCE FORMS, AND MEANINGS

The statistics and case studies from chapter 1 show that many American Indians and Alaska Natives are speakers of English and that encounters with English discourse—brought about by the media, by English-centered schools, businesses, and political institutions, and by the presence of non-Indians—are unavoidable features of daily life, even for those who are not speakers of that language.

But these statistics and case studies say very little about the *knowledge of English* that guides Indians and Alaska Natives when they participate—as speakers, listeners, or observers—in these encounters. My purpose in this chapter is to examine the English used by Indians and Alaska Natives in such settings and to explore the characteristics of sound, word structure, sentence form, and meaning that those codes contain.

To prepare this chapter, I reviewed published descriptions of Indian English grammar and discourse, organizing the findings from those studies around the inventory of "socially diagnostic phonological and grammatical features" that Wolfram and Fasold (1974: 124–36) have proposed for nonstandard American English as a whole and modifying and amplifying that inventory as the data required. I found Fletcher's (1983) review of the Indian English literature and the "error analysis" typologies in sources like Cook and Sharp (1966) and Kuhlman and Kalactaca (1982) to be helpful in this regard. I admit, however, that the final selection of topics for this chapter draws heavily on the themes that I have explored in my own research.

I realize that scholars have used a variety of methods to gather data for Indian English analysis (such as informal observation, small group discussions, individualized interviews, paper-and-pencil tests, documentary analysis) and that scholars have asked speakers from different segments of speech communities to participate in their studies, often without noting those differences in background or their effects on the analysis and conclusions. For these reasons, I include comments on research method and data quality as I discuss examples in this chapter and draw comparisons between them.

THE SOUNDS OF INDIAN ENGLISH

Most scholars who explore the sound systems of particular Indian English codes orient their research around the contrasts between Indian English and standard English phonologies. I am going to follow this approach to organize the information in this section. That is, I am using these contrasts to pinpoint the sound segments and sequences used by speakers of particular Indian English codes and to identify characteristics of English pronunciation shared by speakers from different speech communities. These comparisons will show that, on the whole, sound systems of Indian English rearrange sound contrasts found in standard English usage, but contain very few sound segments that are completely alien to standard English phonology. The comparisons will also show that ancestral language sound systems may or may not predict the characteristic features of pronunciation for a community's Indian English codes.

Vowels

Vowels and vowel sequences found in Indian English varieties differ from those in standard English in at least two areas. First, standard English contrasts between front unrounded vowels and between some front and central unrounded vowels are not always maintained in Indian English. Fletcher (1983: 5) notes that four vowel segments in standard English—[ə] "c*u*t," [æ] "c*a*t," [e] "b*e*t," and [a] "f*a*ther" (that is, higher low, central unrounded; low front, unrounded; mid front unrounded; and low central unrounded)—are pronounced quite differently in many Indian English varieties because "each of the six pairwise combinations of these vowel phonemes fails to contrast in some American Indian language." Similarly, Cook and Sharp (1966) report that Navajo students will exchange [i] and [e], [iy] and [i], and [ey] for [e] (that is, high front vs. mid front; high front long vs. high front short; and mid front long vs. mid front short), particularly when the sounds in question occur in word-medial position. The Navajo language contains segments similar to [i] and [e] and also maintains a contrast similar to English [i] and [iy], so the reworking of the standard English distinctions in Navajo English is not "due to a lack of familiarity with a distinction between the sounds themselves," Cook and Sharp conclude (1966: 22).

TABLE 2.1   Selected Vowel Segments in Standard
and Isletan English

Example	Standard English	Isletan English
v*i*llage	[I]	[i]
pe*o*ple	[Ii]	[i]
h*i*s	[I]	[I]
pu*e*blo	[E]	[ɛ]
th*ey*	[EI]	[E:]
wh*e*re	[Eh]	[ɛ]

Source: (Leap, 1973:280–82)

Unlike the case in Navajo English, adult speakers of Isleta English regularly distinguish between these vowel segments. However, the contrasts they use when making those distinctions do not necessarily parallel those found in standard English, as the examples in table 2.1 suggest.

Penfield-Jasper (1977: 32) observed similar realignments of standard English vowel segments in the English of Mohave, Hopi, and Navajo students in Parker, Arizona (Colorado River Tribes), but found greater overall regularity in the correspondences between Indian English and standard English vocalics at this site than is attested in Isletan English data:

> The general configuration is that vowels shift, usually in the process of lowering. That is in all varieties of (Indian English) examined here, vowels shift at least one degree, usually lower, than their counterparts in standard English. These shifts do not always occur, but they occur often enough to make any particular variety of (Indian English) audibly distinct from (standard English). . . . The shifts are not always complete in the sense of moving from one phoneme to another, but seem to vary along a gradual scale between two positionally related vowel sounds.

In other words, and her observation applies to other varieties of Indian and non-Indian English as well, the pronunciation of any vowel segment varies, speaker by speaker and situation by situation; hence the symbols in Penfield-Jasper's transcriptions represent only the "mid-point values" within a range of vowel qualities and do not indicate the only phonetic quality the vowel in that word may receive.

Several of these examples—use of the same vowel for *his* and *he's* in Navajo English or for *village* vs. *people* in Isletan English—show that Indian English speakers also assign different values to the contrasts between "short" and "long" (or "lax" and "tense") vowel segments found in standard English. The merger of standard English contrasts between back unrounded vs. rounded vowels (e.g., Isletan English [u] for "wo*u*ld" and "comm*u*nity") and of other distinctions in vowel quantity also occur frequently in their English.

Not all Indian English codes show similar revisions in vowel quantities, however. Tsimshian English speakers lengthen vowel segments before voiced consonants (which commonly occurs in standard English) but also apply length to vowels before voiceless consonants as well. Jean Mulder (1982: 99–100) traces this "widening of the environment associated with this feature to the contrastive status which length has in the community's native language." What results is a new class of evironmentally lengthened vocalics, distinct from the vowel/semivowel sequences found elsewhere in English, as well as a new set of rules governing the assignment of vowel length in this English variety.

Kotzebue English is also characterized by a "nonappearance of some English diphthongs" (Vandergriff 1982: 143–47). Speakers pronounce *place* with [E], instead of [EI], and *I'll* with [a] rather than [ai]. Surrounding consonants may condition these changes in vowel quality, though Vandergriff holds that the close relationship between vowel length and stress found in Kotzebue Inupiaq is a more likely source for these segments. For example, he associates the presence of [ai] in *awhile*, but not in *I'll* in a Kotzebue English sentence like *I'll be waiting her for awhile* to the placement of primary stress within the overall sequence, suggesting that in a sentence with a different stress pattern, the lengthened medial vowel in *awhile* would also change. Apparently, Penfield-Jasper's (1977) references to "shift by degree" and "gradual scale" in Colorado River Tribes student English apply to conditions of vowel lengthening in Kotzebue English and, perhaps, to conditions in Tsimshian English as well.

Vowel systems in Indian English may also contain features not commonly reported in standard English usage, but which resemble vowel properties from the speakers' ancestral language tradition. In some cases (e.g., Keresan English "inserted [ə]" and Indian English "tone" constructions, as discussed below) these features add segments to the Indian English vowel inventory or reconfigure existing vowel patterns and syllable structures. In others, the additions merely complement and extend vowel contrasts already established within these codes.

Consonants

J. D. Fletcher notes (1983: 5–6) that the restrictions on occurrence of consonants and consonant clusters in word-final position, as well as the standard English contrasts between voiced and voiceless stops and between voiced and voiceless alveodental spirants (the **then** vs. **thin** distinction), receive quite different interpretations in Indian English codes. Indeed, almost every discussion of Indian English phonology I have found, regardless of the speakers' tribe or ancestral language background, reports evidence for at least one of these conditions within the study's database. Those studies also report evidence of the replacement of some consonant segments by other segments or of other reductions in the overall number of consonant segments and consonant contrasts.

Mulder's (1982: 100–101) description of the consonant inventory in Tsimshian English suggests the complex restructuring of the standard English consonant system that can emerge under these circumstances. In this variety of Indian English:

1. The labial fricatives [f] and [v] are sometimes realized as the labial stop [*b*] [blænk] "Frank," [baylət] "Violet." This substitution is much more frequent in personal names than in other areas of vocabulary.
2. The interdental fricatives [θ] and [ð] often occur as alveolar stops [t] and [d], respectively—[də] "the," and [nortlænd] "northland."
3. The voiced [z] is sometimes devoiced—[pi:s] "peas," [disayn] "design."
4. The liquid [r] is frequently realized as the lateral liquid [l]—[məli] "Mary" and [lut] "Ruth," or deleted—[mætə] "Martha." This substitution is also much more frequent in names than elsewhere.
5. The two affricates [č] and [ǰ] are generally pronounced as [ts] and [dz], respectively—[tsikn] "chicken" and [dzi:n] "Jean."
6. The voiceless alveopalatal fricative [š] is almost always pronounced as [s]—[fɪs] "fish," [su] "shoe."
7. The voiced alveopalatal fricative [z] sometimes occurs as [s]—[visn] "vision" and [mesə] "measure."
8. The velar nasal [ŋ] generally is realized as [ŋ], but occasionally it is realized as [n]—[θiŋkin]. This substitution generally occurs at a syllable boundary.

Mulder's wording suggests that these changes in the standard English consonant inventory are not binding on all Tsimshian English speakers. We do not know, from her description, whether the variation is influenced by speech setting, by speaker background, or by grammatical environment. But her comments suggest that Penfield-Jasper's reference to "gradual scale" and "shift by degree" may also be relevant to consonant phonology in this Indian English variety.

In most of these cases, Mulder explains, the consonants at issue in this restructuring of standard English phonology have no counterpart in the sound system of the community ancestral language (Sm'algyax). This situation prompts speakers to substitute a (more familiar) phoneme from Sm'algyax for the "missing" sound. Many of these substitutions and other modifications in this listing are also attested in the varieties of Indian English used at other sites, so ancestral language phonology may not be the only source for the Tsimshian English consonant pattern.

For some Indian English varieties, ancestral language phonology may have no effect on such restructuring at all. According to Alford (1974), for example, Cheyenne English speakers realize the standard English word initial [θ]/[ð] contrast by substituting the corresponding stop segments, yielding *dem* for "them" and *tin* for "thin." As in Tsimshian, Cheyenne does not have a [θ]/[ð] contrast in its consonant inventory; and while it has a *t* (voiceless alveolar stop), there is no corresponding *d* segment. Without making elaborate claims about Cheyenne-to-English structural analogy and back-formation, Cheyenne phonology cannot be the source for the Cheyenne English speakers' [*t*]/[*d*] contrast.

Nasal consonants, resonants, and laterals often receive special treatment in Indian English phonology. Speakers of some varieties interchange [*m*], [*n*], and [ŋ] in specific words and phrases (e.g., the use of [*m*] or [ŋ] in place of [*n*] in Northern Ute "sandwich") or in all environments; others use one of these sounds as a "cover segment" and eliminate the three-way nasal contrast altogether and may extend that segment to replace occurrences of *r* and *l*.

Cook and Sharp (1966: 23) report that some Navajo English speakers give "ma'am" as *mæn* and "bring" as *briin* (with a lengthened, tensed vowel rather than a vowel-semivowel sequence receiving nasalization from the following sequence.) Alford (1974: 5) notes the absence of [ŋ] in Cheyenne English leads speakers to intensify contrasts in vowel quantity, so that words like *singer* (given in Cheyenne English as *siynɚ*) are still distinguishable from words like *sinner* (*sInɚ*). In addition to the *samwič*/*saŋwič* usage just cited, speakers of Northern Ute English substitute [*n*] for [*l*] (hence *wank*, and sometimes *want*, for "walk").

To conclude this discussion of Indian English consonants, I need to mention instances where speakers use sound segments that are not commonly found in English language settings but that resemble items found in ancestral language phonology. Usually, these segments create additional contrasts within the consonant inventory of the Indian English variety, though their presence may also influence the code's sound system in other ways.

Glottal stops—a pause or "catch" in the speech flow created by a rapid closing and opening of the covering over the voice box (the glottis) is a sound segment whose presence in Indian English is particularly interesting. Speakers of some regional dialects of (non-Indian) English use glottal stops in place of [*t*] or [*d*] in word-medial position, but even then, the occurrence of that segment in ordinary conversation is quite limited. Cook and Sharp (1966: 25) and Alford

(1974: 6) note the presence of glottal stops in Navajo English and Cheyenne English. Their comments suggest that speakers of these codes regularly use glottal segments in the following environments:

- when the corresponding standard English word or phrase has word-medial [t] or [d];
- in syllable-final position before an internal juncture; or
- as an onset or augment before a word-initial vowel.

For Cheyenne English, such usage results in sentence constructions like *Floy'ha' on a re' ha'* (Alford 1974: 6), which sound "choppy" and "syncopated" to non-Indian listeners and reinforce negative conclusions about other areas of the speaker's English skills.

Pitch, Stress, and Juncture

Scholars have not paid much attention to the suprasegmental features of Indian English. However, the limited information available shows that these features contribute substantially to contrasts with standard English—and to contrasts that distinguish Indian English codes from different tribal communities.

Penfield-Jasper's (1977) comparisons of Mohave, Hopi, and Navajo English phonologies show how each of these varieties has a different set of rules governing stress placement and note that listeners use differences in stress placement to help them identify an Indian English speaker's tribal background. Accordingly, she links variety-specific stress placements at this site to the influence of stress assignment rules in the speakers' ancestral language tradition. But the unique properties of Indian English suprasegmentals are not necessarily a result of Indian language "interference," as Steven Stout shows in his (1977) study of stress placement in Keres English from Santa Ana pueblo, New Mexico.

Stout identifies two stress qualities in Santa Ana English (SAE), primary and weak, and notes the close relationship between the placement of primary stress and the location of an internal juncture: primary stress occurs on the first vowel following major junctures (marked with / and # in his transcriptions.) Once placed in that position, stress may (variably) then be back-copied to the last vowel preceding that juncture, provided at least one weak-stressed vowel separates that vowel from any other preceding vowel with primary stress.

Under these rules, the SAE equivalent of a standard English sequence like *Yes, Steve, we do* is:

[... # yéys + ə + stív / wíy / dÚ # ...]

where the vowel segments of [yɛys], [wiy], and [dU] receive primary stress because of their location after the [/] juncture, and [stiv] receives primary stress due to back-copying.

Once SAE speakers assign primary stress according to these rules, stress quality then conditions several other features. For one thing, the assignment of pitch in SAE follows the pattern established by stress contrasts: "high" pitch coincides with primary stress, "lower" pitch with weak stress. Under this arrangement, there can be many more pitch contrasts per sentence than there are in standard English, though pitch contours also have briefer duration in this code.

There is a stress-governed alternation between vowel segments, such that one segment (e.g., [i, u, æ, a, ɨ]) occurs under primary stress and a related segment, lower in tongue height than its counterpart (e.g., [i, U, Æ, ɔ, ə]), occurs in places where weak stress is otherwise assigned. ([E] and [o] do not participate in this alternation, because of the amount of surface-level variation that other SAE rules associate with these segments.) As a result, a speaker's pronunciation of the same word may show considerable variation, in vowel quality and in other areas, from one occurrence to the next.

The rules of SAE stress placement have an additional effect on the sound pattern of this English variety: note the presence of the [ə] in the sentence cited above. Since the [ə] segment occurs with weak stress, [ə] rather than [ɨ] is the appropriate phonetic quality for this vowel. [ə] makes no contribution to sentence reference in this case, though its presence does contribute to the non-Indian English speakers' belief that SAE speakers "hesitate," are "unsure of their words," or "are reluctant to express themselves" when speaking in English.

The occurrence of a [ə] in this position is anything but arbitrary and certainly does not reflect any weakness in the speaker's English skill. The segment occurs at the point in the sentence where a weak stress must occur, before primary stress can be back-copied from [wiy] to [stiv]. Apparently, while the back-copying process is dependent on weak-stress placement for its occurrence in some areas of SAE surface structure, back-copying can also become the incentive for weak-stress placement in other surface structures.

The SAE rules of stress/pitch assignment are quite unlike those governing similar phenomena in other English varieties, and this raises the possibility of an ancestral language basis for these rules. Published descriptions of Keresan grammar do refer to a close relationship between stress and pitch (Davies 1964: 63; Miller 1965: 17–18). What scholars say about these phenomena bears little resemblance to Stout's analysis. Moreover, while there is vowel harmony in Keres grammar, neither proximity to word-boundary nor associated suprasegmental features affect the alternations of vowel-pairs, in the sense reported for

SAE. And back-copying of primary stress across internal junctures is not attested in Keres grammar at all.

There may be ancestral language influence contributing to SAE stress/ pitch assignment, but it appears doubtful, from the evidence, that Keresan grammar should be considered the primary source for these details.

While the reports are not extensive, comments that scholars have made about pitch-juncture (hereafter, intonation) contours suggest that these features can also be a source of code-specific contrast. Penfield-Jasper (1977: 34–45) found little difference in the intonation contours from her Mohave, Hopi, and Navajo English samples, though the overall contrasts with standard English intonation (and with intonation in Keres English, in the sense just described) were quite vivid:

> [Intonation contours are] more level with fewer pitch changes than in standard English. . . . Most conspicuous was the absence of standard English question intonation patterns. In three of the four questions [used to elicit data from] the sample, Indian English pitch was heard either as level or dropping, never with the rising pitch common to standard English.

I infer that Indian English intonation contours are generally somewhat distinct from those of standard English, given the observations of non-Indians that Indian English speakers talk in subdued tones, show little expression or emotion in their voices, speak in a monotone, or speak in a singsong voice. Non-Indian schoolteachers make these comments, and so do others who interact regularly with Indian English speakers in contexts characterized by unequal distributions of power. There is overlap, and possibly reinforcement, here with the rules of verbal etiquette that structure discourse in these settings; the interplay of phonology and pragmatics here has not been examined, to my knowledge, in any study of Indian English intonation.

"Tone" in Indian English

Tone contrasts—instances where pitch values become assigned to particular vowels and vowel clusters and not to more inclusive suprasegmental contours—occur in many American Indian languages; accordingly, the possibility that tone in some way becomes integrated into Indian English phonological structure needs to be explored. To my knowledge, no scholar has reported evidence of such phenomena in the English of any tribe. (Whether scholars have looked for evidence of tone in Indian English is another matter entirely.)

Penfield-Jasper comments that non-Indians often find Indian English to have a monotonous melodic quality; how tone contrasts might contribute to this impression remains to be explored.

WORD AND SENTENCE STRUCTURES

Noun Inflections

Noun inflections in Indian English characteristically differ from those found in standard English usage in two ways: a lower frequency of plural and possessive suffix marking than found in other English codes and the indication of plural and possessive references through word combinations and other constructions.[1]

Mary Rita Miller (1977: 86), for instance, reports that among eleven-year-old Pima Indians, "no allomorph of the plural is more than 50% operational. While the /z/ and /s/ allomorphs appear at that age at about the same proportion, Pima children of eleven used the /z/ allomorph of the plural only 13% of the time." The non-Indian children in her comparison sample were already showing complete mastery of English plural inflections by age eight. Beverley Olson Flannigan (1984a) gives examples of "deletion *or double marking*" of plural nouns in Pine Ridge/Rosebud (Lakota) English:

> *You find some other, two different thing, each one ...*
> *Here is a worksheet, one of the worksheet ...*
> *Sometimes it's almost 500 dancers, man and women together.*
> *There's two way of talking.*
> *One of that word is ...*

These show that Lakota English speakers use number-words, as well as the standard English suffix, to indicate plural reference for the modified noun.

Similar constructions regularly occur in other varieties of nonstandard English and in the "errors" of persons learning English as a second language; they can also be part of the regular development of a speaker's first-language English fluency, as Miller's comments imply. But there is reason to believe that influence from ancestral language tradition may also contribute to the occurrence of these constructions—at least in some Indian English settings.

First, the combinations of word-final consonants that mark plural and possession on English nouns may involve consonant segments or clusters that do not regularly occur in those positions in ancestral language sentences. Miller

(1977: 87) sees evidence of such Pima language phonology in the plural marking patterns of Pima student English reported above. Similarly, as I explain in chapter 3, some of the restrictions on plural-related, final-position consonant clusters in Isletan English resemble the restrictions that Isletan Tiwa grammar places on its final-position consonants.

Second, the process of noun inflection in American Indian languages is much more complex than in English, because these constructions indicate noun class membership, subject/object relationships, and other details of reference and sentence function. Number and possession may be indicated in those constructions or represented through entirely different means. The use of number-words, rather than suffixes, to indicate plural reference in Flannigan's Lakota English sentences can be explained in terms of these parallels. In San Juan pueblo English "for nouns preceded by a quantifier, as in *four books* or *many chairs*, the frequency for plural absence was higher than for other nouns; however, when the noun is a measure noun, such as *dollars*, *weeks*, or *inches*, the rate was lower" (Wolfram et al. 1979: 283). Number-marking options in San Juan Tewa grammar are closely tied to the noun class system, which distinguishes nouns of similar composition (e.g., unique structures, organized sets, unformed aggregates) from nouns that are differently composed. The patterning in Wolfram et al.'s data suggests that number-marking in San Juan English allows speakers to classify English nouns along similar lines.

Distinctions between "Mass" and "Count" Nouns

Indian English speakers, regardless of language background, add plural markers to mass nouns—*alphabets, furnitures, homeworks*—or use count nouns without an accompanying plural marker. Since I have just discussed some of the conditions surrounding absence of plural marking, I focus the comments in this section on "mass" noun constructions.

Pat Kwachka (1988) has explored in some detail the treatment of these constructions in Koyukon English. Data from the speech samples she collected show that Koyukon English speakers recognize the difference between "mass" and "count" nouns and place plural markers on 9% of "mass nouns" they use in daily conversation. Importantly, the mass nouns in that "marked" category are largely the same for all speakers:

> Because these nouns are everyday vocabulary (e.g. furniture/furnitures, home-
> work/homeworks) their appearance is frequently and therefore perceptually
> salient. This salience may explain the false impression that the mass/count noun

distinction has not been incorporated into the L(ocal) E(nglish) grammar. However, since mass nouns are classified as such 91% of the time, and the 9% core also appears stable, it is probable that many of the latter group are becoming permanently reclassified as "count" nouns. This reclassification is by no means limited to [speakers of] Middle Yukon English; even [non-Indian] teachers have been overheard assigning "homeworks."

(Kwachka 1988: 28)

It is possible that the something like "local restructuring" of the "mass"/"count" noun distinction Kwachka describes may also be unfolding in other Indian English speech communities; scholars may note the presence of the "mass" noun "problem" in other speech communities, but I am not aware of studies exploring this feature in any detail at other locales. Kwachka's explanation for the stereotypes associated with this usages in the Koyukon area is certainly worth exploring in that regard.

Articles and Demonstratives

Indian English speakers use articles and demonstrative pronouns quite differently from standard English speakers. For some Indian English speakers, articles simply do not occur in noun-based English constructions—for example, Navajo English *They find bone in deep yard* or *He asked shopkeeper for sheep* (Cook and Sharp 1966: 25). Developmental errors may be the cause of these constructions, but influences from other sources may also be relevant here. Such deletions often occur, for example, when there are no elements comparable to the English article in the speakers' ancestral language, though other rules from ancestral language tradition may encourage article deletion in Indian English even when similar elements regularly occur in that tradition.

Speakers of Northern Ute English, for example, are more likely to delete articles from their English noun constructions if the noun occurs in the sentence predicate, and much less likely to do so if the noun is in subject position and identifies the sentence's primary actor (or agent). The standard English definite article the is the item most likely to be deleted or retained under this pattern.

There are no "articles," as such, in the ancestral language of this speech community; however, there is a noun-related linguistic process—*topicalization*—whose similarity to definite article constructions in standard English is worth examining.

Topicalization is the linguistic process that identifies the focus of discussion in a given sentence. Usually topicalization involves movement of the item indicating that focus to the front of the sentence; affixes or other support material may also be added to the item, to indicate its special function in the sentence.

Sentence subjects are regularly topicalized in Northern Ute grammar, especially when the subject noun specifies the sentence agent. The topicalization marker occurs at the end of the construction being identified in these terms; and the construction may be relocated to the beginning of the sentence, though this movement is not obligatory. (Variable use of this option is one of many points of speaker-level diversity found throughout Northern Ute discourse, as explained in the speech community profile in chapter 1.)

There are also ways to topicalize the noun that functions as sentence object in Ute, but doing so, especially in the presence of an identified agent, reconfigures sentence reference as a whole (in a fashion comparable to passive/ergative references in other languages) and calls for additional changes in grammatical structure. And the grammatical marker indicating topicalization in this case has a different form from the marker indicating subject/agent topicalization.

The syntax of definite article placement/deletion in Ute English coincides with Ute language topicalization structures in at least two ways. First, the Ute English contrast between subject article retention and predicate article deletion allows speakers to maintain Ute language preference for subject-topic over object-topic sentence constructions in their English conversations. This contrast also lets speakers distinguish in formal terms between subject-topic references and object references in Ute English sentence structure, just as is the case in Ute language sentences. These similarities make it important to examine closely the meaning of Ute English sentences where object nouns *retain* definite article marking, as I will do below.

Demonstrative usage in Indian English also reflects a range of grammatical functions and influences that are not always relevant to standard English grammar. In cases where ancestral language tradition requires formal indication of the distance (spatial, temporal, or social) between speakers and the persons, objects, or actions that they are discussing, the form of the English demonstrative may supply similar cues in Indian English settings, redefining the contrasts otherwise associated with the English *this/that* distinction. Such is the case in Isletan English, where speakers intensify stress/pitch assigned to the demonstrative, to indicate particularly close (*this*) or distant (*that*) relationship to topic reference. Isletan Tiwa grammar provides distinct lexical items to indicate these contrasts; shifts in suprasegmental patterns do not occur.

Indian English demonstratives may also introduce points of reference that have no correlate in English language tradition at all. Marie-Lucie Tarpent

(1982) and Jean Mulder (1982: 104–5) account for Tsimshian English *them* constructions in these terms, in sentences like:

> *Beatrice is by them, Joanne's.*
>   (Mulder, 1982: 104)
> *Don't play with them John.*
> *Them Fred's having a party tonight.*
>   (Tarpent 1982: 118)

As Tarpent points out, the speakers' use of *them* in such sentences parallels the occurrence of the plural marker *dim* in Tsimshian, which, when used in combination with a proper noun (e.g., *dim Fred*), indicates reference to the named individual and to others who commonly associate with that individual. Hence the Tsimshian English sequence *them Fred* could refer to a fishing crew (*What time **them Fred** leave the harbor?*), students in a school classroom (***Them Fred** alway sits in the back of the room, causing trouble*), or members of a particular household (***Them Fred's** having a party tonight*). Features of context and topic already established in the conversation cue the listener to the particular type of social relationship *them Fred* usage is designed to convey.

Tarpent also notes that younger speakers of Tsimshian English consider these sequences to have singular reference, rather than plural or collective ones. For the most part, these are not speakers of their ancestral language and are letting the number marker of the noun override the implicit reference to number in the case marking on the determiner. Because of their familiarity with the ancestral language, older speakers of Tsimshian English treat *them Fred* as a collective plural reference, though doing this adds a new, demonstrative-like function to the list of functions associated with the third person plural English pronoun in this English variety.

Wolfram and Christian (1979a: 156) found sequences containing *this* followed by a plural noun in the English of San Juan pueblo:

> *This worms, they get into your body.*
> *It's about this Indians.*
> *this modern homes*
> *one of this days*

Faced with similar constructions in Isletan English, I argued that the nouns in these constructions identify items that are part of a structured set, not items that exist independently and are only arbitrarily connected. Isletan Tiwa grammar assigns noun references with such a focus to a particular category within its noun class system and marks nouns within that category accordingly. Other languages in the Tanoan language family, including San Juan Tewa, make similar distinctions in their noun class systems. So I interpret the San Juan English *this* + *NOUN* constructions in those terms.

Wolfram and Christian suggest that the phonological details of the demonstrative modifier should not be overlooked in this analysis. Speakers of San Juan English regularly devoice final-position voiced consonants of standard English and merge standard English high front tense and lax vowels ([i] and [I]) into a single sound segment. Under these conditions, speakers pronounce *this* and *these* (phonetically, ([ðɪs] and [ðiz] in standard English) as [ðɪs]—which is the pronunciation they give to the *this* demonstrative in the examples just cited. So it is possible that such constructions "should be viewed as lexical merger derived through a phonological process rather than as an underlying grammatical difference" (Wolfram and Christian 1979a: 156). Another reading of these data is also possible: the clear evidence of phonological merger within these constructions makes it unlikely that ancestral language lexical contrasts is the only cause, or the primary cause, for these sequences.

Pronouns and Pronominal Constructions: Pronoun Deletion and Gender Marking

Many of the characteristics associated with Indian English pronoun constructions resemble conditions already described for noun and determiner usage in these codes. Particularly significant in this regard is the absence of pronoun forms in constructions where standard English grammar requires them. Evidence of deletion shows up in every variety of Indian English for which documentation is now available. Importantly, however, pronoun deletion does not occur in all sentence environments, and the conditions specifying the locations favoring deletion are not the same in all codes.

Penfield-Jasper has examined these details as they apply to Mohave English grammar (1980: 73), and I am going to look carefully at her analysis below. Before doing so, I need to make some preliminary comments about pronoun-related gender marking in Indian English.

Indian English varieties do not always maintain the standard English gender distinctions indicated by the third person singular personal pronouns (*he*, *she*, *it*). As a result, gender and number features associated with a speaker's choice of subject or object pronoun do not always correspond with the gender and number features of its antecedent. Such "errors" occurred so frequently in Penfield-Jasper's Mohave English data that she decided to create a set of paper-and-pencil tasks to help her identify the grammatical rules influencing their formation. Her data show that gender/number errors are most likely to occur in Mohave English sentences such as: ——— *likes her, but she doesn't like him*, where the sentence meaning remains ambiguous even after the speaker resolves questions of pronoun gender and number through pronoun choice. In addition, Penfield-Jasper found that other speakers of English (Indian as well as non-Indian) at this site were more likely to use pronouns whose gender reference did not correspond to that of the antecedent noun when those pronouns occurred in constructions at the end of the clause, and much less likely to make such errors when choosing pronouns for clause-initial position; Mohave English speakers use pronouns with noncompatible gender just as frequently in those locations.

Apparently, syntactic constraints are not as important to pronoun-based gender marking in Mohave English variety as they are in other varieties of English used within the same community. Penfield-Jasper does not identify the factors that *do* influence gender-marking patterns for Mohave English speakers. In other settings, scholars have found the treatment of grammatical gender within the speaker's ancestral language tradition to be influential in this regard.

Alford (1974: 6–7) has discussed this issue for Cheyenne English in some detail. As he notes, Cheyenne English speakers are not so much confused by English gender labeling as they are more accustomed to highlighting other features of noun reference in their sentences (e.g., references to living things, things that are sacred, things to which Cheyenne culture assigns other special properties). The gender of the referent, in the sense of the English language-based distinctions in biological sex, is not a relevant descriptive feature under such circumstances,[2] nor is it relevant to the description of nouns in Cheyenne English. Inconsistent ties between pronoun gender and noun referent are an expectable speaker behavior under such circumstances, he concludes.

Alford's claims suggest several ways to interpret the "irregularities" of pronoun-gender in Mohave English. Grammatical gender is an irrelevant factor in the classification of nouns in the Mohave language, much as it is in Cheyenne. In fact, for third person references, neither the verb-related pronominal prefix (Ø) *nor the independent pronoun (n^{y}a)* indicates male/female/neuter contrasts. Learning the gender-marking rules of standard English obligates the Mohave English speaker to master an entirely new principle of reference contrast, something that is largely without contextual support within the speech community's ancestral language tradition.

Alford (1974: 6) identifies a second source for Cheyenne English gender/number-based pronoun "errors." Pronoun markers in Cheyenne (as is the case in other American Indian languages) are verb-related, verb-dominated syntactic categories, so their occurrence in sentence constructions is closely tied to the details of the sentence verb. This arrangement is quite different from English, where pronoun usage is more closely tied to the sentence's nominal constructions. Hence, what appear to be irregularities in Cheyenne English gender marking and other features of pronoun usage may reflect speaker attempts to integrate the "verb-based" pronominal system from ancestral language grammar into English usage.

It is possible that verb-centered constructions may be affecting pronoun-related gender marking in Mohave English, as well. But verb-related syntax is much more strongly evidenced in another characteristic of pronoun usage in this English variety: pronoun deletion.

Penfield-Jasper (1980: 86) noticed at the beginning of her research that Mohave English speakers deleted pronouns from some areas of sentence constructions, but not from others; for example, she found some occurrences of object pronoun deletion in her corpus: *They just put ——— between your teeth.* But the most frequent occurrence of pronoun deletion in this English variety involved subject pronouns, not object markers: Speakers consistently deleted subject pronouns whether they occurred in initial position in English sentences, after initial modifiers, or at the head of a dependent clause located elsewhere in the sentence (Penfield-Jasper 1980: 86):

[ ] shot himself.
But then [ ] woke him up.
There's not many girls [ ] are playing.

(Note: [ ] denotes the location of a deleted pronoun.) Moreover, as long as listeners could establish pronoun referents through contextual details and other clues, Mohave English speakers regularly carried out multiple deletions of subject pronouns within the same complex sentence. Hence her example (1980: 137): *I didn't know it either, [ ] was playing, playing, til the bell rung, [ ] open my book and felt my pocket; [ ] wasn't in there*, where listener inference easily reconstructs the distinction between *I* and *it* references, even though the pronoun forms do not occur, as such, in surface structure.

Penfield-Jasper offers several explanations for this deletion pattern:

○ Mohave English equi-deletion, which allows the second (or additional) occurrence of the same noun or pronoun within the same sentence to be deleted;

○ less stringent pronoun-marking conventions permitted in casual English speech (something not unique to Mohave English, of course); and o the Mohave language grammatical rule that forms "headless" subordinate clauses when contextual details specify the identity of the subject and (in the sense of Alford's argument) the verb affix links the (now-implied) subject to the specifics of the sentence action.

All of these details are relevant to Mohave English subject-pronoun deletion, but I think that a fourth issue—case marking—has greater influence in this regard. Mohave grammar uses case marking to identify, and distinguish between, the functions of the noun constructions in each sentence. Subject pronouns belong to a syntactically more "marked" category in the grammars of most languages, which makes them especially vulnerable to such deletion, and object pronouns (being in the most "neutral" of all cases) much less vulnerable. By assuming that something similar to this constraint is also present in Mohave English, I can account for all of the characteristics of pronoun deletion that Penfield-Jasper identified in this English code, and I can explain why subject pronouns are particularly vulnerable under those rules.

Of course, case distinctions apply throughout sentence structure; they are not applied solely to constructions at the beginning of the sentence. If case is a relevant category in Mohave English syntax, the influence of case marking helps explain why pronoun deletion (and, particularly, subject pronoun deletion) shows up throughout Mohave English sentence structures, unlike the more positionally restricted occurrences of such deletions in the other forms of English used at this site.

Ute student English also contains instances of pronoun deletion; as in Mohave English, subject pronouns are by far the most frequently deleted items within this category, while object pronouns are almost never deleted. However, Ute English speakers use pronoun deletion only after a series of constraints have been satisfied, and none of these are attested for Mohave English, such as:

o the pronoun must precede an AUX-main verb sequence, not just a main verb with AUX suffix;[3]
o the AUX must identify aspect of the verb action, and not just serve tense-marking function (e.g., pronoun deletion is more likely before *modal*-main verb sequences than inflected *BE* or *HAVE* constructions);
o the AUX must otherwise be eligible for contraction or deletion.

When those conditions are met, if AUX is contracted or deleted, then the pronoun standing before AUX may be (but not necessarily will be) deleted.

In other words, while pronoun deletion in Mohave English can be linked directly to case-marking principles, seemingly equivalent usage in Ute English is the result of entirely different grammatical processes—Ute English AUX marking and AUX deletion.

Tense/Aspect Marking

Tense/aspect marking in Indian English grammars is usually quite different from that found in standard English. Frequently reported points of contrast include the following:

- o absence of inflectional endings on simple verbs, verbal participles, and auxiliaries;
- o verb constructions with "past tense" inflections in contexts where "present tense" reference can otherwise be inferred;
- o absence of third person present tense suffix (-Z) in present tense contexts; or, extension of -Z to include all present tense verb forms;
- o extension of past tense suffix (-D) to mark the past tense references for irregular as well as regular verbs;
- o deletion of AUX in complex/periphrastic verb constructions.

Developmental factors and "errors" in second-language acquisition may account for individual items in this list; but other sources for these patterns are also relevant here, particularly the influence of tense/aspect distinctions not commonly associated with standard English grammar.

In Isletan English, for example, tense/aspect marking centers around a contrast between *delimited*, *distributive*, and *continuous* references. Delimited references identify actions that occur only within a particular, definable time

---

EXAMPLE 2.1   VERB-REFERENCE CONTRASTS IN ISLETAN ENGLISH

---

1. *The girl **run** up to me and she **said**: . . .*
   (distributive)   (delimited)

2. *So him and his boys **come** over and **asked** them what they are **doin'**.*
   (distributive)   (delimited)   (continuous)

3. *Well, I guess he **go** to the prarie dog and he **asked** for medicine.*
   (distributive)   (delimited)

4. *She **get** after us that we **were going** to turn into snake.*
   (distributive)   (continuous)

5. *He **went** out to hunt and when night **come** he **howl** again; he **start** the*
   (delimited)   (distributive)   (distributive)
   same thing again.

6. *And you [ ] **talkin'** about just one pine tree.*
   (continuous)

7. *They just, they just [ ] **goin'** by the old ways, yet.*
   (continuous)

---

frame and will not be repeated, as such, once the time frame has come to an end. Distributive references, similar to those found in Black English vernacular (see, for example, Fasold 1969), identify activities that occur only during particular periods, but can occur within any number of such periods. Continuous references, in contrast, play out without any temporal restriction or interruption.

The sentences in example 2.1 show how these contrasts are marked in Isletan English sentences. Each tense/aspect distinction assigns a different form to the sentence verb. Delimited verb references take the tense/aspect suffixes found in other English varieties; as elsewhere, the speaker's choice of suffix attached to the verb base indicates the particular location of the reference in space and time. Not always clear from such usage is the idea that actions so described constitute individually unique events and, once completed, are not expected to occur a second time. The first verb in sentence 5 is one such example. This sentence comes from a longer narrative in which the speaker describes how his new dog behaved on a recent hunting trip. The story-line made clear that the dog had not been hunting before; he was, however, familiar with howling during the evening hours. The speaker accordingly chose verb forms in this sentence to reflect this difference in reference.

Distributive verbs (as shown in the pairings of verb references in sentences 1, 2, 3, and 4, in example 2.1) contain no tense/aspect suffixes in their structures. If the action occurred across some earlier points in time, and has now come to an end, the speaker can add an appropriately focused temporal adverb or an inflected helping verb to the uninflected main verb. Otherwise, and particularly for actions distributed within the period adjacent to the given discourse (as in the examples above), only an uninflected verb base is required. Under this system, speakers use similar verb constructions to designate actions having duration from "recent past" into "present" or from "present" into "immediate future"; compare the meanings of the distributive verbs in sentences 3 and 4. This is another component of Isletan English tense/aspect that is not always clear to outsiders.

Continuous verb references contain a verb base and *-ing* suffix. When additional comments about the position of the activity in space/time are needed, speakers add the appropriate helping verb or one or more temporal adverbs to this construction. Deletion of inflected forms of the verb *BE* occurs in Isletan English, subject to conditions similar to those in Black English and other nonstandard English codes. Sentences like 6 and 7 (example 2.1) are the result of such deletion; contextual details identify the particulars of time reference in such instances.

The tense/aspect system of Cheyenne English (Alford 1974: 6) is organized quite differently from Isletan English. Central in this case is a distinction between manifest and nonmanifest actions, paralleling the animate/inanimate contrast associated with Cheyenne English noun reference and pronoun-based gender marking. When applied to verbs, this distinction reworks the standard English contrast between past and nonpast references, so that the "past," "present," and "future" references that the speaker considers to be concrete, substantive, or otherwise a part of "real" experience fall within one category—usually marked with some form of the -D suffix—while the "past," "present," and "future" references that are speculative, hypothetical, or otherwise *irrealis*-based fall into a second category—usually designated by an uninflected verb. Instances where "past tense" constructions show up in "present tense" reference contexts or "present tense" constructions in "past tense" contexts, are unavoidable under such circumstances, particularly if individual speakers assess the relationship between surface-level morphemics and underlying tense/aspect features in different terms.

Kotzebue English (Vandergriff 1982: 130–38) organizes tense/aspect references by measuring the *completedness* of a given activity. At issue are a series of graded distinctions between references to more continuous, long-term actions and references to more time-restricted actions. Importantly (and unlike both Isletan English and Black English vernaculars) action distributed intermittently within an open-ended period is not highlighted in any way in this system, though actions that occur throughout a specified period can be distinguished from those occurring at a single point in time: *We stayed in Kotzebue for a few days; then we start coming up the Noatak River.* (Hall 1975: 52, cited in Vandergriff 1982: 136). Both of the activities identified in this sentence are "past tense" based, but each had its own duration within past tense reference, as the difference in verb forms suggests. That distinction is then reinforced by the use of the adverbial phrase (*for a few days*) to specify action of longer duration, and the choice of the modal *start* to indicate the beginning of the action that then replaced it.

Not all sentences in Kotzebue English indicate the time frame of action so explicitly. Sentence verbs may occur without inflection to show activities that take place in the past or in the present. Consequently, without contextual cues or other supporting material being added to surface structure, the listener cannot determine the time of action for sentences like: *Leo catch a tomcod* or *He go Norvick* (Vandergriff 1982: 136). However, the listener can determine that the actions in both instances were relatively brief and self-contained; had they been otherwise, the speakers would have included a durative (*always*), inceptive (*start*), conditional (*gonna*), or other modal to index the precise degree of completedness for each reference.

Vandergriff traces these and other features of the Kotzebue English tense/aspect system to an underlying creole language base—a claim that created considerable controversy among researchers in Alaska: see Kwachka's comments (1988: 4)—with additional influences from Inupiaq verb semantics. Bartelt (1982b) traces the tense/aspect features in Apachean English to a similar combination of creole base and Indian language overlay,[4] though the tense/aspect distinctions he finds in these Indian English varieties and the effects of post-creolization on surface forms are quite different from those described for the Kotzebue community.

At issue in Bartelt's description of Apachean English is a three-way contrast:

o action that does not occur before other activities described in the discourse;
o action with duration, occurring before or after the time of the main discourse event; and
o action that has not yet begun.

The latter category includes all references to *irrealis* conditions, regardless of their position in time vis-à-vis the ongoing discourse. Uninflected verb bases, base combined with *-ing* (without helping verb), and combinations of *will/might*, verb base, and *-ing* are the markers speakers use to indicate these distinctions in Apache English sentences.

This three-way contrast intersects with the tense/aspect constraints found in standard English grammar to yield Apachean English verb constructions such as:

1. *Borrowing money and give it to them because they help her a lot when she was sick.*

2. *But he keep on going until he got to the top of the hill.*

3. *After we eat all the goodies, we wanted to eat something. Just turn around there is a refrigerator.*

4. *I live by the beliefs that coming from both the Navajo culture and christianity.*

5. *Here we shopping and went through the town to see things and places.*

6. *Then he will looking forward to the day when he will finish.*

7. *I will becoming a leader the people will be helping by me.*

(Bartelt 1982b: 73, 74, 76, 77)

Examples 1, 2, and 3 are particularly important for this discussion, in that they show how Apachean English uninflected "anterior" references overlap with "past" tense as well as "present" tense distinctions in standard English grammar. As Bartelt (1982b: 72–73) explains, drawing connections with Derek Bickerton's (1975) analysis of similar constructions from Guayanese Creole:

> The Apachean English data seem to show that for many subjects a zero form of the verb marks simple past. In Guayanese, Bickerton (1975) found zero stem forms of active verbs to mean a single action in the past which does not predate any action simultaneously under discussion. With stative verbs, however, the zero stem form signifies non-past. Or, to put it more appropriately, non-anterior is realized as a zero form everywhere, but if one tries to translate this into standard English terms it looks as if the non-anterior zero form means past with actives and non-past with statives (Bickerton, personal communication). Thus, a simple past action and a non-past state form a single non-anterior tense since neither one antedates the main discourse topic under discussion.

For a final example of Indian English tense/aspect distinctions, consider the constraints underlying these contrasts in Northern Ute English. In most cases, speakers of this Indian English variety make tense and aspect references similar to those found in standard English settings. There are, however, two contexts where alternatives to standard usage regularly emerge.

First, speakers use a verb base without inflection or AUX support to indicate instances where action is not restricted to a single point in time. This includes constructions similar to the Isletan English distributive references as well as those resembling Isletan English stative references, since the verb action in those cases—*He always eat more than he should*—cannot be localized in past or present tense contexts exclusively. In this way, Ute English uninflected verb references are quite different from those associated with structurally similar constructions in Apachean English and Kotzebue English.

Ute English speakers' second departure from standard English-based verb structures does not involve time references at all. Instead, it is closely associated with a particular structural constraint that duplicates quite closely the constraints governing tense/aspect marking in Ute language tradition. Tense/aspect markers occur in two positions in that language: suffixed to the verb or combined with pronominal prefixes and other material as part of a syntactically independent AUX construction. Importantly, however, only one of these options—that is, tense marking on the verb or in the AUX, but not in both positions—applies to each clause.

The Ute English equivalent of this rule is evident in two contexts. First, Ute English negated verbs are usually not inflected for any tense/aspect property other than negation, regardless of the time frame of the commentary. (Negation in Ute is an independent element within verb "aspect," and Ute English maintains this principle.) Second, perfective constructions and other English language "helping verb–main verb" sequences usually have tense inflections on the AUX, combined with an uninflected main verb or tense inflection on the main verb and uninflected AUX (and, accordingly, AUX deletion).

Both of these conditions prompt instances in Ute English where the main verb occurs in an uninflected form in the surface structure. Importantly, such constructions do not identify references to distributive action, as they do in Isletan English; nor do they comment on the extent or duration of specified activity in space and time, as is the case for comparable constructions in Kotzebue English. Ute English verb constructions in this form are the result of a general rule restructuring the form that tense marking can take in this English variety; they do not express any single notion of tense/aspect reference.

Adverbs as Tense/Aspect Markers

Adverbial usage is closely linked to tense/aspect distinctions in Indian English grammar. In some cases, adverbs clarify the space/time reference already established in the sentence verb, for example:

We stayed in Kotzebue for a few days, then we start coming up the Noatak River.
   (Kotzebue English; Vandergriff 1982: 136)
He went out on a hunt and when night came he howl again.
   (Isletan English).
Then he will looking forward to the day when he will finish.
   (Apachean English; Bartelt 1982b: 77)

In other cases, instead of just modifying the tense/aspect reference, adverbs provide additional perspectives on this component of sentence reference. Such is the case in Isletan English sentences like the following:

*And they buried that stuff and it is supposed to be buried **yet**.*
*They had a kiva, made out of rocks, **yet**.*
*It had been four years in-between, **already**.*
*That is **already** when they are out of office.*

*He **probably** give out all of the money he is trying to save.*
*And it **usually** be the Navajos attackin' rather than the Comanches.*

Unlike the verb-based distinctions, which specify the duration of the action being described in the sentence, adverbial references indicate the relative position of that action compared to the speaker's position in space and time. The sentences with *yet* indicate action completed at some point before the speaker offered the comment; sentences with *already* suggest actions that are less distant from, and more relevant to, the discourse at hand.

Isletan English adverbs providing such cues occur in one of two positions: sentence final or sentence medial, adjacent to the main verb. As these examples suggest, choice of position also helps the speaker frame sentence meaning. Adverbs in final position indicate comments that, from the speaker's point of view, are verifiable facts: *They had a kiva made out of rocks, **yet***; adverbs in medial position designate comments that, while generally true from the speaker's point of view, may not be accurate statements under certain circumstances: *And it **usually** be the Navajos attackin' rather than the Comanches.*

The pair of sentences with *already* references above show longer description of the political careers of one of the prominent families of the pueblo. Both statements refer to events and actions that occurred prior to the time of the description, but were relatively close to it in space and time. The statement with final position *already* indicated something difficult to refute: there had been a four-year gap separating two events that had been critical to the family's construction of its political base in the pueblo: *It had been four years in-between, **already***. The statement with medial-position *already* indicated something that could not be so readily verified: now that family members' influence over pueblo government had come to an end, the narrator wanted to raise questions about their financial dealings. The narrator was critical of certain transactions that had occurred once the family members returned to private life, but suspected that they were involved in similar transactions prior to leaving office, as well, hence: *That is **already** when they are out of office.*

Adverbial support constructions show up in other Indian English varieties, though not always with the same frequency or narrative power as found in Isletan English. The specific adverbs providing this commentary also differ across varieties. Adult speakers of Northern Ute English, in my observation, use *still*, but not *already* or *yet*, to indicate close connections between the events being discussed and the space/time position of the discussion. Temporal adverbs are employed infrequently for purposes of tense/aspect marking in Papago (Tohono O'odham) English, and the large number of "uninflected" verb forms in Papago student English and the high incidence of "errors" in tense-marking tasks on standardized tests of English language competence (Bayles and Harris 1982: 16–17) are both likely consequences of this condition.

Get as a Verbal Auxiliary

While passive constructions with *GET* rather than *BE* show up in many varieties of Indian English, M. Miller's (1977) study of Pima student English is one of only a few reports that explore the code-specific significance of such constructions in any detail.

Miller found that Pima students at age 8 show little skill with passives in any form; only 2% of them formed passives with *BE* correctly. The frequency of correctly formed *BE* passives increases to 28% at age 9, and to 40% at age 10, although at age 11 the frequency of these constructions declines to 27%. The frequency of nongrammatical passives does not increase at this point, however. The decline in *BE* constructions corresponds to the appearance of *GET* passive constructions like *The fly got bitten by the spider* (1977: 79). Of the passive constructions used by 11-year-old Pima students, 23% contain inflected *GET* rather than *BE* as the helping verb. This is a substantial response rate, Miller observes, given that less than 15% of the students in her sample provided incorrectly formed passive constructions when she elicited them, and one-third of the students made no reply at all.[5]

The 11-year-old Pima students' use of this option, and the decline in the use of *BE* passives linked to it, is particularly interesting to Miller (1977: 35), given the low frequency for *GET* passives among the non-Indian students in her comparison sample:

> ... the *get* passive was little used among the Maryland children who were tested. There were no occurrences of the *get* passive at age seven, three examples at age eight, none at age nine, one example at age ten, five examples at age eleven—one of which was rendered unacceptable grammatically by the presence of an incorrect past participle—and none at twelve or thirteen.

This restricted frequency of *GET* passives within her non-Indian sample contrasts rather dramatically with the findings of other scholars, who note widespread frequency of this construction among elementary school English speakers from various backgrounds. In fact, Miller (1977: 35) notes, "Turner and Rommetveit ... conclude that [the *GET* passive] may be endemic to [vernacular English] with the *BE* passive a product of education." Their observation explains the high incidence of *GET* passives among Pima Indian students, provided we assume that vernacular English grammar does not begin to influence Pima students' English in this area until after students have acquired the *BE*-related construction through school experience. Why this should be the case is not explained in Miller's analysis.

Miller does not provide sufficient information to determine whether *GET* is part of a more inclusive class of Pima English verbal auxiliaries. Such appears to be the case in Isletan English, where the frequent occurrence of sentences like *It got soured* and *Yes, just like Pablo, he got voted in because of his father* show that the Isletan English AUX category includes *GET* as well as *BE* and *HAVE*; and instances of speaker's self-correction like *The people knew Robert will [ ] paid, how Robert will get paid, just because he is leasing it* show that Isletan English speakers apply grammatically controlled AUX deletion to all three members of this category, not just to inflected *BE* in the sense reported for Black English vernaculars (see next section). Perhaps, if similar conditions were also present in Pima English, the complex membership of the class and the number of rules that apply to its members could explain the delayed emergence of *GET* passive constructions.

Copula and AUX Deletion

Isletan English is not the only Indian English variety allowing the deletion of *BE*, *HAVE*, and *GET*. Such constructions are widely attested in Indian country. The conditions associated with these constructions resemble the constraints on *BE* deletion in some Black English vernaculars as described by Labov (1969) and by Wolfram and Fasold (1974: 158–60). That is, deletion occurs in instances where standard English grammar allows contraction of the AUX; and deletion is particularly favored when the AUX is preceded by a pronoun and when the sound segments not affected by contraction (if any) are similar in pronunciation to the sound segments that now surround them. As I explained above, Indian English grammars with AUX deletion rules broaden the scope of the Black English vernacular rule and apply that process to the items in verb constructions in other ways.

In Isletan English, for example, deletion of "linking verbs" as well as "helping verbs" is a common occurrence (see also the examples in the preceding section):

1. *Some of them, they are not given birth. They are just illegitimate. They [ ] no father.*
2. *She [ ] a Red Corn people.*
3. *They [ ] just goin' by the old ways, yet.*
4. *Then the would tell them what law he [ ] broken.*

One instance of copula *BE* deletion turned up in Penfield-Jasper's (1980) Mohave student English corpus and many more such constructions in the English of Mohave adults. The difference in generation-based frequencies suggests that "linking verb" (or copula) deletion may not be significant in Mohave English grammar. However, deletion of "helping verb" *BE* from perfective and passive constructions is quite common for these speakers, regardless of age. Mohave adults particularly favor deletion of inflected *BE* when it precedes a fully inflected present participle.

Copula deletion is also not widely attested in spoken Ute English, among either students or adults; copula deletion does occur frequently in *written* Ute English sentences, however. And AUX elements are regularly deleted in spoken and written Ute English, given the Ute English tense-marking rule that allows only a single tense-bearing element to occur within each Ute English clause. I will have more to say about tense marking in Mohave and Ute English in chapter 3.

Subject-Verb Concord

Standard English grammar requires agreement-marking between sentence subject and main verb. Indian English grammars also allow for subject-verb concord. However, features of pronunciation (particularly, the treatment of final-position consonants and consonant clusters), differences between concord rules in English and ancestral language grammars, and other factors influence the form of agreement-marking and affect the syntax of agreement in other ways.

Cook and Sharp (1966: 25, 27) describe the situation in the English of Navajo schoolchildren:

> Most Navajo nouns do not show number in the noun-word but rather in the verb form. The English plural of nouns is difficult for Navajo speakers for this reason. The regular English *s*-plural, when it occurs after consonants, is especially difficult for the additional reason that the Navajo speaker has difficulty in hearing final consonant clusters and therefore in reproducing them. . . . Forms showing subject-verb agreement in English—*am, is, are; was, were; have, has; do, does,* and third person singular present tense *-(e)s*—cause problems. Examples of common errors are *I were looking for deer; The little needle were pointing to the north; She don't know how to hold on to the horse; Joe asked Billy where he have seen a lamb.*

According to Cook and Sharp's analysis, subject-verb concord in Navajo English is the result of speaker error; they see no reason to assign any grammatical or social significance to these constructions. Stout (1979: 180–81) found entirely different conditions when studying concord patterns in the elementary school student English at Laguna pueblo, New Mexico, where concord marking is closely associated with subject number and type of verb construction: "One of the two constraining principles found was the singular verb form extending variably to plural subject when the verb was *BE* past or present. The other was the plural verb form extending variably to singular subject when the verb (is) NON-*BE* present."

Other features of sentence syntax influenced speaker preference for vernacular (that is, Laguna English) concord in this variety:

> For *BE* verbs, vernacular concord was used primarily with expletive *there* constructions 93.7% and to a much less extent, interrogative construction 22.0%, and collective 19.4% and conjoined 9.1% N[oun] P[hrase]s. . . . For NON-*BE* verbs, *DO* + NEG conditioned predominantly vernacular concord 63.5%. All other NON-*BE* verbs were standard in concord. . . . Noun NP's conditioned greater vernacular concord than pronoun NP's for both NON-*BE* verbs and *DO* + NEG constructions. . . . This conditioning constraint was, however, minimal for NON-*BE* verbs. (Stout 1979: 181)

Certain features of speaker background also come into play here, since Laguna students favored vernacular concord if they:

- ○ came from homes without grandparents or other adults speaking Laguna English as their second language;
- ○ were first-language speakers of English, rather than their ancestral language;
- ○ were male, rather than female;
- ○ lived on the reservation exclusively, with no off-reservation residence experience; and
- ○ were receiving support services in language arts development from the school's Title I program.

Grammatical environment and speaker background also influence vernacular subject-verb concord marking in Isletan English. Here, however, the real "controlling" variable is the reworking of subject-verb concord marking in Isletan English sentences so that speakers can comment more precisely on the details of the subject-verb relationship. In my observations, adult speakers of Isletan English are just as likely to use these constructions as are elementary and secondary school students.

The regularities here show up most clearly in situations of present tense reference. In those cases, if the sentence subject has plural reference and is marked accordingly, then the sentence also occurs in inflected form:

*There are some **parties** that **goes** on over there.*
*Some **peoples** from the outside **comes** in.*
*All the **dances** that **goes** on like that occur in the spring.*
*The **women has** no voice to vote.*
*. . . so that the left or right **sides doesn't** criss-cross one another.*

However, if the subject noun has a singular reference, and is not marked for number in surface structure, the verb is also unmarked:

*Maybe the **governor go** to these parents' homes.*
*About **a dollar a day serve out** your term.*
*This traditional Indian **ritual take** place in June.*
*By this time, this one **side** that are fast **have** overlapped.*
*The **governor don't** take the case.*

Similar concord-marking patterns show up in other varieties of Indian English and persons learning English as a second language often make similar errors when they form English sentences. But one feature of Isletan English grammar gives a site-specific quality to this usage. As I have explained, Isletan English grammar uses uninflected verbs to identify *distributive* action—activities that occur for brief periods during a more extended time span. When such verbs occur in Isletan English sentences, the sentence subject may also be uninflected for number, regardless of the singular/plural status of its reference:

*When the **woman get** together, they have a lot of influence.*
*They leave early in the morning, the **man go** to dig the grave.*
*The little **girl come** upstairs and she said to me: . . .*
*Since the **church close** down, we have been going to mass in Pajarito.*

The overlapping of grammatical rules here is not required in Isletan English grammar. The combination of features is *variable*, influenced by speaker age (older speakers let distributive verb reference determine number-marking on the sentence subject more often than school-aged students), by the degree of formality of the speech setting (more formal discussions prompt more such constructions than do informal discussion), and by the "Indianness" of the topic under discussion (a pueblo-centered discussion contains more such constructions than do discussions dealing with issues of greater concern to outsiders).

The Syntax of Prepositional Phrases

In addition to subject-verb concord marking, Indian English speakers use prepositional phrases to specify the syntax of sentence-level noun-verb relationships. In some cases, the choice of a particular preposition is relevant here, as in Navajo English:

> go **to** *downtown*
> **at** *store*
> *all kinds* **from** *birds*
>
> (Cook and Sharp 1966: 28)

in Mohave English:

> *He got fired **of** the church.*
>
> (Penfield-Jasper 1980: 145)

or Papago English:

> *They were **at** fishing.*
> *Ricky got in such a hurray **on** his zipper.*
>
> (Bayles and Harris, 1982: 17)

Equally important can be the order of components within the phrase, as in Navajo English:

> *the chalkboard **under***
>
> (Cook and Sharp 1966: 28)

or Mohave English:

> *I get **on in** Head Start.*
> ***During at** that time . . .*
>
> (Penfield-Jasper 1980: 145)

or the absence of a preposition within the construction, as in Mohave English:

He lives [ ] that second house.
I was [ ] California.
They go out [ ] night time to shallow waters.
                              (Penfield-Jasper 1980: 144)

Resarchers usually assume, faced with such examples, that the basis for these constructions is ancestral language grammar, not English. Mulder (1982: 105) explains for Tsimshian English:

> The spatial categories of prepositions in *Ts*[imshian] *E*[nglish] are also modeled after *Sm'algyax*. In *TsE*, prepositions frequently have different locational denotations than they do in most English dialects. For example, *Jack is on the table* means that Jack is "at" the table, but not "on" it in the most natural reading; while *Jack is over Johnny's* and *Jack is by Johnny's* means that Jack is "at" or more specifically "inside" Johnny's house. Although more work needs to be done to fully understand the spatial categories of *Sm'algyax* prepositions, it appears that there has been at least a partial identification of the prepositions in English with the locational categories in *Sm'algyax*.

Importantly, however, ancestral language influence over preposition usage does not necessarily lead to finer distinctions in spatial reference in Indian English. Penfield-Jasper (1980: 145, citing Munro 1974: 20) notes that Mohave grammar "has a single locative marker, l^y, which can be translated as a variety of [English language] prepositions, depending on the verb it is used with." She considers the presence of preposition deletion as well as the use of more complex preposition/noun sequences (see the Mohave English examples cited above) to be expectable consequences of ancestral language influences under such conditions.

In other cases, scholars turn to sources other than ancestral language grammar to explain the formation of these constructions. Flanigan (1984a: 92) reports that deletion of prepositions is a common occurrence in Lakota English:

I color [with] this.
We like to ride [ ] horse.
You wanna go [ ] bathroom?
He go [ ] town—he make fire [to] cook.
They live [ ] New York.

(Note: brackets indicate location of preposition deletion in these sentences; filled brackets indicate prepositions added by Flanigan to clarify an otherwise ambiguous meaning.) Her documentary research (1984b) shows that French-speaking traders and their Plains Indian commercial partners used a French-Indian "creole" as their trade language during the eighteenth and early nineteenth centuries. Since preposition deletion is a characteristic of creole languages, she assigns a creole origin to this feature of Lakota English (to tense-shifting and other features of this variety) and sees no reason to base these codes in Lakota language tradition or English-specific sources.

I agree that we should not overlook the influence of trade languages on the history of English in Indian country, and I have more to say on this point in chapter 5. But there are other ways to account for preposition deletion in Lakota English. Developmental factors may be relevant here, especially if these constructions were used primarily by younger speakers of Lakota English. Indeed, some of Flanigan's examples—*We like to ride [ ] horse, You wanna go [ ] bathroom*—may show up in children's English regardless of the speaker's linguistic background.

Case-marking patterns may also be involved here, given that preposition deletion applies to predicate noun phrases only when the primary recipient of the verb action (syntactically the object or the goal) is not specified in the sentence predicate. Hence *I color [with] this* (with the object/goal unspecified, and the instrument indicated without prepositional support). Sentences like *He go [ ] town—he make fire [to] cook* make case marking an especially persuasive explanation, given that the *to* deletion in the second clause applies to a verbal construction (an infinitive, in traditional terminology) and not to a prepositional phrase at all.

Details from the life experiences of the local Indian community can also contribute to Indian English prepositional usage in some instances. Alford (1974: 8) cites Cheyenne English like *Put it on the car* and *Hop on* as two of the various phrases pertaining to automobiles "which reflect a semantic freezing of such phrases from the time when the Cheyenne accepted carts and buggies." Northern Ute English expressions like *Let's ride on your car to Pizza Hut* also reflect the influence of cultural traditions. Such constructions should not be confused with instances (like those cited in the discussion of Tsimshian English, above) where preposition usage parallels ancestral language forms. Regional as well as national non-Indian, nonstandard English usage comes into play here, which explains the widely attested Indian English use of sentences *He is over to the Clarke's*, where *over to* is a variant of *over at* or *at*, and all are alternatives to the more elegant usage involving a participle (visiting) rather than a preposition as its head-word.

Right-to-Left Syntactic Constructions

Comments by researchers exploring Indian English grammar suggest that sentences in some of these codes may be *left-branching* rather than *right-branching* in their syntactic base.

Penfield-Jasper (1980: 86), for example, describing pronoun number/gender reference in Mohave English, notes that personal and possessive pronouns in this Indian English variety show a much higher incidence of gender variation (that is, use of *he* with female references or *she* with male references) when the pronoun in question occurs at the left side of the clause. Pronouns in this position in standard English sentences, being closest to the primary syntactic node of the clause, should be least affected by the influence of other noun phrases in the construction; pronouns at the right end of the clause should be more heavily influenced, accordingly. That the reverse of this pattern occurs quite regularly in Mohave English suggests that sentence formation in this English variety may also work in the opposite (right-to-left, instead of left-to-right) direction.

Grammatical properties of Indian English sentences lend further support to a left-branching basis for some Indian English grammars. In Tewa English, for example, standard English equi-deletion rules regularly eliminate the left-hand, rather than the right-hand, member of each *equi* pair, as in: *Bill is comparing two Indian [ ] the same, and how they are different.* There, and in Mescalero Apache English and Lakota English, the main clause occurs at the right-hand end of the sequence, and with object noun phrase and other modifiers moved out of "sentence-final" position and into "leftward" location in the clause:

They ride bikes is what I see them do. (San Juan Tewa)
There are circle dance songs that we have. (M. Apache)
What he is doing there is he [ ] announcing. (Lakota)

In Arapaho English and Yavapai English, the entire standard English–based word order is regularly reversed, with supporting/modifying materials preceding, instead of following, the subject-verb sequence:

From the family is where we learn to be good. (Arapaho)

or the main verb precedes the subject pronoun:

Where going you? (Yavapai)

It may seem tempting to derive the initial constituents of these sentences through a process of topicalization, rather than to posit a more general claim about fundamental differences in sentence organization. A topicalization argument must explain why a contextually specific and infrequently used syntactic option from standard English grammar becomes more significant in Indian English usage. And topicalization leaves unexplained constructions like Tewa English *Bill is comparing two Indian [ ] the same, and how they are different*, whose syntax has nothing to do with topicalization but everything to do with reversals in the outcomes of expected syntactic processes. Right-to-left branching—traditionally, not a claim made about English grammar—offers a more consistent means of accounting for all of these syntactic constructions. The implications of this claim for the analysis of other Indian English grammatical constructions have yet to be fully explored.

SEMANTICS: VERBAL IMAGERY

Studies of tense/aspect distinctions, subject-verb concord, adverbial usage, topicalization, and other features of Indian English syntax suggest the possibilities of reference that may be open to speakers of these codes. But studies of Indian English semantics have yet to explore these possibilities in systematic detail. For one thing, researchers have not been familiar with the conventions of reference used in the speakers' home communities, such as naming practices, euphemisms and slang, "sacred" vs. "secular" meanings, and strategies for identifying prominent features of the natural environment and social life. This has made it difficult to identify "Indian"-oriented meanings and references when they appear in a speaker's use of English.

Also at issue here is the belief that standard English semantic models are the foundation for meaning and reference for speakers of these codes. For example, some educators believe that, because they "speak English" Indian students count, add, and subtract strictly in terms of a base-10 number system. Such beliefs overlook the influence of community-centered meaning and reference patterns on student mathematics skills, even when there is evidence for such features in the Indian English speakers' word-choices and sentence structure (Leap 1987).

Some components of Indian English semantics have been accessible to researchers, however. One of these components is *verbal imagery*—descriptive statements that add distinctively Indian-oriented references to English discussions. Ancestral language semantic structures, idioms, and other reference conventions common to the tribal membership as a whole, as well as the individual speaker's linguistic creativity, provide the inspiration for these constructions. Indian English and standard English grammars jointly provide the guidelines for their syntax.

Uses of verbal imagery by speakers of different Indian English codes include the following constructions:

○ Alford (1974: 8) reports that on the Northern Cheyenne reservation a young man will tell you that he got a new shirt for his birthday and then add: *but I don't fit it*. Standard English grammar would treat the object (the shirt) as sentence subject, (*It doesn't fit me*), and not the actor (*I*) as is the case in this statement. But Cheyenne English grammar usually assigns actor to subject position; culturally, the resulting construction is "an entirely understandable concept in a society used to being forced to wear hand-me-downs because of poverty. If you don't fit it, someone else might" (Alford, 1974: 8).

○ Recounting what happened when a group of hippies set up camp in the pueblo's plaza one Saturday afternoon, a teenaged male speaker of Isletan English described the appearance of the group leader with this statement *His hair sure was hairy*. Here the speaker submerged the standard English distinction between *head* (the body part) and *scalp* (the external covering for that body part) under the same Indian English lexical item (*hair*), a classification also found in the community's ancestral language vocabulary. The repetition of terms required under this reclassification intensified the speaker's choice of imagery.

○ A teenaged female speaker of Navajo English described the time her evening meal usually begins by noting *I'm eatin' til six o'clock*. This statement is not intended to identify a specific starting point, or ending point, for this event. Such generalizations are difficult to make, given that the items on the menu, the number of participants, the presence of guests, and other contextual factors influence the duration of each meal. What can be indicated in advance is the approximate point during the day during which the event is likely to occur. That is the intended meaning of the reference to "clock-time" and use of the *til* preposition in this statement.[6]

○ Robert Young (cited in Fletcher 1983: 9) notes that speakers of Navajo English restate the ideas of speaker power and control implicit in standard English verbs *have to*, *make*, or *must*:

Rather than say, "I must go there," a Navajo would say something more accurately translated as *It is only good that I shall go there*. Rather than say

"I make the horse run," the equivalent Navajo statement would be more like *The horse is running for me.*

Writers of Indian English also make use of verbal imagery. Such constructions allow them to draw parallels between the meaning of the written text and points of reference from oral language tradition: "The role of marriage, I think is—that one has a real strong heart to face and understand the meaning of marriage" (Bartelt, 1982a: 92). Here *strong heart* is an English translation of the metaphor that focuses Navajo language discussions of this theme. These constructions also allow writers to state community-based perspectives relevant to the discourse theme in terms which non-Indians, as well as community members, will readily understand, as in: "Navajos cannot visit or see an object or animals that are taboos to his religion. Such as, an object of a skeletonal effegies. In the zoo, there are certain animals one can not visit with" (Bartelt 1982a: 92).

PRAGMATICS

The Cooperative Nature of Indian English Discourse

Principles of cooperative discourse—assumptions that help speakers find appropriate, efficient, and effective ways to use language in different situations (see discussion in Levinson 1983: 100 ff.)—are basic to pragmatics systems of all languages. They establish the framework that guides a speaker's use of context marking, turn-taking, and other features of discourse structure and guides the listener's interpretation of these clues to conversational meaning.

The principles of cooperative discourse are not the same for all languages or for all varieties of a given language, as Susan Phillips's studies (1972, 1983) of communication strategies on the Warm Springs Indian reservation have demonstrated.

Phillips worked at one of the on-reservation elementary schools during the period 1968–1973. She observed teacher-student interaction in the classrooms and student use of language in homes, in community settings, and in other out-of-school locales. Some of these students were speakers of English and their ancestral languages; others spoke only English. But whatever the language of choice, my reading of her observations suggests that the following assumptions guide the use of language by Warm Springs children and their parents and other members of their tribe:

   o Face-to-face interaction is the most valued form of interpersonal communication;

o Talking is closely linked to other types of physical activity; talk is rarely the only form of action found in a speech event;
o Speaker age is closely related to speaker skill. To be a good talker, a speaker must be over age 35. Persons under age 35 should be good listeners and defer opportunities for speaking to their elders.
o Listening is a passive activity. Listeners use gaze direction and other indirect cues to show they are paying attention when someone else is talking.
o Speakers direct their comments to all participants in the audience, not to selected individuals.
o Speakers comment on all of the details relevant to the topic under discussion; they make no judgments about the relative importance of individual facts.
o The content-choices of the following speakers, not the first speaker's introductory remarks, establish the direction of discussion.

Language use within the Warm Springs classrooms—an environment controlled by non-Indian teachers and a non-Indian-based curriculum—builds on entirely different assumptions, Phillips found:

o Individualized activity, not face-to-face communication, is the valued form of action within this setting.
o Talk is a self-contained activity; talk occurs independently of other forms of classroom action and should not be disrupted by those actions.
o Age-level has nothing to do with language skill; all persons in the classroom should know how to control talk appropriately.
o Listening is an active activity. Listeners use gestures, direct eye contact, verbal rejoinders, and other clues to show that they understand what others are saying to them.
o Speakers direct their comments to specific individuals, even when speaking before a large audience.
o Speakers stress the main points of their topic and need not dwell on what they consider the unimportant details.
o The first (or primary) speaker establishes the focus for the discussion and regulates the compliance of the following speakers accordingly.

Given such differences between community- and classroom-based approaches to cooperative discourse, it is not surprising that Warm Springs Indian children do not do well in school. Phillips (1983: 126–27) explains:

> The relative use of the visual and auditory channels and the organization of
> participant structures for the presentation of curriculum have been developed for
> the Anglo middle-class child. . . . That organization does not, however, com-
> pletely fit or build on the interactional skills acquired by Warm Springs Indian
> children.

In other words, what Warm Springs students know about English discourse and how
they expect their teachers will participate in such discourse is entirely different from
their teachers' assumptions in these areas. Unfortunately, teachers (and the system
of authority they represent) have the upper hand in these settings and students have
to adapt to their expectations about cooperative discourse if they are to be successful
in the classroom.

   Constraints on discourse and power also influence the cooperative use of
Indian English in other settings. McLaughlin (1991) found a poignant example
of such conditions during his study of the functions of literacy in an
on-reservation Navajo community (north-central Arizona). The speaker in
question, whom McLaughlin identifies as Jimmie Chee, went with other
members of his community one summer to fight a forest fire in Montana. This
was paid labor, and the work was important for a community with a limited
economic base. Unfortunately, Jimmie Chee had an accident, damaged his
thumb, and had to return to his home.

   Several weeks later he received a letter from the Office of Workers'
Compensation (San Francisco) advising: "Your notice of Injury/Illness was
received without sufficient medical evidence to adjudicate the claim. . . . It is
your responsibility to arrange for submission of medical evidence to substantiate
your claim" (cited in McLaughlin 1991: 153). Chee found this a confusing
document, since he had not filed a claim with the OWC and had not asked anyone
else to act on his behalf. But, more importantly, the writer's use of the agentless
passive (*Your notice . . . was received . . .*), choice of vocabulary (*adjudicate,
substantiate*), and other details of text-construction made the letter difficult to
understand, and the suggested remedies for his "problem"—which forms to
send in, what supporting evidence to include—difficult to interpret. So he
decided not to respond.

   Ten days later Chee received a second letter, also from the OWC, which
advised, in part: "It has been determined that the facts of the injury and
employment support Jimmie Chee's contention that he was a federal employee
who sustained a traumatic injury in the performance of duty. You should,
therefore, continue his pay for the period of disability not to exceed 45 days"
(cited in McLaughlin 1991: 153). Again, the writer's use of agentless passives
and other features of syntax created a confusing text, as did the meaning of the

letter, when read literally: Jimmie Chee should continue to give himself disability payments for no more than 45 days.

At this point Chee decided that he needed to discuss this issue with someone who understood the system and could help him plan a suitable response. He went to McLaughlin, who was doing dissertation research in the community at that time. They discussed the problem and concluded that Chee needed to contact the OWC official in charge of his case, so that the identity of his employer could be clarified and Chee could begin receiving disability payments from the appropriate source. A trip to the OWC office in San Francisco, so that Chee could do this through face-to-face discussion, was out of the question. He had to have the conversation by telephone.

McLaughlin and Chee spent the next two weeks planning the conversation—outlining the issues Chee would raise, predicting questions and comments the official would use in the reply, and discussing responses Chee could make to the official's concerns. Using the telephone was itself a new form of discourse for Chee, and part of the planning process included "dress rehearsal" conversations and other activities to orient Chee to this use of English.

Finally, after experiencing some delay in getting through to the OWC official to set the date and time for the telephone call, Chee was ready to state his case. The OWC official called the Rock Point number where Chee and McLaughlin were waiting, and the conversation (as tape-recorded from the telephone ear piece) proceeded as follows:

Chee: Hello.
Official: Good morning. May I speak with, ah, Jimmie Chee, please.
Chee: Yeah, this is he.
Official: OK. This is the office of Federal Employees' Compensation. I am returning a phone call you made to the office.
Chee: Yeah.
Official: OK, may I help you?
Chee: Ah, who is this? Is this Helen [the first name of the OWC official who signed the letters Chee received]?
Official: Yes.
Chee: OK. Well, you sent me a letter on the, August the ninth and August the nineteenth, and I don't really understand what you are saying.
Official: What, um, what do the letters say?
Chee: [clears his throat]. Which one?
Official: OK, see, I, um, you had called up a few days ago, and I requested a case-to-case. It shows on the computer here that it is in there

	but it isn't. So I made a search and I don't have the case. And, um, because of that —
Chee:	[urgent aside to McLaughlin] Dan!
Official:	—I can't, I can't look at the case file and tell you what I have sent to you, so. But I have a note down that you were waiting for my call today at this time, so that's why I'm responding to your call, but, ah, I don't have the case in front of me. You'll have to read the letter to me to give me some idea, you know, what I said. I have too many cases to remember what I wrote you.
Chee:	OK.
Official:	Are they both regarding the same issue?
Chee:	OK, OK.

and Chee handed the telephone to McLaughlin, so he could take charge of the remainder of the exchange.

Chee's use of English during this conversation reflects his unfamiliarity with telephone-based business interaction. But his English also shows a sincere attempt to participate actively and cooperatively in the conversation, even though the assumptions about cooperative discourse are certainly not those guiding the OWC's use of English in this setting.

The OWC official opened the conversation by identifying herself as *the office of Federal Employees' Compensation*; this phrase serves as the syntactic referent for the official's use of the *I* pronoun during the remainder of this conversation. Self-identification in those terms, combined with her constant references to bureaucratic process and administrative procedure, places the OWC official's authority to review data and make decisions at the forefront of the dialogue.

Chee's opening statements show that he is not comfortable dealing with a "faceless" individual: once he has a chance to set the direction of the discussion, he asks: *Who is this? Is this Helen?* With these questions, Chee shifts the tone of the conversation away from the OWC official's attempt at business-only dialogue. That gives him the opportunity he needs to state the purpose of the conversation. He does this succinctly—*You sent me a letter . . . and I don't really understand what you're saying*—using one of the statements that Chee and McLaughlin had carefully rehearsed. And his statement contrasts with the overly detailed commentary that the OWC official constructs when responding to this statement.

Her initial reply to Chee's problem-statement is totally incongruent with that statement's meaning: *. . . what do the letters say?* This reply reiterates the assumptions about appropriate speech guiding her participation in this dialogue:

she is the figure of authority; Mr. Chee is the client. Mr. Chee is the one with the problem, and he has to identify the scope of that problem precisely before she can respond. Her comments about case-to-case, lost files, and computer references restate this position and reinforce her power and his vulnerability. She is being cooperative—she returned the telephone call as she promised she would do. Now it is Chee's turn to take the initiative.

From Chee's point of view, the official's insistence on detached, impersonal dialogue, her emphasis on a single issue ("you tell me the problem, then I'll respond") to the exclusion of other concerns, and her constant shifting of the responsibility for initiating action back to Chee—all of these features conflict with the more personalized approach to communication with which Chee is more familiar and (apparently) more comfortable. Rather than continuing to cope with such an alien discourse, Chee simply withdraws from the dialogue, passing the telephone to someone he knows is more familiar with the conversational strategy the OWC official has chosen to employ.

It is difficult to assess how frequently Indian English speakers' assumptions about *cooperative discourse* influence their participation in English language conversations, since so little attention has been paid to Indian English pragmatics in the literature. There is evidence of such influence in at least two areas of Indian English conversational strategy, however: question-asking and (with apologies to the Western Apache) "giving up on words." I review the evidence in each area in the following sections.

Question-asking

Question-asking is a speech act filled with assumptions about cooperative discourse, though other components of Indian English grammar and discourse also influence the use of such constructions and the assumptions about speaker/listener cooperation associated with them. The "package" of details here often affects communication between speakers of one Indian English code and speakers of other English varieties since "the communicating parties seldom understand that divergent language usage is the source of their difficulty" (Liebe-Harkort 1983: 207).

Liebe-Harkort (1983: 208) explains this situation for White Mountain Apache English:

Direct personal questions are avoided [in White Mountain English] since they are felt to be impolite. However, if they come up and are felt to be an imposition, the answer will often be *I don't know.* (*How old are you?*, asked of a young girl, brought that answer.) What is intended to be conveyed is that one should not have asked; what is often understood is that the individual does not know very much. It follows, then, that *Could you loan me . . . ?*, since it has the form of a direct question, is not a polite way to frame a request, and the imperative is used. Non-Apaches, however, do not feel a command to be a polite request and often react as if they have been insulted.

Speakers of Northern Ute English also regularly avoid the use of direct questions, and they extend this rule of avoidance to cover other forms of questioning. Hence, they prefer to use open-ended statements like *I wonder how come he did that,* instead of a more tightly focused query like *Why did he do that?* and they are much more responsive to questioning when questions are presented to them in this form.

I can explain the appeal of these open-ended statements in several ways. For one thing, use of this wording shifts the questioner to the center of the discussion and diminishes the emphasis on the topic being discussed. Also, this wording allows respondents to comment on the question without having to talk about persons who are not present in the conversation and are thus unable to defend themselves from the respondent's reply or to comment without having to admit that the issue under discussion is not something with which the respondents are familiar. In fact, the wording frees the listener from any need to respond in detail to the question at all. Completing the reference of a simple *Maybe he . . .* sentence satisfies the rigorous turn-taking obligations that questions impose on respondents under such circumstances.

Like Ute English speakers, Lakota English speakers regularly use *I wonder why* or some other sentence-initial augment to introduce their content-oriented questions. But different assumptions regulate turn-taking in this Indian English variety; this lets speakers use these sentence-augments to mark the broad outlines of some concern, without obligating the listener to take any action on the speakers' behalf. A common response to Lakota English *I wonder why . . .* questions is silence.

Request-oriented questions—such as are necessary when students need new writing instruments so they can complete a seatwork assignment—are worded much more abruptly: *Teacher, you must give me a pencil!* For persons unfamiliar with Lakota English usage, such statements take teacher generosity for granted and ignore the social distance that always separates teachers and students in classroom settings. Persons familiar with Lakota community verbal etiquette realize that these statements closely parallel the "imperative verb" constructions in the speakers' ancestral language and that Lakota speakers regularly use such constructions when making requests of kinspeople and other close friends.

Kotzebue English speakers also prefer to begin content-oriented questions with *how come* instead of *why*. According to Vandergriff's analysis (1982: 130), this preference can be traced to two features of Kotzebue English grammar. First, speakers often form questions in the community's ancestral language by placing a question-marker in front of a sentence in declarative form. Kotzebue English questions with sentence-initial *how come* appear to be replicating this pattern in village English grammar. Second, verb constructions involving inflected *DO* or *HAVE* and verbs marked for progressive reference with inflected *BE* occur infrequently in Kotzebue English. This makes it difficult for speakers to apply the rules of standard English question-formation (which depend heavily on *DO*- and *HAVE*-support) in Kotzebue English discourse formats. If Vandergriff is correct here, *how come* constructions in this variety of Indian English are syntactically based and not dependent on pragmatics features at all.

"Giving Up on Words"

One characteristic of Indian English conversations that is very noticeable to non-Indians is the Indian English speakers' use of silence. Keith Basso (1970) has described the conditions that prompt speakers of Western Apache "to give up on words" (Basso's translation of the Western Apache term) in ancestral language settings; silence is an appropriate strategy when, for example, speakers of Western Apache are interacting with strangers or involved in social domains where the assumptions about behavior are not completely clear.

Basso's work has encouraged researchers to explore the discourse-positive functions of silence in other Indian language traditions. His work *should* encourage researchers to raise similar questions about the functions of silence in Indian English discourse. Silence is certainly a viable element in such discourse—at least insofar as school-related English language usage is concerned.

When speech pathologists and other clinicians administer tests of auditory discrimination or make other assessments of Indian student language development and skill, they regularly note that the period between question and response can be two or three times greater for Indian students, compared to that for their non-Indian class- or age-mates. Jack Damico's (1983: 13) study of "functional language proficiency" among Creek students in two Oklahoma Indian communities found 37% of his respondents showing such "question-related response delays."

It is possible that Indian English speakers use response delays when they are unfamiliar with classroom English or have yet to develop their speaking skills in this code. It is just as likely, I think, that such usage reflects something similar to the Western Apache practice of "giving up on words." Silence, hedges, and distractors become features of Indian English discourse in settings that are alien to the speakers' home community and cultural traditions. Non-Indians, or their representatives, are co-participants in those speech events and usually control the opportunities for language use and the guidelines for cooperative discourse within that setting. Change the ground rules and shift the principles of cooperation so the speech event includes (rather than excludes) the Indian English speaker's sense of effective discourse and the use of silence, hedging, and distractors should also decline.

This is exactly what happened during interviews I conducted with Isletan English seventh and eighth grade students during the summer of 1974. My work that summer focused on tense/aspect and AUX constructions in Isletan English. I was able to gather language samples from Isleta and non-Indian students (Anglo and Hispanic in background) participating in a public school–based summer enrichment program, so that I could compare these features of Isletan English grammar to conditions in other varieties of English used in this area of New Mexico. To add some variety to the data-gathering tasks, I included two story-telling tasks. Near the beginning of the interview, I read the student a brief story,[7] filled with images which I thought would be familiar to persons from the U.S. Southwest, regardless of language background: "Once there was a boy named Tom Black. He went to a rodeo and rode a bucking horse. He won a prize—a silver saddle. So he put the saddle in his pickup and then he went home." Then I asked the student to tell the story back to me. All but a handful of students were able to do this without any difficulty, but also without showing much enthusiasm for the task. Note the terse, choppy sentences, the omission of connections between the events indexed in each statement, and the overall "telegraphic" presentation of story-content in the following exchange with an eighth grade female Isletan student:

> Researcher: OK. I am going to tell you a story. I want you to listen real hard and then tell it back to me. OK. [Reads story as cited above]. Now you tell it back to me.
>
> Student: About, uh, a boy named Tom. He went to the rodeo. He was riding a horse and he won a saddle. He put it in the truck and he went home. [Pause.] I don't like stories. [Silence.]

Later in the interview, I showed each student a picture of an animal, sitting on its hind legs, face raised to the sky, howling at the moon. I chose this scene because of its familiar images and asked a seventh grade Isletan student to draw the picture so that the visual imagery would also have local appeal. This time, rather than expecting the student to work within an already formed text, I asked the student to look at the picture, to make up a story about the scene displayed there, and to tell me the story in the student's own words. The young Isletan student who gave such a terse retelling of the Tom Black story responded to this task with much more enthusiasm. She began by establishing comfortable boundaries and guidelines for the task, then she went to work constructing her own narrative based on the picture:

Researcher: Now, tell me a story about this picture. (Shows student a picture of an animal sitting on its hind legs and baying at the moon.)

Student: There is—[pause], this a coyote?

Researcher: I guess so.

Student: A short one?

Researcher: Anything you want it to be, kid.

Student: I can have this animal be a dog or something?

Researcher: Sure. Anything you want. Just tell me a story about this picture.

Student: That'll be a dog, OK? One day the dog was looking up at the sky, and he saw a star fall down. So he carried it and took it to his house, and some other animals came to see what it was. And they looked at it and they said: That's a falling star. [pause] Is that enough?

Examples like these are reminders that the characteristics of Indian English grammar, like the ones described here, are closely tied to conditions of Indian English discourse. To understand these characteristics of grammar requires detailed analysis of situation and function as well as structure. This becomes especially important when describing the connections between Indian English grammar and discourse and the grammar and discourse features in the speakers' ancestral language tradition, and when assessing the diversity of community-specific Indian English codes—tasks I will address in the next two chapters.

PART II

INDIAN ENGLISH AND ANCESTRAL LANGUAGE TRADITION

Many of the characteristics of Indian English grammar and discourse discussed in chapter 2 are closely associated with features of ancestral language grammar and discourse. I have found evidence for such associations in each of the Indian English codes I have studied. That evidence has led me to argue that—whatever the other influences affecting speaker language skills—ancestral language tradition provides the basis for the speakers' knowledge of Indian English grammar and for their use of that knowledge in specific discourse settings.

My purpose in this section is to examine in some detail evidence that supports this claim. In chapter 3 I look at three syntactic constructions, two from Isletan English and one from Ute English, and show how ancestral language grammatical rules provide more powerful explanations for these constructions than do explanations derived from other sources. In chapter 4 I explore features of Indian English grammar that resemble constructions found in other nonstandard English codes, but, when examined more carefully, turn out to be much more closely aligned with ancestral language traditions.

Both of these chapters raise interesting questions about the goals of language description in Indian English research, about the differences between first- and second-language acquisition in particular tribal speech communities, about the processes of language contact and language acculturation in these settings, and about the history and politics of English fluency in Indian country as a whole.

CHAPTER 3

THE ANCESTRAL LANGUAGE BASE

The starting point for these chapters is the idea that rules from ancestral language grammar and discourse, or rules that closely parallel those sources, give Indian English grammar and discourse their uniquely expressive, distinctively "Indian" and tribe-specific properties. I have argued this position steadfastly over the years because, in all of the sites where I have studied these codes, I have found evidence of Indian language influence on Indian English sound systems, word constructions, sentence forms, reference structures, and usage strategies. Importantly, these sites include settings where Indian English speakers are not fluent speakers of their ancestral languages, and where Indian English becomes the only contact speakers have with their tribe's verbal tradition. (I will describe some of these settings in chapter 6.)

Working at multiple sites has also shown me that ancestral language traditions do not always have the same effects on community-specific Indian English codes. In some speech communities, Indian English rules of pronunciation draw heavily on ancestral language sound contrasts; in others, pronunciation closely parallels sound inventories found in local or regional vernacular English, combines principles from both sources, or approximates standard English models. The same range of conditions applies to the degree of ancestral language influence over Indian English tense/aspect distinctions, noun classification, turn-taking strategies, and other details of site-specific linguistic structure. Given that ancestral language skills provided the starting point for the development of English fluency in some tribal communities, while other language traditions played more central roles in that regard at other sites, the same conditions apply to site-specific Indian English histories.

The absence of consistent parallels between ancestral languages and Indian Englishes has led some researchers to reject the notion of an Indian language "base" and to explain the grammatical characteristics of these codes through other means. The more frequently cited arguments to this end include the following.

o *Dialect similarities/diffusion:* Proponents of this position note that speakers of Indian English share many features of nonstandard English grammar and discourse with speakers of African American, Spanish American and other vernacular English codes. The special characteristics of Indian English reflect the diffusion of features across English varieties within a particular historical context or reflect grammatical features shared by all nonstandard English codes. Dillard (1972: 143), for example, notes that there is "little direct evidence for the transmission of Pidgin English—the whites who kept the records being little concerned with the speech of Blacks and Indians—but there is great circumstantial evidence." In Maryland, Virginia, and Massachusetts (and presumably other colonies as well), "Indians had preceded the Africans as slaves and continued to be their fellow slaves for some time, [and] the first attestation of American Indian Pidgin English came ten years or so after the arrival of the Africans." And Wolfram and Christian (1979b), concluding a lengthy discussion of the differences between Indian English varieties from San Juan and Laguna pueblos, draw attention to the similarities in these codes' grammars and point out their parallels with other nonmainstream English codes. Four features are especially important in this regard—multiple negation, cluster reduction, concord, and plural absence. Importantly, they report no reason to posit an ancestral language connection for any of them.

o *Modification of a local pidgin/creole:* Proponents of this position argue that the origins of community-specific Indian English codes lie in Indian language-based or European/Indian language-based pidgins/creoles spoken by members of the tribe at an earlier time. Flanigan, for example, cites a list of dialect features that are "not unlike those observed in greater or lesser frequency, in other nonstandard varieties of American English, including Black English Vernacular, Appalachian English, Chicano English, and others," and concludes that "this variety bears little evidence of direct interference from the ancestral Lakota dialect of the Siouan language spoken throughout the area" (1984a: 84). She cites documentary evidence of a closer relationship between this variety and the trade language used by French traders and the Plains tribes during the eighteenth and nineteenth centuries.

o *Developmental errors:* Speakers of Indian English make the same mistakes as persons from other language/cultural backgrounds when they learn English, and the unique properties of Indian English grammar reflect learning errors that speakers have yet to overcome. Here is how Cook and Sharp (1966:

21–22) summarized this position when describing the problems of Navajo speakers in learning English:

> Many mistakes made by non-native speakers of any language may be attributed to the fact that they do not accurately hear sounds or sound combinations in the new language which are different from or nonexistent in their own language. Many of the mistakes Navajo learners make in English phonology are readily understood from this point of view. . . . Young native-English speaking children have similar difficulties. . . . However, native English speaking children live in an environment peopled by adults who pronounce these sounds correctly, and correct the children's errors, as well, eventually overcoming these problems in pronunciation. Young Navajo children by and large do not live in such an environment but rather in one in which such errors are often perpetuated by themselves and by each other, without correct models or guidance.

o *Semilingualism*: Speakers of Indian English have developed only a partial control over the grammar of English, either because they had only limited opportunities to acquire such skills or because of particular problems in the areas of linguistic competence. In some cases, scholars describe the speaker's ancestral language skills in similar terms, echoing Leonard Bloomfield's (1964: 395) classic description of White Thunder, one of his Menominee informants:

> White-Thunder, a man round forty, speaks less English than Menomini, and that is a strong indictment, for his Menomini is atrocious. His vocabulary is small, his inflections are often barbarous, he constructs sentences of a few threadbare models. He may be said to speak no language tolerably. His case is not uncommon among younger men, even when they speak but little English. Perhaps it is due, in some indirect way, to the impact of the conquering language.

Certainly, these explanations offer useful insights into the conditions of culture contact, of English language learning, and of economic and social opportunity that have become established in Indian country over the last 500 years. And some highlight dimensions of Indian English grammar and discourse that other interpretations of these codes are not able to address.

Yet none of these explanations accounts for the similarities linking Indian English grammars and discourse processes to their speakers' ancestral language traditions. In fact—as the following examples will show—even constructions that appear to result from "dialect diffusion," "faulty language learning," or even "standard English" sources can have close ties to ancestral language tradition and need to be analyzed accordingly.

COGNATE OBJECT PREDICATES IN ISLETAN ENGLISH

Adult speakers of English at Isleta pueblo (New Mexico) frequently make use of cognate object predicates when talking Isletan English.[1] Here are some examples of these constructions, collected during my work at the pueblo (1968–1974) and during follow-up visits to the site:

1. *Lay people do not* **take actual participation** *in church functions.*
2. *They do not know how to* **give a decision.**
3. *You had to* **have** *a* **book-keeping knowledge** *to do that.*
4. *He is supposed to act* **as a protection.**
5. *The dance group* **has no requesting** *for curing.*
6. *He* **uses** *the bow* **as a protection.**
7. *It* **is tradition** *that we eat food at the end of the ceremony.*
8. *It* **has identification** *on it.*
9. *You* **have** *your* **belief** *in the corn.*
10. *They* **have vision of** *the edge of the plaza.*

Isleta English speakers use these constructions in informal, face-to-face conversations and in highly structured speech events. By my assessment, the constructions occur less frequently in the English of younger members of the pueblo (persons under 21), though the frequency increases as they reach adulthood and take a more active role in community life. It is worth noting that this is also the age-level at which these persons' ancestral language fluency begins to expand.

Note that each of these sentences contains an inflected verb and associated noun object. Speakers of other English varieties are more likely to use a single verb instead of verb-noun complex to make the same referent: participate, rather than *take . . . participation* in 1, **know** *book-keeping* rather than **have** *a book-keeping* **knowledge** in 3, and so on; either of these options is equally acceptable in standard English syntax. So it is possible that the occurrence of such constructions in Isletan English reflects nothing more than speaker preferences for idiom or expressive style. Even if this is idiomatic or stylistic usage, Isletan English grammar (as a statement of the speaker's knowledge of language) needs to account for these forms.

Isletan Tiwa grammar makes use of a similar type of verb-noun sequence, as shown in sentences like:

11.	*Tabude u-chachi-we.*	"The governor gives orders."
12a.	*Na k'unin iw-shiw-ya.*	"I am hunting rabbits."
12b.	*Na iw-k'u-shiw-ya.*	"I am hunting rabbits."

13.   *Na, te-p'a-'a-ma.*   "I am irrigating."
14.   *Im- nathe-[ ]-we.*   "I can do it."

To explain the syntax of these constructions, I need to introduce some facts about Isletan Tiwa sentence structure.

There are four word-types in Isletan Tiwa grammar. One of these word-types roughly corresponds to English verbs, and the other three to English nouns. Importantly, items are not "frozen" within these categories. The same grammatical base can be found in several word-types, depending on the meaning that the speaker needs to express and the grammatical construction the speaker feels will best represent it. Hence, there is a verb *u-chachi-we* "(s/he) gives orders" or "(s/he) acts on the basis of authority" composed of base -chachi-, pronominal prefix *u-*, and tense/aspect suffix *-we*. There is also a word in one noun category, *shachide* "someone who is an authority" composed of base -shachi- and a -de suffix; and a word in a second category of "noun base" (marked by *na-* prefix) *nashachi* "authority" (the more general, inclusive attribute that enables political action). Isleta Tiwa speakers do not use the third category of noun, composed of base without additional affix material, to make references to "authority." Words in this category indicate unique, nonreplicable occurrences: for example, *t'e'u* "a clay pot" compared to *nat'e'u* "pottery," with the *na-* prefix also found above.

In most instances, bases found in Isletan Tiwa "noun" constructions can become bases for "verb" constructions, and vice versa, simply through a shift in affixes.[2] But verb-building may also involve other types of grammatical processes. A fully inflected noun (*k'unin* "rabbits") may retain its noun affix and combine with an inflected performative verb base (*-shiw-* "to pursue") to produce a descriptive verb-object sequence like "hunting rabbits" in 12a. Or a noun base without affixes may be joined directly to the verb base (*-k'u-shiw-* in 12b), to produce a base-compound to which verb-affixes are then applied.

The same syntactic processes apply to sentence 13, where the combination of noun (*p'a* "water") and performative verb (*'-a-* "to cause, to bring about") yields an Isletan Tiwa construction "I am irrigating."

The syntax of sentence 14 shows another variation in this pattern. The verb construction contains a base-compound, rather than verb-noun sequence; note that the pronominal prefix *im-* precedes the noun-base (as in 12b) rather than follows it (as in 12a). This suggests that the verb in this compound is an unmarked performative, the result of an Isletan Tiwa rule that allows deletion of "helping verbs" from sentence structures under certain conditions. Note, also, that the *na-* affix on the compounded noun has not been deleted, as is ordinarily the case when "noun" bases occur within these constructions. This suggests that a more inclusive interpretation of "power, force, ability" (similar to *nat'e'u* "pottery") rather than a personalized and more individualized interpretation (similar to *t'e'u* "a particular pot") is the foundation for the reference of the compound.

Table 3.1 summarizes the rules governing the formation of noun-based verb-building—or *cognate verb* constructions—in Isletan Tiwa grammar. The rules operate in the indicated order, as suggested by the Isletan Tiwa examples examined here. According to those data, rule IT 1 is obligatory, but rule IT 2 is optional: following rule IT 1 with rule IT 2 yields constructions like 12b, while bypassing rule IT 2 yields constructions like 12a. Rule IT 3 is also obligatory, though criteria governing the selection of each performative vary with the meaning of each sentence and (as example 14 suggests) in some cases the performative reference does not need to be specified at all.

TABLE 3.1   RULES FOR FORMING COGNATE VERB CONSTRUCTIONS
IN ISLETAN TIWA

IT 1. Select the desired noun reference; assign the appropriate base to the *object* node in sentence deep structure.
IT 2. Copy object base into verb node and delete first copy.
IT 3. Supply performative verb to verb node, as appropriate to sentence reference; then add person prefix and tense/aspect suffix to the verb node to complete the construction.

Keeping these facts in mind, let's return to the Isletan English examples in sentences 1–10. In each of these sentences, the object noun provides the core meaning for the reference, while the "verb" (which in several instances is actually an AUX) indicates only the occurrence of that action. This sounds very much like the reference conditions associated with the "cognate verb" constructions of Isletan Tiwa, and the Isletan Tiwa rules governing these constructions (see table 3.1) apply equally well to these English-based constructions. That is, using sentence 1 as an example (and ignoring the syntax of the modifiers for purposes of this argument), the speaker locates the desired object reference (*participation*) within the object node (as required under rule IT 1):

15.

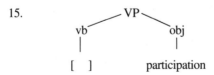

Rule IT 2 is an optional rule; the speaker does not apply it here (however, see discussion of example 8, below). Then the speaker adds the appropriate helping verb (*take*) to complete this portion of the construction, as allowed under rule IT 3:

16.

Similar analysis accounts for the other sentences (2–10) displayed in the corpus of "cognate verb" constructions above.

Discovering a workable parallel between Isletan Tiwa and Isletan English grammar in this case does not mean that the analysis of these constructions is complete. Standard English grammar also allows for sentences with close syntactic and semantic connections between verb and noun object. As described by Fillmore (1966: 85–86), there "cognate verb" constructions fall into three categories:

- o verb with "empty" object NP node:
    17. *John **dreamed** [ ] about a new truck.*
- o verb with object node filled by "copy" of verb base:
    18. *John **dreamed a dream** about a new truck.*
- o pro-verb/AUX replacement of original verb with verb "copy" in object node:
    19. *John **had a dream** about Mary.*

Table 3.2 displays the rules Fillmore uses to account for these English constructions. These rules operate in the order listed in the table. Rule E1 is categorical; that is, speakers always use it when forming these constructions. Rules E2 and E3 are optional. To use rule E3, rule E2 must already have been applied to the given sequence, as in example 19, above. However, as shown in example 18, rule E2 can be applied on its own, without input from E3.

Fillmore's rules, while developed to account for data from standard English, also explain the formation of the Isletan English constructions in

TABLE 3.2 RULES FOR FORMING COGNATE VERB CONSTRUCTIONS
IN STANDARD ENGLISH

E1. Select the appropriate verb reference; locate the corresponding verb base under verb node in sentence deep structure;

E2. Copy verb base from verb node into "empty" object node, and assign appropriate noun affixes to that base;

E3. Replace original verb with appropriate AUX or other "pro-verb."

---

sentences 1 through 10. Again, using sentence 1 as the example, the speaker uses rule E1 to locate the base with desired reference under the sentence verb node:

20.

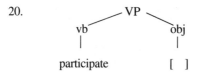

Next, the speaker copies the base under the verb node into the empty object node, as allowed under rule E2:

21.

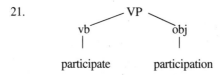

Finally, the speaker replaces the base under the verb node with the appropriate "pro-verb" form, as allowed under rule E3:

22.

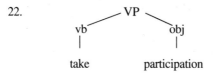

The Isletan English speaker needs to make only one change in the standard English rule inventory (table 3.2), in order to form sentence 1 in these terms: rules E2 and E3, optional in standard English "cognate object" settings, become categorical within Isletan English syntax.

Apparently, these Isletan English constructions can be derived from two entirely different sources. So the next task is to decide if one of these options does a better job of accounting for these constructions or if both options are equally suited to the task.

While the English and Isletan Tiwa rule inventories are similar, they are not identical. Standard English grammar uses the verb as the starting point for these constructions and derives the base of the object construction from the sentence verb reference. Isletan Tiwa grammar, in contrast, uses the object noun as the starting point for the construction and derives the form of the sentence pro-verb from the reference of that noun.

Most Isletan English sentences with cognate verb constructions do not contain structural clues indicating which of these options the speaker followed when deriving those sentences. But *some* sentences do contain such clues. One such example is sentence 23, given during the follow-up discussion surrounding sentence 1:

23. *People participationize in the mass.*

Clearly, the surface-level form of the verb in 23 is noun-derived; the base for the verb construction contains the *-tion* ending that can only be added to nouns in standard English. This is exactly the kind of surface-level construction which could emerge if Isletan Tiwa rule IT 3 supplied an unmarked pro-verb (as it does for example 14 and elsewhere in Isletan Tiwa), or if rule IT 3 became optional, instead of an obligatory stage in the derivational process.

Standard English "cognate-object" rules can also be used to account for sentence 23, but not without substantial modifications in the rule inventory. First, as required under SE 1, *participate* is introduced under the verb node. Next the verb is copied to the object noun and assigned the *-tion* suffix, as specified under rule SE 2. First-copy deletion of the base under the verb node, as specified in rule 3, is then applied; but now, to complete the construction, rather than adding the appropriate "pro-verb" as also specified in rule 3, the inflected noun under the object node is back-copied into the now-empty verb node, with second-copy copy deletion—provisions not anticipated under standard English rule 3 at all.

In contrast, no such adjustments need to be made in the Isletan Tiwa-based rule inventory, in order to account for sentence 23, nor does application of those rules to the sentence add overly complicated intermediate stages to the process of sentence formation of the sort just described. The relative efficiency of the Isletan Tiwa–based explanation strikes me as powerful evidence of an ancestral language rather than standard English basis for the formation of cognate object constructions in this English variety.

Instances of speaker self-correction also contain evidence of a noun-centered, Isletan Tiwa–based derivation for cognate-object constructions in Isletan English. In some cases of self-correction, the object noun is incorporated *as is* into the sentence verb construction, preempting the pro-verb of the original statement as in 24:

24. *They are doing it for commercial, I mean, they are **commercializing** on it.*

In others, the original choice of pro-verb is left intact, while the remainder of the predicate receives further elaboration, in the sense predicted by rules IT 1, 2, and 3:

25. *The dance group* **has** *no* **curing**, *uh, no* **requesting for curing**.
26. *You would* **have** *a* **fiesta**, *uh, a* **preparation** *for the birth of Christ*.

In all such instances of spontaneous self-correction, Isleta English speakers treat the object construction as the component of the sentence that needs to reconfigured. Changes in the sentence verb occur only as a consequence of object-noun alteration and never independently of those changes—precisely what should occur if the form of the sentence verb is secondary to and dependent on the form of the object noun, in the sense specified in Isletan Tiwa grammar.

Additional evidence of a noun-centered, Isletan Tiwa derivation for the cognate object constructions came out of Isleta English-speaking students' assessments of the acceptability of several cognate object sentences. These sentences were part of a larger set of Isletan English sentences these students reviewed; then they made changes in sentence form, as necessary, in order to bring them into an "acceptable" English format. Almost two-thirds of these students proposed no changes at all in the sentences with cognate objects. Those who did propose changes focused their changes around the "cognate object," rather than the verb (e.g., *have vision of* from sentence 10, above became *have a vision of*, *have visions of*, or *have vision at*) or substituted an entirely new verb-object complex for the wording of the given sentence (e.g., *have vision of* became *can see well*). In no case did students propose corrections in the sentence verb independently of changes in the predicate as a whole. Again, this is exactly the outcome that should be expected if the Isletan English–speaking students are evaluating these sentences in terms of an underlying Isletan Tiwa grammatical base.

I conclude, then, that while it is possible to derive the Isletan English cognate object predicates from either of the "source" language traditions, there is much evidence within Isleta English grammar and discourse—noun-based verb inflections, speaker self-correction, comments during formal language assessments—pointing to an ancestral language basis for these constructions, not a basis in English grammar at all.

MULTIPLE NEGATION IN ISLETAN ENGLISH

English language influence plays a more substantial role in my next example—Isleta English multiple negation—and ancestral language tradition has an entirely different effect on Isletan English syntax in these cases.[3]

Speakers of Isletan English, regardless of age and first language background, regularly use a range of nonstandard negation constructions in their spoken (and written) English, as suggested by the following statements from a lengthy discussion of women's and men's roles in pueblo political life:

27. *No, they are medicine men's houses.*
28. *No, no Isleta man does something like that.*
29. *No, you'd never use anything that formal like.*
30. *No, they don't have nothing there.*
31. *No, the woman has no voice to vote.*

All of these statements contain sentence-initial negative onset (*No*). This is the only negative marker in sentence 1. Sentence 2 contains a second negative marker within the subject-position noun phrase (*no Isleta man*). Sentence 3 has the negative form of underlying *ever* in the verb predicate. Sentence 4 has negative marking in the verb (*don't*) and the object construction (*nothing*). And sentence 5 has a negative marker in object construction (*has no voice*) though not within the verb.

Labov's analysis of multiple negation in Black English vernacular (1972) does much to explain the regularities in these examples. According to this analysis, speakers begin the formation of these constructions by placing NEG (a syntactic place-holder associated with sentence-level negative reference in varying ways) in sentence-initial position. Speakers may then map NEG directly into surface structure, as shown in the use of initial *NO* in example 1. However, if there is also an indefinite modifier (e.g., underlying *any* in sentence 2) in the subject noun construction, the indefinite "attracts" the NEG and NEG changes the form of the indefinite (in this case, from underlying *any* to *no*). Then speakers map the NEG-indefinite marker into the surface structure.

If there is no subject position indefinite, speakers may copy NEG from sentence-initial position into the AUX component of the verb construction, then map it directly into surface structure, as in sentence 3. (Initial NEG may be retained or deleted, once the copying is complete.) Or, once they locate NEG within the verb construction, speakers may copy NEG from the verb to sentence predicate; retaining both copies yields the familiar negative concord (or double negative) pattern found in sentence 4. Deleting the verb-based NEG copy, or bypassing that step entirely and copying directly from initial NEG into the predicate, yields the postposed negative construction in sentence 5.

As table 3.3 suggests, there are five syntactic rules involved in the formation of negative sentence constructions in vernacular English, and all five rules apply directly to multiple negation in Isletan English. Labov points out, moreover, that these rules do not have equal status in vernacular English grammar, and a similar range of constraints is present in Isletan English as well. That is, as is true elsewhere in vernacular English, Isletan English grammar requires speakers to copy NEG into the verb construction (rule 3) unless the syntax of the sentence calls for the use of rule 2. Sentence syntax does not require the application of rules 4 or 5, however. In fact, according to Labov's analysis, there are no grammatical constraints favoring the use of these options at all.

It is at this point that Isletan English multiple negation constructions begin to diverge from the more general vernacular English pattern. For Isletan English

TABLE 3.3   Vernacular English Rules for Multiple Negation

E1. NEG location
    1. No, they are medicine men's houses.
E2. NEG indefinite attraction
    2. No, no Isleta man does something like that.
E3. NEG verb-copy
    3. No, you'd never use anything that formal like.
E4. NEG concord
    4. No, they don't have nothing there.
E5. NEG postposing
    5. No, the woman has no voice to vote.

---

grammar indicates quite precisely when a speaker should—or should not—make use of these options. To understand these constraints, I need to introduce some facts about negative sentence reference, and the syntax of negative sentences, within the ancestral language of this community. I will use sentence 6, and the two negative sentences associated with it (7 and 8) as the database for this discussion.

    32. *liwran iw napab se we altar ag* "The ladies put flowers on the altar."
    33. *liwran we iw napab se mi altar ag* negative of (6)
    34. *liwran iw e napab se mi altar ag* negative of (6)

Sentence negation in Isletan Tiwa draws on a multilayered package of syntactic process, under which the corresponding affirmative sentence becomes subordinated to a more abstractly focused syntactic construction containing the same subject reference and an unfilled verb node. This is why, I argue, negative sentences in Isletan Tiwa make use of tense/aspect suffixes (-*mi* in sentences 7 and 8) that regularly occur on subordinate clauses, not the suffixes (in this case, -*we*) that occur on syntactically independent clause constructions.

At a point quite late in the sentence formation process, the subordinate clause is raised into the dominant clause. Raising can produce one of two different structures, distinguished by the presence of a syntactic element not found in the sentence sequence at any earlier stage in this derivation. In sentence 7 (*liwran we iw napab se mi altar ag*) this new element stands between the surface-level subject construction and the verb. In sentence 8 (*liwran we e napab se mi altar ag*) the new element occurs inside the surface-level verb construction, behind the prefix (*iw* in 8) and immediately in front of the noun component (*napab* in 8) of the object-verb base-compound.

Importantly, the position of this element in each sentence coincides quite closely with the speaker's restatement of ideas from the underlying subordinate clause in that sentence. That is, in a sentence like 7, the subject identified in surface structure is being excluded from the activity designated by the subordinate clause verb, and the location of *we-* between subject noun and verb construction anchors this meaning precisely in surface structure. This sentence means: "Someone put flowers on the altar, but the women [*liwran*] were not involved."

A sentence like 8, with the marker located within the verb construction, indicates that the identified subject (also the subject of the subordinate clause) carried out some activity, but the action described by the subordinate clause verb was different from that activity. By this analysis, sentence 8 means: "The women did something, but they didn't put flowers on the altar."

The syntactic differences between sentences like 7 and 8 coincide with substantial differences in sentence semantics. And the *we-* vs. *-e-* distinction, a by-product of syntactic processes that establish these differences in sentence form, is the formal marker of this semantic difference within surface structure. Nothing like the vernacular English NEG copy, postposing, or concord rules is involved in the formation of "negative" sentences in this language. Indeed, there is no NEG in the deep structure of Isletan Tiwa "negative" sentences at all.

All of this makes it difficult to see connections between ancestral language grammar and the syntax of sentence negation in Isletan English. Connections at the level of semantics are another matter entirely. Isletan English grammar allows speakers to form sentence pairs where the difference in syntax can be traced to the speaker's use of single vs. multiple negation. Sentences 9 and 10 contain such a syntactic contrast:

35. *We don't have a word for it.*
36. *But we don't have no word.*

I recorded these sentences during a conversation with a middle-aged Isleta man, a fluent speaker of his ancestral language and active in pueblo politics and ceremonial life. He and I were standing near the pueblo bakery one August morning, discussing traditional Isleta notions of appropriate and inappropriate behavior and their parallels to Western distinctions between "right" and "wrong." I asked: *Is there a way to talk about sin in the Isleta language?* His opening response was sentence 9:

We don't have a word for it. Then he went on to explain that the Isleta language does not have specific lexical items that speakers could use to translate this term, though he knew that Spanish and English provided speakers with ample terms for such references. We talked for a while about different categories of moral and ethical behavior; at times, he shifted from English to his ancestral language, to explain his meaning more carefully. So I said to him: *So you can talk about sin in your language. Yes, we can,* he admitted, *but we don't have no word.*

Also found in Isleta English are instances where speakers contrast single vs. multiple negation within the same sentence:

> 37. *You do not record none of your wills or any of your transactions with BIA.*

I recorded this sentence during an informal discussion in an Isletan home one Sunday after morning mass. Several adult members of the family were trying to explain the intricate relationships that link pueblo government and the Bureau of Indian Affairs. The speaker, a middle-aged woman fluent in Isletan English, the standard English of central New Mexico, as well as her ancestral language, was familiar with the problems of small business operation in a reservation setting. As she went on to discuss the issues she was raising in this comment, I realized that she was telling me two rather different things. First, while Isleta people may have to deal with the BIA in some areas pertaining to inheritance (shifts in claims to land ownership, specifically), Isleta people never make it a practice of filing their wills or other such documents with BIA. Second, while individual members of the pueblo do not have to record business transactions with BIA, pueblo-operated businesses are expected to file such reports and so are the elected officials who are in charge of pueblo government.

Notice how, in both of the examples, Isleta English speakers introduced two types of negative reference into the discussion, and how they used different surface-level constructions to express these differences in negative reference. The constructions in question conform to Labov's rules for NEG concord (table 3.3, rule 4) and NEG postposing (table 3.3, rule 5); yet the motivation for using these rules and the reason for choosing between them in the context of a particular reference are quite closely aligned with the semantic distinctions between *we-* and *-e-* constructions in the Isletan English speaker's ancestral language tradition.

Isletan English multiple negation shows the questions that need to be raised when English as well as the ancestral language tradition contribute to Indian English grammatical rules. In this case, vernacular English grammar supplies speakers with the syntactic foundation for these constructions, while the ancestral language provides speakers with guidelines (in the form of the *we-/-e* distinction) to rework the standard English rule inventory into something more consistent with Isleta language negative references. English grammar plays a more substantial role here than in the cognate object predicates. Even so, the significance of ancestral language influence over Indian English grammar is not diminished in this setting.

DUPLICATED TENSE MARKING IN UTE ENGLISH

The tense/aspect system of Northern Ute English is largely similar to that found in standard English settings. Two features are unique to that tense/aspect system. First, speakers use verb constructions without inflection or AUX support to indicate action not restricted to a single point in time. Second, whatever the tense/aspect commentary they intend to make, speakers include no more than one tense/aspect-bearing marker within each verb construction.

This makes the presence in Ute English of verb constructions like the following somewhat puzzling, in that their syntax violates standard English and Ute English grammatical rules:

38. ***Can*** *you **be** able to do that?*
39. *My sister **has see'd** that movie eighteen times.*
40. *It has to know how much money you **have make**.*

That, plus the relatively low frequency of these verb forms in everyday discourse, makes it tempting to treat these constructions as developmental errors: that is, Ute English speakers use these constructions because they have yet to master completely the tense/aspect marking rules that other speakers of English at their age-level have already acquired.

There are, however, some reasons not to be satisfied with a developmental explanation in this case. For one thing, Ute English speakers at all age-levels make use of these verb constructions, even if they do not use them with great frequency. If developmental errors are the cause of sentences like 1, 2, and 3, many people at Northern Ute reservation have been a party to those errors, and there must be a reason why so some many members of this speech community make these mistakes.

To find out what that reason might be, I decided to include these constructions in my studies of adult Ute English during one of my extended visits to the reservation. It did not take long to notice some similarities in discourse associated with these forms. I rarely heard Ute English speakers use these constructions when talking to other members of their tribe. I was more likely to hear them in speech events involving Ute and non-Indian participants. And in those settings, I noticed, the Ute participants formed verb constructions when replying to questions from non-Indians, not when introducing topics or making commentary on their own.

I was not able to identify the characteristics of these questions until I became part of a English language assessment project at one of the on-reservation elementary schools. The school's Ute language program (the Wykoopah project) was the sponsor; the participants whose English skills were to be assessed included the second and third grade Ute students and their non-Indian classmates receiving bilingual instruction that year (1981–1982).

Wykoopah staff decided to use the *Bilingual Syntax Measure* (Burt, Dulay, and Hernandez-Chavez 1975), as the data-gathering instrument for this project, since (according to reports from other Indian bilingual programs) the colorful pictures, the amusing cartoon characters, and other elements of format made this instrument much less intimidating to Indian students compared to other language assessment instruments. Much as the Wykoopah staff had hoped, all of the students (26 Utes, 22 non-Indians) participating in the assessment did seem to enjoy working with *BSM*.

In many areas, the Ute students' English language skills were comparable to those of their non-Indian classmates. Most of the points of contrast were consistent with features of Ute English grammar and discourse found elsewhere in the speech community. One of those contrasts was duplicated tense marking. Several of the *BSM* questions (see table 3.4) elicited such constructions from the Ute participants, while the non-Indian participants did not use such constructions in those cases.

TABLE 3.4   UTE STUDENT USE OF DOUBLE-VERB INFLECTIONS ON THE *BSM*

BSM Question	Sample Response
3. Why do they want food ?	*They are starve.*
13. What would have happened to his shoes if he hadn't taken them off ?	*They would get took.*
17. Is the man all wet?	*He is dried.*
22. What happened to the king's food?	*It got ate.*
23. What would have happened if the dog hadn't eaten the food?	*The king would have aten it.*

Notice that all of these questions focus on conditions or situations that *might* occur at some unspecified time in the future, depending on circumstances yet to appear, or *might have* occurred at an earlier point in time had conditions been different.

These questions expect the respondent to supply precise opinions about uncertain outcomes, to speculate about events not under the respondent's control, or otherwise to deal in conditions contrary to established fact.

This is a big task for any elementary school student, but it presents even greater problems when students come from a language and culture background like that at Northern Ute. The rules of English discourse allow, and in some cases encourage, speakers to engage in such discussion. But Ute language tradition is not so tolerant in this regard. Ute verbal etiquette discourages speakers from commenting on conditions over which they have no control; it devalues speaker attempts to substitute fantasy or fabrication for fact; and it prohibits speakers from making assertions when they are only partially familiar with the issues at hand. If speakers find they cannot avoid making such comments, they include one or more syntactic qualifiers (similar to English *perhaps*, *maybe*, etc.) in their statements and add a special suffix or sequence of suffixes to the verb construction; the presence of these markers ensures that the hypothetical and experientially unreal (*irrealis*) quality in their commentary will not be ignored.

Speakers of Ute English can include qualifiers like *perhaps* or *maybe* in their sentence structures when they are expected to refer to such conditions during an English conversation. But, because speculation is such a familiar component of English discourse, the presence of these qualifiers does not convey the same sense of *irrealis* reference and create the same degree of contrast with experientially based sentence references as is the case for the comparable forms in the Ute language tradition.

Ute English speakers can also draw on the rich inventory of "hedges" (e.g., *I don't know*, *Can't really tell*, *Could be*) commonly found throughout non-Indian English discourse or simply say nothing at all, when faced with requests for "unreal" commentary. But if they do so, Ute English speakers violate another rule of Ute (and Ute English) discourse: the obligation to respond directly when someone asks a question and not to avoid the task.

Considered in these terms, duplicative tense marking provides speakers of Ute English with an effective strategy for addressing all of these problems. The sequences themselves resemble the structural form of the ancestral language verb—*irrealis* affix added to regular tense/aspect marker—found under comparable discourse conditions in a Ute conversation. And because the structures are different from verb constructions found in "ordinary" Ute English discourse, duplicative tense marking allows speakers to distinguish speculative statements from statements more firmly grounded in fact, and listeners are able to distinguish speaker intentions in this regard as well.

Assuming that duplicative verb constructions are developmental errors may account for the presence of these verb forms in Ute English; such an assumption does not, however, shed any light on the significance of these forms within Ute English discourse.

SOME CONCLUDING REMARKS ON METHOD

My purpose in this chapter has been to examine connections between the ancestral language tradition and Indian English grammar and discourse. I have focused the discussion around the idea that Indian English has an *ancestral language base*, because I want to suggest that the influence of the ancestral language tradition in these cases *must not* be overlooked, even when—as in the examples discussed here, the linguistic characteristics of these codes can be accounted for through other means. In fact, as a starting point for my research, I assume that an ancestral language tradition underlies *all* features of Indian English grammar and discourse, and then I design data gathering and analysis to help me support, or refute, that claim.

Sentences like the following are important to the discussions in this chapter:

23. *People participationize in the mass.*
37. *You do not record none of your wills or any of your transactions with BIA.*
39. *My sister has see'd that movie eighteen times.*

These sentences contain constructions that can be directly associated with ancestral language grammatical rules and can be explained in terms of (non-Indian) English grammar much less successfully.

I realize that the ancestral language tradition is not the only source for the linguistic features found in Indian English grammar and discourse. Assuming that there is an ancestral language base to Indian English constructions—which is the underlying premise in this chapter—does not rule out the possibility that other language traditions may be involved in these constructions. Indeed, deciding whether a feature of Indian English grammar or discourse is exclusively ancestral language–based, derived from some other source, or constructed through some combination of ancestral and other language sources is a recurring problem in Indian English research.

Similarly, developing guidelines that will help people make such decisions is an equally problematic component to such research. In this chapter, for example, I made these decisions by asking which explanation accounts for the given construction in the most straightforward and most productive fashion. Hence, I consider Isletan English cognate object constructions to be ancestral language based, because I need to make only minor modifications in the Isletan Tiwa verb-object copying rules to account for those constructions, but I have to make greater modifications in the standard English rule inventory to reach the same goal.

Similarly, even though the constructions violate Ute syntactic rules, I consider the Ute English duplicated tense-making patterns to be ancestral language based. By drawing this conclusion, I show how speakers of Indian English adapt ancestral language knowledge to meet speaking needs in the contemporary speech community. Otherwise, to account for these data, I am forced to make some claims about the Ute English speakers' problems in English language learning that exceed the scope of my database and paint derogatory pictures of the on-reservation speech community.

CHAPTER 4

DIVERSITY AND CONTRAST

In this chapter I continue my discussion of the ancestral language basis of Indian English grammar and discourse. Here I want to focus on several features of Indian English grammar that are also widely attested for nonstandard English as a whole:

o restrictions on final-position consonants;
o unmarked past tense;
o copula (linking verb) deletion;
o multiple negation.

The grammatical basis of these features has been discussed in some detail for Black English vernacular and other nonstandard American codes. The problem is that the conclusions reached in those studies are not always applicable to conditions in American Indian English. As I showed in chapter 3, Isletan English speakers use copying and deletion rules identical to those in Black English grammar to form sentences with multiple negatives (e.g., *No, they don't have nothing there*). But Isletan English grammar applies additional constraints to these rules, allowing speakers to introduce distinctions in negative reference (e.g., *You do not record none of your wills or any of your transactions with BIA*) that are not ordinarily found in English conversations. This makes the functions of multiple negation in this Indian English code quite different from those in other vernacular English contexts.

Isletan English is not the only Indian English code that assigns ancestral language functions or other, community-specific meanings to features of nonstandard English grammar and discourse. I draw on examples from a range of Indian English varieties in this discussion, because I want to show contrasts between code-specific constructions, as well as contrasts between Indian and non-Indian English usage as a whole.

FINAL-POSITION CONSONANT DELETION

A frequently reported feature of spoken Indian English is the special treatment given to consonants and consonant clusters when they occur in word-final position or in front of some word-internal boundary. In other forms of nonstandard English, the rules that apply to segments in these positions are quite straightforward. As Wolfram and Fasold describe it (1974: 139), while no nonstandard English variety requires deletion of consonants in such positions, many varieties *favor* consonant deletion under those circumstances, particularly if the consonants in question are voiceless or voiced alveolar stops [*t*] or [*d*], and if one or more of the following constraints also apply:

o   the beginning segment of the following syllable is a consonant rather than a vowel;
o   the consonant in question occurs after an unstressed vowel;
o   the consonant is not part of a past tense suffix;
o   the segment is part of a past participle or an adjective derived from a past participle.

Overall, [*d*] (the voiced alveolar stop) is more favored for deletion; it is especially favored if it occurs in a final-position consonant cluster followed by a plural, possessive, or third person present tense marker.

These are not the constraints governing the treatment of final-position consonants or consonant clusters in American Indian English. While Indian English speakers may delete consonants in word-final or related positions, it is much more common to find that they devoice consonants in those positions or modify their pronunciation in other ways or combine devoicing and/or modification with segment deletion. Moreover, Indian English speakers regularly apply these options to a large class of consonants, or to all consonants in final position, not primarily to [*t*] and [*d*].

Here are some examples of final-position consonant phonology in particular Indian English codes. These examples come from site-specific studies of the spoken English of American Indian students. I recognize that developmental factors may be influencing the patterns I describe here; but the differences in site-specific usage and the contrasts between these details and those in other varieties of vernacular English make it more likely that ancestral language grammar or other community-based constraints on English are the primary sources for these details.

Isletan English

Consonant contrasts that regularly occur in other English varieties are neutralized in final position in the Indian English of Isleta pueblo (New Mexico).[1] That is, speakers give the same pronunciation to the final consonants in word pairs like "cup" and "cub" or "got" and "God." In both cases, speakers devoice both consonants, relax the muscles in the throat when pronouncing them, and do not add offsets or make other modification to the sound quality. In addition, when sequences of two or more consonants occur in final position, the number of consonants in those sequences may be reduced; speakers give "hunt" as *hun*, "contest" as *contez*, "hunts" as *hunz*, and so on.

Two rules of pronunciation apply here, neither of which reproduce the conditions described for other (non-Indian) vernacular English codes. As shown in table 4.1, the first rule (R I-1) deletes the final element of any group of consonants standing in front of a word-internal or word-final grammatical boundary. The second rule (R I-2) requires that all consonants remaining in final position after the application of this rule be devoiced and assigned weak muscular tension. The pronunciation of any final-position Isletan English consonant or consonant cluster can be affected by these rules.

TABLE 4.1
FINAL-POSITION CONSONANT OPTIONS IN ISLETAN ENGLISH

	"cup"	"cub"	"hunt"	"hunts"	"contest"
	-p#	-b#	-nt#	-nt#s#	-st#
by R I-1	n.a.	n.a.	-nØ#	-nØ#s#	-sØ#
by R I-2	-b#	-b#	-nØ#	-nØ#z#	-zØ#
	cub	*cub*	*hun*	*hunz*	*contez*

Note the differences between the derivations of "hunts" and "contest" under these rules. The final [t] of "contest" is subject to deletion because it is the second of two consonants in front of a grammatical boundary (marked as # in the notation I am using here). The final [s] of "hunts" is not deleted, however, since the grammatical boundary separating verb base from verb suffix stands between the [nt] sequence and [s]; the [t] in that cluster is eligible for deletion under rule 1, since it is the member of that consonant cluster standing in front of a grammatical boundary. Hence the derivation *hunz* in table 4.1.

Northern Cheyenne English

Speakers of Cheyenne English (Montana) treat final-position consonants somewhat differently, according to Alford's research (1974). The number of consonants affected by final-position constraints—[*t*], [*d*], [*r*], and [*l*]—here is much smaller compared to those affected by rules I-1 and I-2 in Isletan English. However, the options in pronunciation allowed under these rules are much more diverse in this case. Cheyenne English speakers pronounce underlying final "*d*" as [*t*], ['*t*] ([*t*] with glottal stop onset), ' (unaccompanied glottal stop), or as [ø] (no consonant closure whatsoever). They pronounce underlying final "*t*" as [- '], or leave the segment without modification. They either delete final position "*l*"and "*r*" entirely or leave them unaffected by phonological process; glottal onsets or reflexes of "*l*" or "*r*" never show up in final position in Cheyenne English.

Alford does not specify conditions that favor a speaker's use of any one of these options. But he provides enough information to show that an ordered (if highly variable) set of rules guides the speaker's treatment of final-position consonants in this code.

TABLE 4.2
FINAL-POSITION CONSONANT OPTIONS IN CHEYENNE ENGLISH

	d	d	d	d	t	t	l	l	r	r
Ch-1	n.a.	'd	'd	n.a.	n.a.	't	n.a.	n.a.	n.a.	n.a.
Ch-2	n.a.	n.a.	'Ø	Ø	n.a.	'Ø	'Ø	n.a.	Ø	n.a.
Ch-3	t	't	n.a.	n.a.	n.a.	n.a.	n.a.	n.a.	n.a.	n.a.
	t	't	'	Ø	t	'	Ø	l	Ø	r

The rules themselves are displayed in table 4.2 and can be summarized as follows: the first rule (Ch-1) allows any consonant in word-final position to receive a glottal onset. The second rule (Ch-2) allows a word-final consonant to be deleted. The third rule (Ch-3) devoices any consonant in this position. Speakers may apply either rule Ch-2 or rule Ch-3 to a given derivation, either in conjunction with or independently from their use of rule Ch-1. However, they do not apply both of these rules to the same derivation.

Note that Cheyenne English speakers apply these rules to [*d*], [*t*], [*l*], and [*r*] only when the segments occur in absolute, word-final position. There is no modification of these (or any) consonants when they occur in front of word-medial grammatical boundaries, as is the case for the [*t*] in Isleta English "hunts" and elsewhere in that code. The rules apply when [*d*], [*t*], [*l*], or [*r*] is the final segment in a final-position consonant cluster; but because these are the only consonants subject to modification in that position, the overall integrity of final-position clusters is largely unaffected by these rules. Thus, the Cheyenne English *huntz* is the equivalent of Isletan English *hunz*, and either *contes'* or *contest* could correspond to Isletan English *contez*.

Northern Ute English

Speakers of Northern Ute English give an entirely different treatment to these words.[2] Unlike the case in Isletan and Cheyenne English, Ute English speakers do not delete final-position consonants; rules of pronunciation in this Indian English variety allow speakers to *retain* the integrity of these segments. However, they also allow Ute English speakers to devoice these consonants (rule U-1) and to give them weakened muscle tension (rule U-2), to apply these modifications to all consonants in final position, not only to [*t*] and [*d*], and to do this whether the segments occur individually or as members of a consonant cluster. These modifications are not obligatory, but speakers use these options so frequently that non-Indians consider this one of the unique linguistic features of this code.

As in other Indian English codes, grammatical boundaries define "final position" for these rules. Here, however, "final position" includes base-final as well as word-final boundaries. Among other things, this constraint gives [*l*] and [*r*] a particular status under these rules. If [*l*] or [*r*] is the first segment of a final-position consonant cluster, devoicing and weakening do not apply to the [*l*] or [*r*]. This constraint holds even when [*l*] or [*r*] is in base-final position and the remaining element(s) in the sequence are components of the word suffix. Hence the [*r*] in the final sound cluster of Ute English "doors" is not affected by devoicing or deletion, even though it stands in front of an internal morpheme boundary, though the [*r*] of "door" is quite likely to fall under the influence of these rules.

Rules U-1 and U-2 frequently occur with two other Ute English rules of pronunciation, each of which gives further elaboration to the sound pattern of this Indian English code.

Ute English speakers have the option of altering the position of the junctures (phonologically significant "breaks" in the speech flow) that occur in English word and sentence structures (rule U-3), particularly if, by doing so, the English language sound sequences become more closely aligned to the syllable patterns found in Ute language tradition. As a result, Ute English speakers may give an English sentence like "he didn't eat it" as: [*hil + dl#n + t#il + t#it*].

The relocation of juncture positions (marked by [+] in these examples) converts a series of distinct, self-contained morphemic elements into a larger, phonologically interconnected whole. The staccato cadence of this sequence (e.g., *he-din-tee-tit*) is quite unlike anything found in the other varieties of English spoken in northeastern Utah, which also adds to non-Indian perceptions of the distinctiveness of this code.

Of course, rules U-1 and U-2 still apply to the word-final grammatical boundaries (marked as # in this transcription). So the [*nt*] cluster of [*dl#n* + *t#*] is devoiced and weakened, even though the shifted [+] boundary divides this cluster into two independently pronounced sound segments.

Juncture shifting is not an obligatory process in Ute English grammar, but I have found that Utes who use this rule in English conversations can be grouped into one of three categories:

1. Older Northern Ute adults who are first-language fluent in their ancestral language, who learned English after they learned Ute, and who consider English to be of secondary importance in their language inventory. Almost everyone in this category is age 60 and over.
2. Northern Utes who learned English from persons in category 1. This includes children and in some cases grandchildren of those in category 1; usually, persons in category 2 are not speakers of Ute.
3. Northern Utes, regardless of age, who speak or do not speak their ancestral language, may or may not know standard English, but use Ute English selectively in public domains to express their affiliation with Ute tradition.

Importantly, Ute English speakers apply juncture shifting to any Ute English phonological sequence, including those where rules U-1 and U-2 have not been (or will not be) applied, and they may apply this rule more than once to that sequence. In some cases, use of this process creates "new" medial or final sequences composed of a single consonant or consonant cluster but no vowels. English phonology does not permit such a "syllable" pattern, and neither do phonological rules of Ute language tradition. So when such instances arise, an additional Ute English rule of pronunciation introduces a ə, ł, or other "reduced" vowel segment (rule U-4) to accompany the isolated consonants and complete the syllable structure. Like rule U-3, rule U-4 may be applied more than once to the same sequence. Unlike rule U-3, rule U-4 is obligatory: it applies each time sound sequences formed through the process of Ute English sentence constructions produce "syllables" without vowels.

The interaction of these final-position consonant rules produce Ute English sequences that are quite different from those found in other varieties of vernacular English. For example, these rules reconstruct a word like English "birds" ([*bɚd#z#*]) in the following way. Rule U-1 devoices the [*d*] and [*z*] before morpheme boundaries, and rule U-2 weakens degree of muscular tension associated with those sounds: [bəɗ #z̧#]. Some speakers (frequently those in the three categories identified above) then shift the position of the word-final phonological juncture to convert this into a two-syllable word: [bə + d#z#]. Rule U-4 automatically supplies the necessary vowel for the "second" syllable: [bə + ɗ #z̧# ɫ#]. Then some speakers apply rule U-3 a second time, to break up the syllable initial consonant cluster: [bə + ɗ # + z̧ ɫ#]. Rule U-4 then supplies a vowel to the + d# + sequence: [bə + d# ɫ# + z# ɫ#], producing a three-syllable sequence for this word.

Similar application of these rules converts standard English "she's walking" [(šiɫ#z# + wahk#in#)] into Ute English: [šiɫ + z# ɫ # + wah# + ki + n# ɫ#].

Pima English

Entirely different rules govern final-position consonants in the spoken English of elementary school Pima students from the Salt River reservation of south-central Arizona (M. Miller 1977). Pronunciation patterns that emerge under these rules provide some of the clearest evidence that Pima students speak a distinctive variety of English.

For example, the treatment of final-position consonants in Pima student English is sensitive to some, but not all, instances of suffix inflection. Consonant deletion is likely when the word-final consonant indicates plural reference (-s, -z, or -iz) or past participle (-d, -n) morphemes; importantly, the third person singular present tense morpheme does not fall under the influence of this rule, nor do instances where plural or participle suffix follows base-final consonant.

Sound alternations and replacements, rather than modification of single features of pronunciation, are also frequently associated with consonants in word-final position. This includes:

○ alternation of voiced and voiceless stops, affricates, and fricatives, making voiceless consonants the consonants with most frequent occurrence in final position.
○ alternations of affricates (č, ǰ) and fricatives (š,z), and replacements of affricates by fricatives, making fricatives the Pima English consonants with most frequent occurrence in final position.
○ alternations of palatal fricatives (š, ǰ) and alveolar fricatives (θ, d) and replacement of palatal fricatives by alveolar fricatives, making [θ] and [d] the fricatives with most frequent occurrence in final position.

o merger of final [*n*] and [ŋ], with [*n*] used as the corresponding sound for both segments in Pima English surface structures.

In other words, speakers of Pima (student) English regularly collapse distinctions in point and manner of articulation when pronouncing final-position consonants in their English variety. One result is a large number of Pima English homonyms of the sort identified for Isletan English above; note, however, that the rules of pronunciations creating those homonyms are entirely different in each case.

Mohave English; Comparisons between Indian English Codes

Penfield-Jasper's studies of Mohave English (1977: 29–31) show another set of restrictions on final-position consonants in American Indian English. Here speakers regularly *delete* consonant segments in word-final position, provided one of the following requirements also applies (rule M-1):

o the consonant is the second member of a cluster and a nasal consonant is the first member of that pair;
o the consonant functions as a verb suffix marking "simple" past tense; or
o the consonant occurs directly after a vowel or semivowel and stands in front of a word boundary.

Mohave English speakers may, however, handle final-position consonants differently in some cases. Fricatives, eligible for deletion under rule M-1, are more likely to be devoiced than deleted; to receive a devoiced offset and no further modification (especially if the fricative is [-*z*]); or to receive the offset in combination with segment devoicing (rule M-2). Stops in final position more regularly receive devoiced offset, but are usually not devoiced themselves (rule M-3).

These Mohave English rules differ from the final-position consonant restrictions described for other Indian English varieties in this chapter; particular points of contrasts are worth noting here. Unlike the case in Isleta English and Northern Ute English, the Mohave English rules apply only to consonants in word-final position; consonants in front of mid-word grammatical boundaries are not affected by this rule. Mohave English speakers apply these rules only to certain consonants, whereas speakers of Isleta English and Northern Ute English make adjustments in any consonants occurring in final position, as defined by the rules of their grammar. Mohave English speakers favor deletion in instances where the consonant in question functions as a past tense marker. Pima English speakers specifically exclude past tense segments from the corresponding rules in their English variety; in fact, for most Indian English codes, restrictions placed on final-position consonants do not take into account the functions those consonants serve.

Penfield-Jasper's own research highlights additional contrasts between Indian English codes and explores the social implications of these differences. One of her research goals was to gather data that would show how differences in Indian English specify a speaker's tribal background. Parker, Arizona, was an ideal site in this regard, since members of the Colorado River Tribes come from three different language, culture, and political traditions (Mohave, Navajo, and Hopi). "It became apparent," she writes, "while working on this reservation that one could easily tell the tribal identity of an individual by the way in which he [or she] speaks English" (1977: 25). She began to notice such differences herself while working in one of Parker's elementary schools and decided to arrange her data-gathering activities so that she could explore the linguistic basis for these contrasts.

To do this, she asked Mohave, Navajo, and Hopi students at the school to read a selected English text out loud,[3] tape-recorded their reading, and transcribed the tapes verbatim. She tabulated the frequency of occurrence/deletion for final-position consonants in each student's reading of the selection. Then she pooled these data to determine occurrence/deletion frequencies for all students from each tribal background in her sample.

She found that speakers of Navajo and Hopi English favor deletion of word-final consonants when the consonant indicates simple past tense (in the sense allowed under rule M-1, above) and that Navajo students carry out deletion at the same level of frequency as do Mohave students (83% of the time), compared to the Hopi students (66%). At the same time, both Navajo and Hopi students applied offsets to final-position consonants almost twice as often as did Mohave students (as in rules M-2 and M-3) and applied them just as frequently to fricatives as to stops, rather than primarily to stops. Finally, Navajo and Hopi students deleted single, unaccompanied consonants much more frequently (Navajo students 39%, Hopi students 45%) than did Mohave students (5%).

According to these findings, rules similar to Mohave English M-1, M-2, and M-3 are also present in the Navajo and Hopi English used at this site. Yet there are differences in the frequency with which speakers of each English variety actually apply these rules to consonants in word-final position. Apparently, it is these differences in rule use, not merely contrasts in the details of rule inventory, which contribute to the listener's recognition of tribal background–related Indian English contrasts reported for this site and to the persistence of tribally specific Indian English codes under what might otherwise appear to be circumstances that would promote linguistic acculturation and grammatical convergence.[4]

The 5% deletion rate for single consonants in Mohave student English may seem unusually low, especially in comparison to the more substantial rates of single-consonant deletion found in the English of their Navajo and Hopi classmates. My reading of the constraints on rule M-1, and of the scope of rules M-2 and M-3, suggests reasons for this outcome. Under these constraints, Mohave English speakers delete consonants in word-final position only in instances where contextual clues will help listeners retrieve the fact of deletion. Where this will not be possible, modification of consonant form through devoicing or addition of a devoiced offset becomes a preferred treatment for these segments.

Modification rather than deletion is also the preferred treatment for final-position consonants in Ute English; a closer look at conditions in these two varieties provides another opportunity to see how different uses of a "similar" feature of pronunciation lead to more general contrasts between Indian English codes.

Some of the differences at issue here have to do with the types of modifications that apply to word-final consonants in each of these codes. Mohave English grammar (rules M-2 and M-3) allows for the introduction of voiceless offsets to accompany final-position stops and, though less frequently, final-position fricatives. There are no offsets, as such, in Ute English. The closest parallel is the introduction of additional vowel segments (rule U-3) during the (optional) reorganization of Ute English syllable structures as described above. Speakers introduce these extra vowels after designated consonants and often, because of the influence of Ute language phonology, the vowels are devoiced as well. It might be possible to argue, on structural grounds, that the Ute English "postfinal"-position vowel segments and the Mohave English "postfinal"-position consonant offsets are the same linguistic phenomenon. But to do so requires an elaborate restatement of the relevant grammatical rules that would be difficult to justify descriptively.

Substantial differences also underlie the deceptively similar use of final-position consonant devoicing in these two Indian English varieties. In Ute English, devoicing involves a straightforward change in consonant pronunciation, applicable to any single consonant or consonant sequence standing before a morpheme boundary. The rule in question also assigns weak muscular tension to the devoiced consonant and to any consonant in final position that is already devoiced.

In Mohave English, according to Penfield-Jasper's description, use of the corresponding process is more restricted. Just as offsets occur primarily with

TABLE 4.3

ACTUAL FINAL-POSITION CONSONANT DEVOICING COMPARED TO POTENTIAL DEVOICING IN FOUR
INDIAN ENGLISH VARIETIES

| | Speaker's Indian English Background | | | |
	Mohave	Ute	Hopi	Navajo
No. locations where devoicing could occur	42	134	42	42
No. cases of devoicing in those locations	19	27	19	12
Frequency of occurrence of devoicing	45%	20%	45%	28%

final-position stops, devoicing occurs primarily with final-position fricatives. Taken together, these two rules reinforce the distinction between these general categories of sounds, a contrast that has importance elsewhere in Mohave English—and ancestral language—phonology.

The more restricted scope of the Mohave English devoicing rule does not mean that final-position consonant devoicing occurs any less frequently in Mohave English, compared to Ute English. Quite the opposite conditions hold, according to the data in table 4.3.[5] Even though they were working with rules restricting devoicing to a smaller number of environment types, Mohave English speakers still made use of consonant devoicing more than twice as often as did Ute English speakers. Thus there is good reason to believe that the contrasts in rule use displayed in table 4.3 are not the result of chance factors or an artifact of the testing process, but due to specific patterns of pronunciation relevant to each English code.

San Juan English: Comparisons with Non-Indian Varieties of Non-standard English

Wolfram and Christian's (1979a: 164–79) study of consonant deletion in the English of San Juan pueblo, New Mexico, reveals conditions similar to that in Cheyenne English (and some varieties of non-Indian English) in that [t] and [d], much more frequently than other consonants, are likely to receive special treatment in this position, d more so than [t]. Unlike Cheyenne English, the rules that apply to San Juan English [t] and [d] do not apply to [r] and [l]. Reading their analysis against other comments in this section shows other characteristics of final-position consonant deletion unique to San Juan English:

- ○ San Juan English allows for devoicing as well as deletion of consonant segments in word-final position. But speakers apply only one of these processes to a sound segment or cluster in final position. They never use these rules in sequence, as is the case in Isletan English grammar. And they never apply these rules to consonants standing before word-medial grammatical boundaries.
- ○ The deletion or devoicing of final *t* and *d* occurs most frequently in San Juan English when [*t*] or [*d*] is the first segment in a consonant cluster, and much less frequently when [*t*] or [*d*] occurs alone. Number of final-position consonants or position in a cluster does not affect deletion/devoicing in Isleta, Northern Cheyenne, or Northern Ute grammar.
- ○ If the segment that begins the following word is a consonant, deletion of the final-position consonant segment is highly favored in San Juan English; consonant devoicing occurs only infrequently in this condition. Other Indian English varieties use devoicing with much greater overall frequency.
- ○ San Juan English speakers favor devoicing over deleting when the final-position consonant occurs in a syllable with an unstressed vowel. Devoicing is particularly favored if the consonant occurs in sentence-final position or as the last item in some other extended phonological sequence. Other Indian English varieties apply devoicing to final-position consonants with much fewer restrictions.
- ○ In some instances, speakers replace [*d*], but not [*t*], with ['] (glottal stop). The most common occurrence for this replacement is the medial [-*d*-] of "didn't." Importantly, ['] replacement does not occur in "couldn't," "shouldn't," "wouldn't," or other negative contractions, suggesting that the San Juan English [*d*/'] alternation may be specific to the pronunciation of certain words and not, as in the case of Cheyenne English, the result of a more broadly focused phonological rule.

Wolfram and Christian's findings result from an analysis of community-based oral interviews conducted in (San Juan) English by members of the San Juan community. Members of the interviewers' family and friends were the participants in those interviews, which minimized the artificial use of language in the speech event. They then tabulated the frequency of occurrence of final-position consonant deletion and devoicing throughout these texts and used other linguistic and social variables to organize those data for broader interpretation. Their findings on [*d*] deletion are especially rich in this regard (see table 4.4).

TABLE 4.4

Treatment of Syllable Final *D* in San Juan English

Age	___V		___#		___C	
	dev.	del.	dev.	del.	dev.	del.
10-19	17.3	4.1	51.5	2.0	49.4	22.8
20-39	18.9	0.0	41.7	0.0	37.2	28.3
40-59	26.9	1.0	41.5	0.0	50.0	16.9
60-older	33.3	0.0	63.8	0.0	42.5	21.8

Source: Wolfram and Christian (1979a: 194).

According to this analysis, San Juan English speakers aged 10–19 devoiced 17.3% of the total number of final-position [*d*] segments occurring before following vowels (indicated as ___V in table 4.4), and deleted 4.1% of the [*d*] segments in that environment. San Juan English speakers aged 60 and higher devoiced [*d*] in that position almost twice as frequently (33.3%), but made no use of segment deletion.

Conditions change somewhat when word-final [*d*] occurs before a following consonant: here 10- to 19-year-old San Juan English speakers devoiced [*t*] and [*d*] almost 50% of the time and deleted [*d*] almost 23% of the time; speakers aged 60 and older used these options at nearly identical frequencies—42.5% and 21.8%.

Two things about these statistics interest me. First is the inconsistent association in San Juan English between devoicing/deletion options and speaker age. Age-level has proven to be an important sociolinguistic constraint in non-Indian nonstandard English and in some varieties of Indian English as well. At San Juan pueblo, however, [*d*] devoicing before vowels is age-sensitive, but [*d*] deletion is much more uniform across age-levels. This suggests that some factor, widely shared within the San Juan speech community, may be neutralizing the effects that age-level would ordinarily be having on language diversity in this setting. Shared fluency in the tribe's ancestral language is a likely candidate in that regard: in particular, final-position consonants in that language may be modified in various ways but are rarely deleted.

The second interesting thing is the difference between the frequencies of [*d*] devoicing and deletion in San Juan English, compared to those in other nonstandard English varieties also studied by Wolfram and Christian. The pattern in San Juan English, as previously reported, favors devoicing of a final consonant when the segment precedes a following vowel; consonant deletion has only a limited occurrence in that position. According to the statistics in table 4.5, San Juan English usage in this regard resembles the treatment of final-position consonants by working-class African American English speakers

TABLE 4.5

<small>TREATMENT OF SYLLABLE FINAL *D* IN SAN JUAN ENGLISH AND OTHER</small>

<small>VARIETIES OF ENGLISH</small>

	Devoicing		Deletion		Replaced by other segments	
	__V	__C	__V	C	__V	__C
Middle-class white English	0.0	0.6	1.3	3.7	1.3	4.3
Working-class Black English	8.3	41.0	11.5	26.4	19.8	67.4
Puerto Rican English	2.6	18.3	20.6	57.4	23.2	76.2
San Juan English						
10–19	17.3	50.2	4.1	14.8	21.4	65.0
20–39	18.9	38.0	0.0	23.4	18.9	61.4
40–59	26.9	48.3	1.0	13.5	27.9	61.8
60–higher	33.3	48.8	0.0	15.4	33.3	64.2

Source: Wolfram and Christian (1979a: 197)

from Detroit, much more so than it does the treatment of such consonants in the English of Puerto Ricans from Harlem (New York City) or in the English of white, middle-class English speakers from Detroit. Whether this is a random occurrence or reflects some more inclusive fact about San Juan English and Black English vernacular remains to be determined; but the data in table 4.5 certainly refute the commonly held assumption that all nonstandard English varieties share a similar inventory of final-position consonant rules.

Other Conclusions

I end this section with two additional comments about variability and diversity in this area of Indian English grammar.

First, while the point of this chapter is to look at similarities and differences between Indian English and other nonstandard English codes, the examples I have discussed here have shown how greatly Indian English codes can differ among themselves, even on something as seemingly insignificant as word-final consonant phonology. Some of this diversity can be traced to influences of ancestral language traditions, in the sense discussed in the preceding chapter. While ancestral language phonology rarely maps directly into Indian English in this regard, particular rules may provide guidelines for the modification of these sounds or sound sequences or otherwise contribute to this area of Indian English pronunciation. As my examples have shown, other linguistic principles also come into play here; some are common to many varieties of (Indian and non-Indian) nonstandard English, while others are found only in Indian English settings or are unique to particular Indian codes.

In the past, persons who have made casual observations about Indian English in school settings or other domains have reported that speakers commonly "drop their consonants at the ends of words" or "fail to pronounce final sounds carefully." Such generalizations do not do justice to the variety and complexity of rules of pronunciation found in Indian English grammars; researchers and classroom teachers make misleading judgments about speaker English skills, and contribute to the maintenance of stereotypes when they repeat these statements or allow others to do the same.

UNMARKED PAST TENSE

Unmarked past tense is a second feature that Indian English varieties share—or *appear* to share—with other nonstandard English codes. At issue here is the use of uninflected verb forms —*Last year, we **go** to the fiesta* (Wolfram 1984: 31)—in instances where speakers of standard English explicitly indicate past tense reference within the verb construction—*Last year, we **went** to the fiesta.*

Absence of tense inflection in such instances may indicate the speaker's unfamiliarity with the standard English distinction between present and past tense references or unfamiliarity with the constructions that ordinarily indicate those contrasts in English sentence structures. But uninflected verbs are not always indications of poorly developed grammatical skills. Speakers of some Indian English codes use past-tense-oriented adverbs, rather than verb suffixes, to specify time of action under these circumstances (see chapter 2); they indicate "tense" by including other types of descriptive material (the initial *last year* in the example just cited) in the sentence construction. Indian English speakers can also rely on contextual clues, including references to time of action in adjacent sentences, or on a more general appeal to listener inference maintained throughout the text to establish time-reference for particular comments. Rules of pronunciation may also contribute to tense-marking forms, particularly in instances where Indian English grammar already gives special treatment to final-position consonants and consonant clusters.

In other words, while absence of verb inflection certainly is a violation of standard English tense-marking rules, alternative approaches to tense/aspect marking may be prompting speakers to form such constructions—and alternative notions of "tense" may be involved here as well. The following examples examine some of these alternatives and their consequence for tribe-specific Indian English syntax in greater detail.

San Juan Pueblo and Laguna Pueblo

Wolfram (1984) explores unmarked tense constructions in the English varieties spoken at San Juan and Laguna pueblos, New Mexico. The ancestral languages of these communities belong to totally unrelated language families (Tewa and Keresan, respectively); language differences and other contrasts in cultural background and social context made these two communities particularly valuable settings for comparative research.

At issue in Wolfram's paper are instances where speakers of San Juan and Laguna English do not use tense marking on sentence-level main verbs, constructions with uninflected *BE* as copula or progressive marker or constructions with *HAVE, DO*, or one of the English modals. At the same time, temporal adverbs, past tense inflection on an accompanying verb, or other details accompanying the unmarked verb forms make clear that the verb in question refers to action that occurred at some earlier time.

Wolfram's (1984: 48) review of these constructions shows that the tense-marking systems used by speakers of these codes have been restructured in a way which "systematically differs from mainstream varieties, and that [these systems] cannot simply be considered as a faulty approximation of the mainstream variety." Characteristics of this restructural system include:

1. Verbs need not be inflected for past tense. Speakers can establish reference through the presence of a temporal adverb or a past-tense-inflected verb in an associated sentence construction:

o *Remember that time they **fight** for Unge, well, it was because there were some mens that could use their strength and they knew where the Indian from the pueblo belong.*

2. Speakers may use "present tense" verbs in "past tense" contexts, in instances of historical or other narration, provided they have already established past tense reference (through verb inflection or some other means) in an adjacent clause;

o *They all **speak** in Indian when we first started school we had to learn it, the English, in school.*

3. Speakers favor an uninflected tense marking if the verb reference describes an ongoing, habitual action rather than a completed one.

o *We usta go in the wagon with my family, boys **help** their daddy . . .*

As these examples suggest, more than one of these constraints may influence the surface form of a verb construction at the same time. Moreover, different speakers of San Juan or Laguna English use uninflected verbs in these contexts with different rates of frequency. Factors prompting such variation are presented below.

Wolfram recognizes that other factors may be contributing to the formation of these uninflected verb constructions. For example, final-position segments in both English varieties can be the focus for consonant deletion, producing the appearance of uninflected verb constructions even when speakers intended verbs to have tense-bearing suffixes. However, as careful study of the rules of pronunciation in these English varieties has shown (Wolfram and Christian 1979b: 299–321; see also the summary for San Juan English earlier in this chapter), speakers of these varieties are more likely to favor consonant cluster deletion when the cluster occurs *inside* a morphemic segment, while they delete consonant clusters that cut across morpheme boundaries much less frequently. This makes it impossible for verb-tense markers and other grammatical suffixes to occur in the primary environments affected by these rules.

Historical/second-language acquisition models offer a more satisfactory explanation for these forms, Wolfram suggests. He assumes that earlier forms of English used in these communities contained a streamlined set of surface-level markers, as is often the case in the earliest stages of second-language acquisition. Next came a stage where speakers introduced surface-level tense marking into their newly acquired second language, with constraints from their ancestral language as well as from English governing tense inflection in these cases; this was followed by a third stage where English constraints began to take precedence over ancestral language constraints and the incidence of unmarked past tense began to decline.

The distinction between habitual and completive verb references, which speakers carried over from their ancestral language traditions into their English in stage 2,[6] continued to be maintained by some speakers in stage 3. The influence of that distinction, combined with the speakers' use of temporal adverbs and associated verbs to establish tense references in other instances, helps explain why older members of these speech communities (those in the 60 and over age categories in table 4.6) apply uninflected past tense marking in "cluster verbs" much more frequently than they do to other past tense verb inflections. (That older speakers of San Juan English make greater use of this option than do older speakers of Laguna English is not surprising, given the code-specific differences in treatments of final-position consonants discussed in the preceding section.)

In contrast, younger members of these communities acquired the more standardized English of stage 3, and their use of uninflected past tense verbs only in certain environments (primarily, those identified at the opening of this section) reflects a decline in ancestral language influence over their English. This, Wolfram concludes, accounts for the general decline in frequencies of tense-marker absence across age categories, as displayed in table 4.6.

TABLE 4.6

FREQUENCIES OF PAST TENSE DELETION IN THREE ENVIRONMENTS
IN SAN JUAN PUEBLO ENGLISH AND LAGUNA PUEBLO ENGLISH

	Lexical clusters (ex: *cold*)	Cluster verbs (ex: *messed*)	Noncluster verbs (ex: *bent*)
10–19 years			
San Juan	49.4%	12.1%	1.7%
Laguna	37.1%	9.4%	3.0%
20–39 years			
San Juan	57.1%	38.5%	6.8%
Laguna	37.6%	16.3%	4.3%
40–59 years			
San Juan	55.3%	36.2%	13.6%
Laguna	35.7%	12.5%	10.7%
Over 60 years			
San Juan	88.2%	81.3%	16.5%
Laguna	32.6%	28.0%	21.2%

Adapted from Wolfram (1984: 36).

Pima English

Miller reports (see preceding section) that Pima English grammar *favors* the deletion of final-position consonant clusters and the reduction in the overall variety of single consonants that may occur in final position.[7] However, this does not prevent Pima English speakers from distinguishing between present and past tense references in verb constructions. In fact, Miller finds that Pima students use several different strategies to indicate this contrast in their English:

○ Some Pima students altered the voicing quality of the final consonant on the verb base to specify past tense reference, while leaving the consonant unaltered in present tense domains. In other words, syntactic environment alone may influence the speakers' treatment of final-position consonants in this variety.

o   In other cases, Pima students indicated past tense reference by adding a consonant or vowel-consonant sequence to the verb base, then shifting the voicing quality or some other feature of the added consonant to make it consistent with consonants that regularly occur in word-final position. Here, in effect, speakers combine the standard English past tense marker with Pima English pronunciation to specify tense reference.

o   In still other cases, Pima students indicated past tense reference by altering the core vowel in the verb base as well as adding a suffix. A similar tense-marking rule applies to certain irregular verbs in standard English; speakers of Pima English have expanded the scope of this rule so that they can apply it to a much larger category of regular as well as irregular verbs.

Importantly, and very much in contrast to conditions Wolfram found for speakers of San Juan English and Laguna English, Miller reports no evidence that Pima English speakers use temporal adverbs or other descriptive phrases to specify past tense reference in unstructured conversations. However, since their tense-marking rules allow them to specify past tense reference within the structure of the sentence verb, use of such supplementary material elsewhere in the sentence may not be necessary.

Miller reports some instances of uninflected verbs with past tense reference (e.g., verbs without past tense marker) in Pima English. These constructions reflect the rules governing pronunciation of final-position consonants that apply to any syntactic construction in this English variety; at the same time, they have a very limited occurrence in Miller's data, compared to the speakers' use of the tense-marking strategies listed above. This suggests to Miller that speakers who apply consonant deletion to past tense verb constructions have not yet mastered the rules of tense marking for Pima English. The fact that older Pima students are less likely than younger Pima students to use consonant deletion in these settings adds further support to this claim.

Importantly, while Miller finds an infrequent occurrence for uninflected tense marking in Pima English, her data show that 11-year-old speakers of this variety use uninflected verbs rather than verbs with some form of the past tense (*-ed*) suffix at approximately twice the frequency reported by Wolfram for 10- to 19-year-olds at San Juan pueblo and at nearly three times the frequency reported for 10- to 19-year-olds at Laguna pueblo. Additional data from San

Juan and Laguna (table 4.6) show that the incidence of uninflected tense marking *increases* with speaker age at those sites; Miller, as noted, finds exactly the opposite age-related pattern among speakers of Pima English and cites entirely different factors (developmental/acquisitional, rather than historical/language contact) to account for these details.

Mohave English

Uninflected past tense is one of several constructions with uninflected tense-marking in Mohave student English, according to Penfield-Jasper (1980: 82–83, 116–26).

- o Uninflected verbs in present and past tense contexts:
  He just flip.
  They tell me when I was five years old.

- o Uninflected past participles and fully inflected helping verb:
  He just got mash.

- o Deleted helping verb and fully inflected past participle:[8]
  I [ ] seen it.

- o Uninflected *DO*-support in negative constructions.
  He don't know what to do.
  She don't want to go through there at night.
  (Note: Sentences surrounding these examples are in the present tense.)

She found similar uses of uninflected verb forms among adult speakers of Mohave English:

> *That's the bunch that run away.*
> *After he got the papers, he never make a speech.*
> *When he walk down, he happen to find . . .*

Instances of deleted helping verb and fully inflected past participle (pattern 3, above) are not widely attested in her adult corpus. In fact, these constructions show up in adult Mohave English only in instances (as above) where *see* is the main verb. The adults' use of uninflected past participles and fully inflected helping verb (pattern 2, above) is also considerably lower compared to that of the Mohave students she observed. Both findings suggest that developmental factors could be influencing the students' use of uninflected verb forms in Mohave English.

But if this is the case, the influence must be highly selective, since Mohave student English contains very few of the constructions that indicate language development problems in other varieties of nonstandard English (e.g. *he knowed* or *who gots*). This suggests that, as a group, these students have mastered the details of English language verb construction in the fashion appropriate for their age-level. If so, while developmental factors could be influencing the tense-making choices of certain students (e.g., the age-related variation that Miller reports for Pima student English), it is likely that influences from other sources have greater effects on the tense-marking constructions in these students' English.

Especially important in that regard are the Mohave English restrictions on final-position consonant sequences discussed earlier in this chapter. Unlike other Indian English varieties, Mohave English grammar favors the deletion of the second of two consonants in word-final position if the consonant has a past tense function in sentence syntax. However, consonant deletion accounts for only a portion of the uninflected verbs in present and past tense contexts; and it does little to account for the constructions in other cases cited above.

Under such circumstances, it is worthwhile considering whether ancestral language grammar and/or influence from the grammars of other nonstandard English codes might be influencing the tense-marking patterns in Mohave English.[9] Support for this claim can be found by looking more closely at the underlying system of tense reference in this English variety.

First, let me recast the description of Mohave English uninflected verb constructions in structural terms (see table 4.7). I add to that list two other patterns (5 and 6) to indicate forms of the verb permissible under standard English tense-marking rules, options that speakers of Mohave English also employ under certain circumstances.

A review of these patterns shows that the presence of unmarked tense on the verb base (indicated by Ø in table 4.7) is closely tied to other details of verb construction. That is, if Ø occurs on the verb base, either the AUX occurs with tense-bearing suffix or there is no AUX in the construction at all.[10] If Ø does not combine with the base (because the verb *is* inflected for tense), there is an associated AUX construction only if the speaker is using standard English grammar to guide tense-marking usage. Otherwise, if a tense-bearing suffix occurs on the verb base, then there is no AUX in the verb construction.

Clearly, the tense-marking patterns in Mohave English are constructed somewhat differently from those found in standard English settings. The use of main verb suffix deletion could be a Mohave English reflex of the generalized

TABLE 4.7
UNINFLECTED VERB CONSTRUCTIONS IN MOHAVE ENGLISH

Category	Description	Structure
1	uninflected verb in present and past tense contexts	VB - Ø
2	uninflected past participle and fully inflected helping verb (Note: SX includes -Z and -D)	AUX-SX VB - Ø
3	deleted helping verb and fully inflected past participle	Ø VB - N
4	uninflected *DO*-support and uninflected main verb in negative constructions	DO - Ø NEG VB - Ø
all of which are used in addition to two standard English tense-marking patterns:		
5	inflected verb in present and past tense contexts	VB - SX
6	inflected AUX and inflected verb base	AUX - SX VB - SX

-ed deletion rule found in other nonstandard English codes. However, one of the key constraints on that rule is the favored deletion of final-position consonant clusters (that is, base final and suffix *d*) when the following word begins with a vowel, and Penfield-Jasper reports no evidence of such preferences or of any favoring of tense-marking patterns in particular phonetic environments. Moreover, many of the patterns in table 4.7 do not have correlates in other nonstandard English grammars—which suggests that the source for the patterns may lie outside the domain of "nonstandard English," as traditionally defined.

Ancestral language influence is the more likely source of influence in that regard. According to Pamela Munro's research (1974: 8–9) critical features of the Mohave tense/aspect system include the following:

○ Mohave speakers regularly distinguish between "true" and "hypothetical" references. final *-k*, *-m*, and *-pc* indicate statements the speaker judges to be true, and *-Ø* (that is, suffix absence) indicates statements which the speaker considers to be hypothetical.

○ "True" statements can be translated with present and/or past tense references in standard English; usually, speakers offer those statements without tense commentary in Mohave speech settings. They add material to the clause, when reference to a specific tense is necessary.

○ "Hypothetical" statements translate as standard English future tense references; second person hypothetical constructions translate as English "imperative" constructions.

o To indicate a contrast between standard English "simple" vs. "perfect" references, speakers add $-n^y$ to the direct object of the verb; usually, this puts the $-n^y$ suffix in second position in the syntactic structure. In other syntactic positions, $-n^y$ corresponds to the English definite article (*the*) and/or indicates a shift in sentence action from indefinite (unmarked) to more definite tense reference.

There are striking similarities between the tense/aspect distinctions of Mohave, as Munro describes it, and Mohave English, as displayed in table 4.7. Particularly important in that regard is the use of marked/unmarked base forms to indicate the general tense/aspect focus of sentence reference, along with the addition of special markers to the sentence form (Mohave n^y, Mohave English AUX) when a more precise comment on tense reference is desired. Since adult speakers of Mohave English are speakers of Mohave or have learned English from persons who were first-language speakers of Mohave, it is not surprising to find structural similarities between these codes. It is more surprising to find Mohave children, who are usually not fluent in their ancestral language, maintaining such a system in their English. It is likely that they learned the system as part of the "package" of information transmitted to them when they acquired their (first-language) fluency in Mohave English. I will examine other instances where young people "learn Indian" when they "learn English" in chapter 6.

COPULA DELETION

Nonstandard English grammars generally allow speakers to delete forms of inflected *BE* from sentence constructions when inflected *BE* functions as a "linking verb" within sentence reference; for example, *I know it good when he ask me* (Smitherman 1977: 7); *They over there all the time* (Wolfram and Fasold, 1974: 158). Copula deletion is not a requirement of nonstandard English syntax: no speaker of English uses this rule in all sentences, and some groups of speakers use it much more frequently than others.

Scholars explain these constructions through one of several arguments. Some, working with Black English vernaculars, cite the absence of *BE* in West African languages and West African–based English pidgins and see *BE* deletion and other features of Black English as part of an "African linguistic tradi-tion . . . modified on American soil" (Smitherman, 1977: 15). Others consider the absence of *BE* as evidence of the speaker's failure to understand that the items identified in such sentences—*it* and *good*, or *they* and *over there* in the examples above—are connected in some way. Still others point to the similarities in the conditions in which *BE* deletion occurs—in William Labov's now famous observation (1969), where standard English can contract, nonstandard English can delete. By this analysis, *BE* deletion is not an artifact of historical experience or an indication of defective cognitive process; instead, it is one component within a widely shared "package" of syntactic rules, whose influence over sentence forms varies greatly, code by code and speaker by speaker.

All three of these explanations seriously underestimate the complexity of copula deletion constructions in American Indian English.

Ute English

Deletion of inflected *BE* is a noticeable characteristic of Northern Ute English; it is one of the features that distinguishes this English variety from the English used by non-Indian residents of this part of Utah. I found one-third of elementary school students from this tribe regularly using such constructions while participating in structured language elicitation tasks, telling stories to teachers or friends, or conversing in unstructured speech settings. This is comparable to the percentage of adult Ute English speakers using this construction in structured interviews and informal settings. The remaining members of both age-groups also used this construction, though at a much lower frequency.

The grammatical environments that favor *BE* deletion in Ute English are the same for all speakers: *BE* may be deleted in situations of linking reference (*A is B*), but deletion is more likely to occur when *BE* functions as a "helping verb" (auxiliary) within a present or past progressive construction (that is, *A is/was B-ing*) or in other instances where speakers cast the main verb in participial form. Importantly, Ute English speakers treat surface-level verb constructions with *HAVE*, *DO*, and *GET* and other English modals in similar terms. That is, as suggested by the sample constructions in table 4.8, *any* "helping verb" accompanying a main verb in participle form is a candidate for deletion in Ute English.

The data in table 4.8 agree with the conditions governing *BE* deletion elsewhere in nonstandard English, and broadening the scope of *BE* deletion to include "helping" as well as "linking" verbs does not weaken the relevance of this argument. But the central place assigned to phonological deletion in this claim creates problems for analysis in a Ute English setting since (as explained earlier in this chapter) Ute English rules of pronunciation allow for devoicing of final-position consonants, but not for the deletion of consonants from that position. This makes it unlikely that the deletion of *BE* and other "link-

TABLE 4.8
SAMPLE UTE ENGLISH CONSTRUCTIONS WITH AUX DELETION

Ute English	Standard English
1. Deletion of inflected *BE*	
He [ ] cleaning.	*He **is** cleaning.*
2. Deletion of auxiliary *HAVE*	
They [ ] been in the water.	*They **have been** in the water.*
3. Deletion of modal *WOULD*	
They [ ] [ ] shrunk.	*They **would have** shrunk.*

Note: These examples come from Ute student responses to the Bilingual Syntax Measure (Burt, Dulay, and Hernandez-Chavez 1975) part of the instrumentation used during the 1982 assessment of Ute student language skills at the on-reservation elementary school. They suggest the three types of "linking"/"helping" verb constructions that regularly occur throughout Ute English; I have cited additional examples of such constructions elsewhere in this volume.

ing"/"helping" verbs in Ute English sentences is based in a phonological process and suggests that some other component of Ute English grammar is the likely source for this usage.

Note, however, that the presence of a generalized "linking"/"helping" verb deletion rule at any location in Ute English grammar is somewhat problematic: "linking"/"helping" verbs are usually the tense-bearing segments in English sentences, and deletion of these segments removes a primary source of information about tense/aspect from surface structure. The significance of "linking"/"helping" verb deletion becomes clearer when analyzed in terms of the ancestral language grammar.

The linguistic category *tense* in the Northern Ute language is constructed quite differently from the corresponding category in standard English. For one thing, *tense/aspect* is the more appropriate label for this component of the grammar, since spatial as well as temporal dimensions are designated in these references. Hence, instead of being expansions of a more fundamental reference to the time-position of verb action, distinctions like *progressive* vs. *continuing* action are themselves key points in Ute language tense/aspect reference. There is a distinct marker for each of the tense/aspect options that can occur in Ute surface structures; adverbs express such references only in the presence of the appropriate tense/aspect markers, never on their own.

Tense/aspect markers regularly occur as suffixes on main verbs, but are not restricted to that position. They may also be suffixed to subject or object nouns, added to sequences of noun and postposition, or combined with subject/object reference prefixes and other markers to form an independent syntactic segment. Only one constraint applies to the placement of Ute tense/aspect markers: while tense/aspect markers may occur at any position in the sentence, only *one* such marker can be assigned to that sentence.

Accordingly, there is nothing in Ute grammar that resembles the English language combination of tense-bearing "helping verb" and main-verb-as-participle. Either the verb carries the tense/aspect marker appropriate for sentence reference or the AUX occurs elsewhere in the sentence and the (uninflected) verb stands alone.

It is possible, under such an arrangement, that a single clause will not contain a complete picture of tense/aspect reference relevant to its meaning. Here lies the syntactic basis for the distinction between independent and subordinate sentence constructions in Ute discourse: independent clauses are self-contained, where tense/aspect reference is concerned. Subordinate clauses draw on the tense/aspect commentary already established in some adjacent (independent) clause to complete their reference in this area.

Now let's return to the sample constructions in table 4.8. Sentences with "linking"/"helping" verb deletion may violate standard English expectations about tense marking, but they conform quite closely to the restrictions placed on tense/aspect marking in the Ute language tradition. To complete this parallel, note that Ute English -*ING* (category 1, table 4.8) and -*N* (category 2, table 4.8) mark particular tense/aspect distinctions under this system; verbs with these suffixes do not need "helping" verb support in order to express a "complete" tense/aspect reference. That claim is also consistent with the Ute language tradition—and offers another example of how familiarity with Indian English grammar orients speakers to the ancestral language reference and point of view.

Mohave English

Penfield-Jasper (1980: 148–51) found evidence of "linking"/"helping" verb deletion in Mohave English, though individual speakers varied considerably in their frequency of use of such constructions. Unlike in Ute English, however, variation in frequency is determined, in part, by the function served by the "linking"/"helping" verb in the given sentence. Deletion of "linking" *BE* occurs more frequently in the English of Mohave English–speaking adults than children. Deletion of *BE* in other syntactic settings occurs with comparable frequency across generational categories.

This is exactly the opposite pattern from that found in Ute English, where deletion of "linking" *BE* occurred less frequently than deletion of "helping" verbs for all speakers using this syntactic option. Also unlike Ute English, Mohave English "linking"/"helping" verb deletion does not appear to be connected to ancestral language grammatical rules. The Mohave language equivalent of *BE* supplies information not provided by any other segment in the clause; if anything, Mohave grammar works to preserve *BE* reference in surface structure.

Rather than positing an ancestral language source for these constructions, Penfield-Jasper proposes to study these constructions in terms of their discourse functions. Her observations of Mohave English usage in speech event settings suggest that use of *BE* deletion (and deletion of other "linking"/"helping" verbs) reflects the speaker's sense of the relative informality within the speech setting: a more informal context elicits a higher rate of deletion than does a more formal one. The speaker's rate of talking English in the speech setting (regardless of relative formality) may also influence decisions in this regard.

Worth considering, then, are reasons why the ancestral language grammar, which has so much influence over other areas of Mohave English, is not influencing the "linking"/"helping" verb deletion pattern in this English variety.

There are several ways to account for this situation, each of which holds interesting implications for the study of Indian English as a whole.

First, we can assume, following the argument developed by Labov (1969) and others, that *BE* and the associated "linking"/"helping" verbs are candidates for deletion in *all* nonstandard English codes. Ancestral language or other "source" language grammars may reinforce this generalized feature of vernacular English grammar (as is the case in Ute English), but they cannot inhibit the occurrence of these constructions. Under this explanation, Mohave grammar may favor the retention of *BE*, instead of its deletion, but the ancestral language preference will have little effect on the "inherently variable" properties of this feature of Mohave English syntax.

Equally important here is a second argument, which questions whether all ancestral language grammars will affect local Indian English codes in comparable ways. Ancestral language transfer is not the only element, or even the primary element, shaping Indian English grammar in all cases. Since the ancestral language correlates for inflected *BE* and related "linking"/"helping" verb constructions in Ute and Mohave are so different, there is every reason to expect that those categories will influence Indian English grammar in different ways, if they are transferred across language traditions.

According to this argument, the importance of *BE* in Mohave grammar does not automatically predict the importance of comparable constructions in Mohave English. Detailed analysis of Mohave English will provide the database to that end and, in the process, make it unnecessary to propose before-the-fact predictions about likelihood of ancestral language influence in any area of Indian English grammar.

MULTIPLE NEGATION

Multiple negation involves the use of more than one negative marker to indicate negative reference within a sentence, as in Isletan English *You do not record none of your wills or any of your transactions with the BIA*. As I explained when I discussed the meaning of this sentence in chapter 3, Isletan English grammar contains rules of negative location, copying, and postposing similar to those found in Black English vernacular and in other nonstandard English codes; but the influence of ancestral language semantic contrast leads speakers to draw on these rules selectively, so that they can introduce into English discourse finely honed contrasts in negative reference not reported in other nonstandard English settings—for example, the difference between *(you **don't** report)* ***none*** *of your wills* vs. *(you **don't** report)* ***any*** *of your transactions*.

In this section, I discuss sentence-level negative constructions used by speakers of two other Indian English codes, providing additional examples of diversity and contrast in this area of Indian English syntax.

Laguna English

Stout's (1979: 66–124) analysis of negative sentence constructions in the English of Laguna pueblo, New Mexico, offers interesting contrasts to the conditions in Isletan English grammar. Stout worked for several years (1977–1981) as an English language arts instructor at the elementary school on the Laguna reservation (50 miles west of Albuquerque). Developing profiles of Laguna student English language needs was one of the features of his job description. To construct these profiles, he observed student language use in classrooms and on the playground, interviewed students in small groups and in one-on-one settings, and talked to parents and community members about educational concerns. Where possible, he collected speech samples from students and family members, though he centered his analysis (the basis for the comments that follow) around the English language skills of Laguna students in grades four, five, and six.

Laguna English negative sentences contain the range of syntactic options reported for Isleta English, Black English vernacular, and other (non-Indian) nonstandard codes, such as:

o Postverbal negative concord:
   We don't got no pick.
   I don't want no boys to hear.

o   Preverbal negative attraction:
    *Nobody hardly picks him in . . . to, um . . . like if they have
    a team they don't try to pick him.
    Then no police didn't catch us.*

o   Negative postposing:
    *There is no practice.
    Because he had no feathers.*

o   Ain't constructions:
    *Everybody ain't looking; it's only us.
    Gol, my brother's real good in marbles; he ain't lost a game yet.*

In Isletan English, speakers treated negative postposing and negative concord as contrastive constructions, each contributing its own type of negative meaning within sentence reference. In Laguna English, social and cultural constraints guide the speakers' use of these constructions and semantic considerations are not relevant in this regard at all.

Ain't constructions, for example, are quite rare in Laguna student English. On the whole, students used *ain't* in less than 12% of the sentence environments where *ain't* constructions could occur, a frequency considerably lower than that reported for non-Indian nonstandard English: 25% of the speakers are the sources of the *ain't* usage in Stout's corpus; the remaining consistently used contracted *BE* and *NOT* (*He's not going*) as their verb form in such environments and avoided *ain't* constructions altogether.

Laguna students who share *ain't* usage had other things in common. Most of them were male, in the sixth grade, and not enrolled in the school's Chapter I (remedial language arts) program. Most lived in the same village on the reservation. All had lived away from the reservation during some period of their lives. And they are all monolingual speakers of English who grew up in homes in which grandparents (who presumably would be speakers of the ancestral language) were not in residence.

Similar background features characterized Laguna students who favored the use of negative concord and postposing. These students were predominantly male and lived in the same on-reservation communities. Most had lived away from Laguna for some time, and all came from homes where grandparents were not in residence.

Students in this social/culturally defined category used negative concord in more than 70% of the sentence environments where the construction could occur. Stout raised this criterion to 80%, to see if any of these background variables would continue to be associated with negative concord users under those circumstances. One variable did: absence of grandparents in the home.

Stout explains the association of this variable with high incidence of (nonstandard) negative usage in several ways. Presence of grandparents overlaps strongly with use of ancestral language within the home. This prompts Laguna students to turn to non-Indian adults to find models for English usage—teachers and school authorities, church officials, government workers. Such persons are unlikely to be speaking nonstandard English negation constructions in reservation settings.

But Stout also reports that, according to the comments of pueblo members, Laguna people who are fluent in their ancestral language have greater proficiency in English than those who are monolingual speakers of English. Stout's own observations support this claim. To the extent that Keresan-speaking grandparents and parents use English in the presence of their children, the English their children hear in the home is less likely to contain features of nonstandard English grammar, reinforcing the language models they find in outside sources. Children coming from homes where the ancestral language is not spoken are less likely to be exposed to such models and the English they acquire would differ accordingly.

It is not clear from Stout's comments whether rules of ancestral language grammar influence the formation of nonstandard negation in Laguna student English. If anything, given that students who use nonstandard negation most frequently tend not to be Keresan speakers or to come from homes where Keresan is spoken, ancestral language grammar appears to be promoting a more standard English usage in this case and not, as is the case at Isleta pueblo, promoting alternatives to standard usage.

A brief review of the rules of negative syntax in Keresan grammar shows why such an unexpected outcome might emerge here. According to data in Davis (1964: 114–18), Keresan speakers copy the subject/object prefix and tense/aspect suffix usually found on the main verb to a preverb auxiliary and then add one of several special suffixes to the verb base. The resulting sequence is not an unusual configuration for this language. Keresan speakers regularly employ it to indicate statements of volition ("I wish/want . . .") hortatory expressions ("I urge you to . . .") and other references to contrary-to-fact conditions.

Keresan negative sentences do not have the distinctive syntactic structure of the sort assigned to negative sentences in English. But persons accustomed to forming negative sentences according to Keresan-based grammatical rules will find the standard English emphasis on negative postposing to be a familiar syntactic process, and the nonstandard English copying of materials into multiple points in the verb and predicate structure to be in direct conflict with Keresan rules.

Mohave English

Multiple negation is present in Mohave English sentence structure, though the usage here is quite different from that reported for Isleta and Laguna English. According to Penfield-Jasper's analysis, ancestral language grammar has very little influence over this area of speaker English proficiency. She used formal elicitation techniques to measure Mohave students' reactions to the "acceptability" of different types of negative constructions, then observed Mohave students talking English in formal and informal speech settings to determine how frequently they formed negation concord sequences and other nonstandard negative constructions.

Her analysis of these data suggests that nonstandard negation occurred just as frequently in the oral English of Mohave students as it does in the oral English of other Indians and of non-Indians from the same community.

Analysis of specific types of negative constructions—NEG-attract, concord, and postposing—showed higher incidence of concord than postposing (as at Laguna), but a widely based distribution for postposing, involving many more verbs than *BE* and *HAVE* (as at Isleta). Overall, however, her data show multiple negation in Mohave English replicating the usage patterns found in other nonstandard English varieties, not reworking those patterns in tribally specific, innovative ways.

CONCLUSIONS

The examples presented in this chapter suggest several general observations about diversity and contrast in American Indian English.

First, each of the features of Indian English grammar described in this chapter contrasts in some way with conditions in standard English grammar. Such contrasts are hardly surprising, given the range of linguistic, social, and historical influences that have contributed to English grammar and discourse in Indian country. Standard English tradition is but *one* source, and certainly not the only source, for those influences. This makes it important, when standard English grammar does not serve as the model for Indian English sentence structure, to specify as clearly as possible which details are providing speakers with guidance in that regard.

Second, the features described in this chapter show that American Indian English varieties do not always conform to widely held expectations about nonstandard English grammar—nor should they. Black English vernaculars, Appalachian English, Puerto Rican nonstandard English, and other nonstandard English codes are unique language traditions; each is a product of the historical, social, and cultural experiences of its speakers, which overlap, but certainly do not replicate, those of American Indians and Alaska Natives. This is why the characteristics of Indian English grammar and discourse presented in chapter 2 are quite different from the examples of "unique grammatical usage" and "phonological variation" presented in, for example, John Baugh's study (1983) of *Black Street Speech*.

All too often, I think, researchers studying nonstandard American English have downplayed historical and social experience and focused attention solely on the surface-level sentence forms. They see evidence of copula deletion or multiple negation in several varieties of nonstandard English and assume that these are features of all nonstandard English codes. Structural similarities do not necessarily indicate similarities in grammatical process or similarities in significance for discourse. To conclude otherwise is to disregard the very details that make Indian English codes, and other varieties of nonstandard English, important components of local community life.

Finally, it goes without saying that Indian English grammars differ in their own right, site by site and (in some cases) speaker by speaker. Just as there is no single nonstandard English, so there is no single Indian English code. If anything, tribal and community-based variability is the norm in these settings. In part, such diversity reflects the unique properties of each community's ancestral language and cultural traditions, though other factors are involved here as well—some of which I will identify more precisely in the historical discussion in the following chapter.

PART III

HISTORY AND FUNCTIONS

Until now, my discussion of Indian English has focused on the structural characteristics of these codes, highlighting features of Indian English grammar and discourse that regularly show up in tribally specific varieties of English and features that have a more limited, variety-specific distribution. I have shown how the ancestral language tradition influences features in both of these categories. Differences between Indian English and other varieties of non-Indian, nonstandard English can be explained in the light of the ancestral language base and differences between particular Indian English codes can also be explained in those terms.

The ancestral language base also raises interesting questions about the history of English in Indian country and about the functions served by English within contemporary tribal speech communities and at earlier points in time. How did these Indian language–based English codes come about? Who spoke them, and for what purposes? And why has fluency in these codes been maintained and passed from generation to generation, even in settings where ancestral language fluency remains uninterrupted and where other varieties of English are also viable elements in community life?

These are some of the issues I want to explore in the next two chapters. Chapter 5 explores the historical contexts surrounding the emergence of English fluency in Indian country. At issue in this discussion are the events that prompted individual tribal members to become speakers of English (some of which have to do with the politics of language pluralism already established within Indian speech communities) and the events that shifted the focus of English fluency from individual speakers to the tribal membership as a whole (most of which have to do with non-Indian political themes). For many tribes, these shifts have occurred quite recently. And for them, ancestral language retention in the face of competition with English has become problematic. Indian English fluency, as I will show here, offers interesting solutions to that problem.

Chapter 6 examines some of the functions associated with English, and fluency in English, within contemporary Indian speech communities. Of interest throughout this chapter are the circumstances under which community members use Indian English, rather than standard English or some other regional English code, to address these functions and those under which they use Indian English to meet speaking tasks associated with ancestral language fluencies in earlier times.

CHAPTER 5

THOUGHTS ON THE HISTORY OF INDIAN ENGLISH

There have been speakers of English in Indian country since the founding of the Jamestown colony (southeastern Virginia) in 1607. The date may be somewhat earlier, if Dillard (1972) is correct about shipwrecked sailors spreading a maritime-based English "pidgin" along the Atlantic coast during the earliest years of exploration in the Americas. But the presence of English in Indian country did not lead to an automatic acceptance of English fluency on the part of the tribes; ancestral languages continued to be the codes-of-choice for many tribes until the middle of the twentieth century: even today, students from Navajo, Mississippi Choctaw, Crow, some of the pueblos, and other tribes enter kindergarten or grade school for the first time with only nominal fluency in English.

My purpose in this chapter is to consider the conditions that led to the emergence of English fluency—specifically, fluency in ancestral language–based varieties of English—within tribal speech communities. Particularly important to this process were the English-only language policies in the federally operated off-reservation boarding schools. But other factors, ranging from the traditions of language pluralism in Native North America to patterned migration between reservation and urban areas since World War II were also influential in this regard, as I will explain below.

SOME COMMENTS ON METHOD

My intent in this chapter parallels the *sociolinguistic restatement of ethnographic materials* proposed in Hymes (1974: 12) and illustrated in Dubois and Valdez-Fallis's studies of Mescalero Apache, Spanish, and English language contacts (Dubois 1977a, 1977b; Valdez-Fallis 1977). Dubois and Valdez-Fallis

(1976) have proposed the term *historical sociolinguistics* for this type of research, emphasizing that the questions they ask when reading the historical documents and other source materials are quite similar to those they ask when doing ethnography of communication in the field.

I am following the same approach in this chapter—using the description and commentary in historical documents to answer questions about the emergence of English fluency in various locations throughout Indian country, and about the social, cultural, and political factors that influence these outcomes. Recent events in Indian/non-Indian contact have been described in many sources, though language dynamics have rarely been used as the framework for interpreting those events. I have also drawn from the published materials on tribal language histories and related themes, when such materials were available, to discuss conditions at earlier times. But to broaden my database, I turned to descriptions of language use within contemporary tribal speech communities and extracted historical meaning from the ethnographic details in those descriptions. My interpretations of those data assume that the social organization underlying tribal life in the precontact period was more egalitarian than stratified and that expectations about appropriate language use and other rules structuring public and private discourse were also consistent with an egalitarian-centered community politic. In my experience, such expectations underlie principles of conversational structure, approaches to oratory, and other notions of "good speaking" found within contemporary Indian speech communities; to the extent that documentation on this point is available, similar expectations were relevant to those communities during the earliest years of the contact period, as well.[1]

ANCESTRAL LANGUAGE DIVERSITY AND
TRIBAL MULTILINGUALISM

When the Europeans first came to North America, there were more than five hundred American Indian and Alaska Native languages. Today at least two hundred of those languages are still widely spoken within Native speech communities. Some are as different in grammatical form and rules of discourse as Russian and Chinese, Burmese and Bantu, or English and Arabic. Others share features of form and meaning, either because they were the direct descendants from a common (or "parent") language spoken at some earlier time (much as Spanish, Italian, French, and other Romance languages are descendants of Latin), or because frequent speaker interaction and other situational factors led to similarities in grammar and discourse (which researchers call *linguistic acculturation*) in spite of differences in family background.

Researchers consider languages that are descendants from a common parent language to be members of the same *language family*. It is difficult to estimate the number of language families in Native North America before European contact. Today there are at least twenty such language families plus a series of individual languages (or *language isolates*) not known to be related to any other American Indian/Alaska Native language or language family, but which probably had such connections at earlier points in time.

In some cases, speakers of languages in the same language family lived in the same geographic area—Choctaw, Chickasaw, and other Muskogean language speakers in the U.S. Southeast; Isletan Tiwa, San Juan Tewa, and other Tanoan language speakers in central and northern New Mexico. In other cases, speakers of related languages could be found in different regions—speakers of Algonquian languages in the northeastern United States, in eastern Canada, around the Great Lakes, and on the Great Plains, with more distant relatives in California, Oregon, and (perhaps) elsewhere on the Northwest Coast; speakers of Athabaskan languages in the U.S. Southwest and in northwestern Canada; speakers of Siouan languages in the U.S. Southeast, Ohio River Valley, the western Great Lakes, and across the Plains; speakers of Uto-Aztecan languages from southwestern Oregon into eastern Utah and Colorado and from Idaho into central Mexico.

Thus in *every* area of Indian country tribes who spoke related languages could be living next to tribes speaking languages with entirely different family backgrounds. Intertribal communication under these circumstances (whether for trade, political negotiation, or other purposes) involved one or more of the following strategies:[2]

1. Members of different tribes talked to their neighbors in their own ancestral languages if both languages were members of the same linguistic family. This was the case for Northern Ute and Chemehuevi (Southern Numic languages from the Great Basin), for Isleta and Taos (Tiwa languages from north-central New Mexico), and for Choctaw and Chickasaw (Muskogean languages from the U.S. Southeast). This assumed that people were willing to adjust expectations about grammar and discourse so that they could interpret the neighbor's language choices correctly. Speakers learned how to make those interpretations either by observing conversations and developing their own sense of the relevant points of contrast or by seeking training from some more experienced speaker of their language. Older speakers (over 65) of Northern Ute, Isleta, and Choctaw regularly include anecdotes to this end when telling stories about their childhood.

2. If neighboring languages were not closely related—as was the case for Isleta (Tanoan) and Laguna (Keresan) pueblos in central New Mexico, Makah

(Wakashan) and Quinault (Coastal Salish) on the Washington coast, or the Iroquois and Algonquian tribes in the northeast—tribes learned the language(s) of their neighbors and developed guidelines to determine which tribe's language was the appropriate means of conversation in any speech setting. The decisions were not the same in all cases. Among the Eastern pueblos, for example, hosts commonly spoke with guests in the guests' ancestral language; for tribes on the Northwest Coast, guests (or, at least, the spokesperson[s] for that party) were expected to talk with their hosts in the language of the host community.

3. Tribal leaders designated one of the languages widely spoken in the region to serve as their code for intertribal communication, and tribes not already familiar with that language became familiar enough to use it for such purposes. This appears to have been the case for Choctaw/Chickasaw, which became a *lingua franca* for the tribes of southern Alabama, Mississippi, and Louisiana who were not already speakers of a closely related language. Importantly, as Crawford notes (1978: 7–8, 30–32), tribes were already using Choctaw/Chickasaw as their regional code prior to the emergence of the Creek confederacy and the beginnings of Spanish and French colonization. Taylor (1981: 178) suggests that Ojibwa and Peoria, both Algonquian languages, may have served as *linguae francae*, respectively, for Algonquian and Siouan speaking tribes in the Great Lakes area and for tribes from diverse language backgrounds throughout the Mississippi River Valley.

The approach to communication presented in the first two of these strategies is reciprocal and egalitarian. Communication in such terms does not make unfair or one-sided linguistic demands on any of the participating tribes. *Linguae francae* could also be a mechanism for egalitarian linguistic exchange if, as in the examples cited here, the tribes whose languages served this function did not use this arrangement to centralize and extend their own political power. But there were instances where *linguae francae* became associated with conditions of intertribal political inequality. John Lawson (cited in Crawford 1978: 5), reporting on his travels in the Carolinas at the beginning of the eighteenth century, wrote that the Tuscarora:

> the most powerful Nation of these Savages scorns to treat or trade with any others (of few Numbers and less Power) in any other Tongue but their own, which serves for the *lingua* of the country, with which we travel and deal; as for example, we see that the *Tuskeruro's* are most numerous in North Carolina, therefore their tongue is understood by some in every Town of all the Indians near us.

Note that it is the "*most powerful Nation*" that insists on using its own language in dealing with others who are "of few Numbers *and less Power*" (emphasis mine).

The same association between linguistic privilege and political inequality was found in the Creek expectations that neighboring tribes brought into the Creek confederacy would use Creek as the language of political exchange, regardless of their ancestral language background.

But also interesting in Lawson's comments is the following statement: "their tongue is understood by *some* in every Town of all the Indians near us." Apparently, fluency in Tuscarora, and perhaps other *linguae francae* created under similar political circumstances, was not a communitywide linguistic skill. Instead, certain members of each tribe mastered the language of more powerful neighbors, and provided mediation and translation on behalf of the home community. This approach to intertribal communication is quite different from the more open-ended, interpersonal exchanges associated with strategies 1 and 2 above; even in those settings, however, tribes could find it useful to have certain persons prepared to speak on behalf of the entire membership, when formal discussions with outsiders were required.

NON-INDIAN LANGUAGES AND TRIBAL MULTILINGUALISM

European colonization affected every facet of tribal life in Native North America, including ancestral language skills and communication strategies. Whether the conditions of contact involved trade, political negotiation, open hostility, or some combination of those conditions, the coming of the Europeans forced tribes to add new items to their ancestral language vocabularies, to learn new languages, to find new reasons for intertribal communication, and to develop opportunities for communication with outsiders.

It is important to remember in this regard the range of European languages with which the individual tribes had to contend during the colonial period. English came to the "New World" during this period, but so did Spanish, French, Portuguese, German, Dutch, Swedish, and Russian. None of these languages was in any sense internally uniform. There were distinct regional, social, and other "dialects" in the speakers' home countries, and speakers of different dialects found their way to the New World and brought their own ways of speaking colonial languages with them.

Moreover, interaction and communication between speakers of colonial dialects and members of Indian speech communities took many forms, and the language skills exchanged and acquired through these settings varied greatly, site by site and speaker by speaker. Dozier (1956) shows, for example, how differences between Jesuit and Franciscan approaches to missionization produced entirely different patterns of Spanish-Indian language pluralism among the Yaqui (who used Spanish extensively in the presence of Spanish-speaking missionaries and colonists) vs. the pueblos (who refused to speak Spanish in the presence of non-Indians, even after they became fluent in that language).

In addition to introducing European languages to the tribes, European colonization also produced changes in ancestral language usage patterns. Particularly serious in that regard was the wholesale extermination of tribal communities or of key figures in tribal political and intellectual life—strategies used in some areas of the U.S. Southeast and in California to establish colonial rule rapidly and thoroughly. Where conditions of colonialism were less extreme, some Indian languages began to be spoken more widely under European influence and patronage. Taylor (1981: 178) writes: "It is certain that Ojibwa became a lingua franca thanks to its use by the fur companies, whose employees were often native speakers of some Ojibwa dialect (Chippewa, Algonkin, Saulteaux) and whose local officials, as often as not, had Ojibwa wives." Mobilian, already an established means of intertribal communication in southern Alabama, Mississippi, and eastern Louisiana, became the French and Spanish colonists' code-of-choice for French and Spanish communication with those tribes; through this process, Mobilian acquired new vocabulary and a "simplified" sentence syntax, indicating that pidginization of this indigenous language was also a part of the contact process.

Entirely new linguistic codes also emerged in some of these settings, through a synthesis of European and Indian language grammars and rules of discourse. Examples include Michif, an Algonquian-French-based code originally spoken by Chippewa and Cree peoples living in Canada and used today by members of the Turtle Mountain Chippewa Tribe (north-central North Dakota) and in the Metis communities in Canada (Thomason and Kaufman 1988: 228–33); a French-Siouan code, used for purposes of economic exchange by French traders and tribes living west of the Great Lakes area and across the Plains long before non-Indian settlements appeared in those areas, whose influence on English use within Lakota (and possibly other Plains Indian) speech communities may have extended well into the twentieth century (Flanigan 1982); an Algonquian-English pidgin used by the tribes on the northeastern coast (Leechman and Hall 1955), which may have been influenced by the Portuguese-based maritime "pidgin" discussed at length in Dillard (1972); an Indian-Spanish language, Chileno, used by tribes from California to Puget Sound (Callaghan, cited in Taylor 1981: 181–82); Chinook jargon, whose grammar made use of linguistic processes common to any number of languages, indigenous and European, rather than from a single language source (Silverstein 1972) and a "trader Eskimo" that shows connections to Danish and English as well as evidence of indigenous language grammatical processes (Stefansson 1909).

Michif is unique within this listing, in that people are still fluent in this code. More generally, fluency in the other European-Indian "pidgin" languages continued under specified conditions and for specified periods, then began to decline. Flanigan (n.d.: 16, citing Spicer 1962) notes that the English-only policies at the federally operated off-reservation boarding schools were particularly instrumental in eliminating fluency in the French-Lakota pidgin, even though by that time speakers had added enough English vocabulary to the code to be able to use it in conversations with English-speaking outsiders.

That there were non-Indian speakers of these language "hybrids" is apparent from these brief descriptions, though how extensively non-Indians used these languages outside of particular economic and political settings of interest to individual speakers, or how long such usage was retained, is difficult to assess in most cases. Flanigan observes that the French speakers of the French-Siouan pidgin were traders and missionaries, who would never have been present in large numbers within a Native speech community for any prolonged period. Thomason and Kaufman (1988: 231) write:

> the ethnic heritage of most Michif speakers is Cree: we know of no evidence that large groups of French speakers ever learned to speak good Cree, but many Cree speakers did (and still do) speak French. This means that the French part of Mitchif must have been incorporated into a Cree matrix by Cree speakers [through] a process of wholesale grammatical replacement of Native Cree nominal structures by French ones.

In these cases, and possibly others, the European-based European-Indian codes may have been vehicles for limited egalitarian exchange (pattern 2, from the precontact period), but were more commonly used as mechanisms for communication in settings of political and linguistic inequality (similar, perhaps, to the tribes' use of Tuscarora in the Carolinas).

Two other nonindigenous language traditions contributed to language diversity among the tribes during the colonial period and western expansion that followed it, and both had particularly powerful effects on the knowledge of English taking shape in Indian country during this period. First were the varieties of nonstandard English that are the antecedents to today's Black English vernacular, introduced into the Indian Southeast in the early years of the seventeenth century as a result of the slave trade and the commercial ties between the southern colonists and the Caribbean. Second, though somewhat later (mid-nineteenth century), were the many forms of "Pidgin English" introduced into the Indian West by the Chinese laborers who helped build the railroads and worked in the mines.

Forms of Black English vernacular spread from the Southeast into the West due to several factors, such as: (1) intertribal slave trading, whose networks moved African American slaves from the Atlantic coast toward the Mississippi Valley and beyond; (2) tribal willingness to extend sanctuary to escaped slaves (usually these were not tribes involved in slave trading); (3) voluntary migration by recently freed former slaves into Indian country, to establish homesteads in "unclaimed" territory; and (4) interaction between tribes (and their members) and the Buffalo Soldiers, units of African American soldiers stationed at strategic military posts throughout the West during the U.S.-Indian military conflicts of the later nineteenth century and afterward.

Each of these arrangements placed speakers of some form(s) of African American English into close contact with tribal communities or with particular segments of those communities. In some cases, contact became a basis for long-term relationships between these parties; more commonly, it appears, connections were less enduring. Even so, Dillard's (1972: 139–63) review of documents from the eighteenth and nineteenth centuries finds enough parallels between Indian English and Black English usage to suggest that some degree of convergence between linguistic traditions must have developed in these settings, whatever the conditions or duration of contact. Brackettville (Texas) "Seminole" (see chapter 6) and related codes were one outgrowth of these exchanges; some of the structural similarities between Indian English and Black English vernacular, even in settings where ancestral language grammars have assigned entirely different functions to those features, may have been another.

Chinese and Chinese-English "Pidgin English" had important, if frequently overlooked, influences on some of the Indian English language traditions that emerged in the U.S. Southwest. The "gold rush" of 1849 brought over 60,000 Chinese people to California; and more than 130,000 arrived during the period 1868–1877 (Brandt and MacCrate, n.d.: 2, citing Chu and Chu 1967: 37, 39–40, 85) to work in the mines or to assist in the construction of the railroads. Forms of Pidgin English, based on the maritime code that had helped to shape the earliest forms of Black English vernacular and had such an impact on tribal speech communities along the Atlantic coast Pidgin English, were already widely used in the seaports of Asia and on the ships that brought these workers to the West Coast. Some of these workers learned Pidgin English during those voyages (or had learned it in the seaports back home), and that code became the means of communication with their crew bosses and (when workers came from different language backgrounds) among themselves.

As Chinese family members followed their kinspeople to the West Coast, families moved inland to continue working for the mining companies or the railroads. Some, over time, were able to start businesses, particularly in areas—like those on or near Indian settlements—where competition with other non-Indians was not so severe. All of these activities brought Chinese people into sustained contact with tribal peoples, many of whom were as unfamiliar with English (and Chinese) as the Chinese were with Indian languages. Chinese Pidgin English became a workable code-of-choice in such settings, and over time individual tribal members became proficient in these codes. Browne (1868: 390, cited in Brandt and MacCrate n.d.: 3) reports the following exchange between a Paiute tax collector and a Chinese worker:

> *Me Piute cappen. Me kill plenty Melican man. Dis' my lan'.*
> *You payee me, John. No payee me, gottom me killee you.*

Brandt and MacCrate's comments show that this was not an isolated linguistic incident. Importantly, as this example suggests, the English used in these exchanges is not similar to nineteenth-century Black English vernacular, though speakers of that code had reached Paiute country before 1868. Nor does it reflect principles of ancestral language grammar that characterize Paiute varieties of Indian English. The Paiute tax collector is speaking Chinese-based Pidgin English; if he learned the code, other members of his tribal community may have done the same.

ENGLISH FLUENCY AND TRIBAL MULTILINGUALISM

By the time (1860s) that railroad construction began in earnest in the American West, English had already become the primary language of the non-Indians living east of the Mississippi River and in the eastern areas of the Great Plains and had joined French, Spanish, and the various ancestral languages (and, in some cases, had replaced those codes) as language(s) of daily experience for tribes in the eastern and north-central states. Also by this time, English-speaking traders, missionaries, military personnel, railroad/mine workers, freedmen and women, and other settlers had moved into the Plains, the Southwest, and the Northwest Coast (areas explored and colonized by persons from other European language traditions): tribes whose previous encounters with English had been limited were now interacting with speakers of English on an increasingly regular basis.

We know from anecdotes like Browne's (the Pidgin English of the Paiute tax collector, just cited) that individual members of some tribes became fluent in English (in some form) as a result of such interaction. But while tribes may have had access to English during the latter half of the nineteenth century, the familiarity with English that emerged during this period did not necessarily displace ancestral language skills or disrupt the strategies for multilingual communication that individual tribes had long maintained.

For example, once individual members of a tribe became proficient in English, those persons could serve as translators for Indian/non-Indian speech settings; this meant that tribal leaders (or their representatives) did not have to learn English in order to negotiate with outsiders, but could continue to use their ancestral language in those discussions, much as had been the case in intertribal negotiation in previous times. If there were no speakers of English within the tribe, speakers of Indian languages associated with the military forts, religious missions, and trading posts now being established throughout the West could provide translation services. And if Indians and non-Indians were fluent in a third language—French in some areas of the Plains, Spanish in the U.S. Southwest, Russian in the islands off Alaska's southwestern coast—tribal leaders (or their spokespersons) could use that language as the basis for negotiation and bypass the need to use English in these settings entirely.

Young people's language skills were even less likely to be affected by the presence of English in their home/tribal community. Certainly Indian young people became more aware of English during the latter half of the nineteenth century. Conversations with English-speaking non-Indians took place in public settings and young people had opportunities to observe how tribal leaders or their delegates used English and other languages to exchange ideas, bargain, and reach consensus on particular themes.

But these discussions were between adults; they were not opportunities for speaking openly to young people. Hearing adults use English in these settings did not necessarily prompt young people to develop proficiency in English on their own. In the 1860s, teachers working in on-reservation schools still reported that their students came to school unfamiliar with English pronunciation, vocabulary, and sentence forms and that special efforts to provide them with English skills were required. And as late as the 1890s, administrators in on-reservation mission schools still favored using the students' ancestral language as the language for initial instruction since their students' English skills were not sufficiently developed for this task. Ironically, concern over the same issues led federal policymakers to *reject* ancestral language education in favor of English-only classroom instruction for Indian students. Since these students were not learning English in home/community settings, they argued, alternative opportunities for language learning had to be provided for them.[3] By the end of the nineteenth century, the off-reservation boarding school program had become the federal government's policy-of-choice to this end.

THE OFF-RESERVATION BOARDING SCHOOLS
AND THE RISE OF INDIAN ENGLISH

The idea for the off-reservation boarding schools came out of the work of Lieut. Richard Henry Pratt, a U.S. Army officer whose success in developing innovative educational programs for freed African Americans after the War between the States led him to propose making similar educational experiences available to American Indians.[4] In 1879, with the support of the U.S. Congress, he created the Carlisle (Pennsylvania) Indian school, whose curriculum combined the civilization/work ethic orientation of the Hampton Institute (a federally funded school for freedmen in Virginia) with Pratt's personal commitments to education through military discipline and rigor.

Initially, students were brought to Carlisle from reservations all across Indian country, and the success of its program led to the creation of additional boarding schools at Haskell, Kansas; Chemawa, Oregon; Chilocco, Oklahoma; Albuquerque, New Mexico; and other sites across Indian country. Unlike Carlisle, these schools were located in areas close to students' homes. But except for that change, the plan for Indian education established at Carlisle and summarized in the school motto—*To civilize the Indian, get him into civiliza-tion. To keep him civilized, let him stay* (cited in Reyhner and Eder 1989: 80)—became the blueprint for education in all of the federal boarding schools.

Central to Pratt's plan for "get[ting] him [*sic*] into civilization" was the "outing" system.[5] Under this system, Indian students were placed in (non-Indian) homes, where they received room and board while they attended classes at the school and gained practical work experience on the family farm or other commercial enterprise. Pratt assumed that the knowledge and skills that Indian students acquired through these experiences—and through their firsthand exposure to Christian family values—would help students find employment (presumably, in a non-Indian environment) once they left the boarding school; if they returned to the reservation, the knowledge and skills could also help them improve the quality of life within their home/tribal community.

By 1879 mission schools were in operation throughout the Indian West, and some of the students who came to Carlisle and other boarding schools may first have attended mission schools and were already familiar with non-Indian assumptions about appropriate behavior within the classroom. For them, "outing" may not have been an enjoyable experience, but at least they understood in advance some of the expectations on which this system was based.

But more often, judging from the reports of graduates from these schools, Indian students were unfamiliar with life in the non-Indian world when they first arrived on the boarding school campus. For them, the boarding school curriculum had to do much more than provide academic services to Indian students.

The best way to do this, Pratt and his colleagues decided, was to operate these boarding schools as tightly controlled, highly regimented, and self-contained institutions, where every phase of student life was to be closely monitored and no activity left without supervision. School policy determined what type of clothing students wore, what food they ate, what time they were sent to bed, and what time they were awakened. Christian religious instruction was mandatory, and the curriculum reinforced that instruction with its emphasis on Euro-American values—ideas that the "outing" system translated into practical experience on a day-by-day basis.

Student language choices were subject to a particularly rigorous regulation at these schools. The ground rules were simple: speaking in an Indian language or any language other than English was a punishable offense. Punishments included whippings, having one's mouth washed out with soap, and solitary confinement. The boarding school's English language instruction was equally heavy-handed in its design. In today's terms, the approach would be described as *total unstructured immersion*: the students were surrounded on all sides with English-only discourse, were drilled in correct use of grammatical inflections and sentence forms, and were expected to apply the patterns they memorized through rote-learning in daily language settings. Unlike the case in some of the mission schools, no attempt was made to integrate what the students already knew about the ancestral languages, or might have known about English, into the teaching/learning process, or even to present the rules of English grammar through a structured, appropriately sequenced curriculum plan. Instead, school policy assumed that students would become proficient users of English if the school gave them sufficient opportunities to hear, acquire, and practice those skills. And school authorities made certain that every facet of the boarding school experience—including the "outing" system—directed students toward that goal.

Indian student descriptions of boarding school life and boarding school language policies assure us that conditions in these schools were severe, intimidating, and (under some circumstances) life-threatening. We can understand why, under such circumstances, students who had not been proficient in English when they arrived at these schools became speakers of English in these settings. It is important to realize, however, that learning English did not always come at the expense of the students' ancestral language proficiency, nor did it indicate that Indian students were now devaluing the importance of ancestral language fluency in their lives. In fact, some Indian students became quite adept at creating school-related opportunities within which they could speak their own languages without threat of reprisal, even as they were acquiring English. Here are two examples of these strategies.[6]

An Ojibwa woman returned to her home in Wisconsin after her first year at boarding school to discover that she had forgotten (her word) her own language. Her family refused to speak to her in any language but Ojibwa throughout the summer, and she soon regained her fluency. That experience convinced her to do everything she could to retain her Ojibwa fluency during the coming school year. The problem was that there were no speakers of her language in her classroom (third grade) or her dormitory, so opportunities for conversation were quite limited. She did have ample opportunity to go off by herself for prayer and meditation (religious instruction being a major theme in the federally operated boarding schools, as noted); since the Creator understood Ojibwa as well as English, she decided to use her personal devotions to address her linguistic as well as spiritual needs. The woman telling me this story chuckled at this point in the narrative, as she recalled how pleased the school staff members were with her "new" interest in religion, and how delighted her family was when she returned home the following summer with her Ojibwa fluency intact.

Navajo students found they had to cope with a somewhat different set of conditions when they attended boarding schools. The problem was not an absence of Navajo speakers: there were always students who spoke Navajo in the schools, and usually the school staff included Navajo-speaking adults who monitored student behavior closely in every school setting. To speak Navajo under these circumstances meant they had to conceal their conversation; but given that the boarding school was a distinctively non-Navajo environment, it was also important that they select a context for secluded conversation that would itself be compatible with Navajo traditional discourse. So, said the Navajo elder telling me this story, he and his friends searched the campus for "the right place" to talk their language—and very soon, joined the school's track team.[7]

Examples like these suggest that Indian students in boarding school settings did what minority-background students have always done in mainstream-controlled educational settings:[8] they created their own student-centered, school-based, *boarding school cultures*—guidelines, practices, and rules for living to help them make sense out of the requirements imposed by the school environment and respond appropriately to expectations. And if ancestral language maintenance could be a part of boarding school cultures, so could strategies promoting the development of student-based, school-related English fluency.

Here are some samples of boarding school English used by Indian students attending Carlisle Institute during its first two years of operation (1880–1881) (cited in Schuchardt 1980: 30–37).

Selection 1 (Pueblo, male, May 1881):
My dear friend: I am going to write to you this morning very good school. All Indian boys play the arrow shooting up birds tree very nice sing yellow bird. Very beautiful rain down ground, green grass very nice. I very happy in Carlisle school very kind write letter me. Indian boy not much write letter, my hand write very nice to learn.

                                        John Shield, Pueblo at school nine months

Selection 2 (Cheyenne, sex unstated, May 1881):
Desert is covered with sand and rocks and is nothing grows there because is no rain there and is very dry country and very hot and no trees no grass there and I think must so poor country and must stop I got sor figer I write.

Selection 3 (Sioux, male, December 1880):
My dear teacher: I am going to write to you I want this morning a little English to tell you and my work and my school which one good tell me. I guess and your good teacher because that every day my heart is very cheerful the time this morning I must try to write to you more that is all. From your loving friend that is me. Philip.

Selection 4 (Kiowa, male, June 1881):
Now dear brother Yellow Hair our mother ands other rest friends all pretty well and all want to see you very much. Only one cousin die last spring. Now this I am so sorry to tell, your dear wife got other young man, never mind brother, good many other nice girl yet not see all friend yet some time way of good way. Pretty soon the Kiowa all move away to making medicine house and also Cheyenne making medicine house three times. I want you write to me soon if you can. Good bye god bless you be a good boy. Your dear brother. P.C.Z.

Selection 5 (Sioux, female, August 1881):
My Dear Three Stars: I want to write to you again and I have cheerfully to work all the time and to learn everything. I have accomplish a pair pants and coat too, every day because I can build the pants and coat too. I have work in 13 months in tailor trade, and I never become tired. We are perputual cheerfully attending school every day. We are trying long

. suffering and hard think. Now I can able write letter this time that is all to say, write soon. From your cousin Clarence Sioux—that is me.

The letters were written by Carlisle students for publication in the school newspaper. One of the editors explained the purpose of this newspaper in the following terms:

We know that this is a small paper. It is the smallest paper that we ever saw. We are going to try to make it good. We put everything in this paper that the Indian boys write for us. Not any white man's writing but all the Indian boy's writing. Some speechs and some letters . . .

Hugo Schuchardt published a selection of these letters in an article exploring the pidgin/creole affinities of nineteenth-century American Indian English. He found six linguistic features occurring with great frequency in these texts:

1. Omission of the *s* in the third person plural present (*she know*, *she give*);
2. Noun and pronoun as subject markers (*My father he*, *the people it*);
3. Use of personal pronoun for the possessive pronoun (*he name*);
4. Confusion [*sic*] of *he* and *she* (*my horse her name*);
5. Contrast of imperfect auxiliary (*was*) with the perfect *have*, to distinguish imperfect from past completive references (*I was stayed*, *you both were came*, *he was smoke*);
6. Absence of *to be* in the present tense, when followed by a gerund, adjective, or adverb (*I continuing*, *I just thinking*, *I very happy*).

All six are familiar elements in nonstandard English grammar, and some—particularly the imperfect construction in 5—do show close connections with pidgin/creole languages used elsewhere around the world. However, my review of the data in Schuchardt's corpus suggests that the features in his list do not appear with the same frequency in all texts. Moreover, his list captures only a portion of the complexity of usage, and knowledge of language, which these texts contain.

Left without comment, for example, are syntactic constructions like:

Very beautiful rain down ground (selection 1; right-to-left expansion, inflected *BE* deletion, and use of preposition as verb form);
is nothing grows there because is no rain there and is very dry country (selection 2; deletion of redundant clause-initial subject noun phrase)

> *I want this morning a little English to tell you and my work and my school*
>   (selection 3; unmarked relationships between predicate noun phrases)

These cannot be explained simply by reference to pidgin/creole linguistic features. Also overlooked are instances of choices in word and sentence:

> *your good teacher because that every day my heart is very cheerful*
>   (selection 3)
> *We are perputual cheerfully attending school every day.*
>   (selection 5)

and text-internal style shifts between Indian English vernacular and standard English usage:

> *Now this I am so sorry to tell, your dear wife got other young man* vs. *I want you write to me soon if you can. Goodbye god bless you be a good boy* (selection 4).

Neither of these can be explained satisfactorily by reference to universals of pidgin/creole grammar.

To me, it seems more reasonable to suggest that these students were drawing on a range of linguistic (and cultural) skills as they constructed these compositions; the pidgin/creole grammatical process may have contributed to that end, but so did other types of language skills with which these students were familiar.

Certainly, the English language instruction that these students were receiving in the classroom was also influential here, as were the attempts of school staff to model appropriate English usage in other settings across the campus. *How much* influence standard English actually had in shaping the outcomes of this process is another matter entirely. If standard English had been the primary influence on the Carlisle students' knowledge of English, then there should be much more evidence of such constructions—or of attempts to approximate them—in the linguistic structures of these compositions and the frequency of such constructions should be much more uniformly displayed throughout the sample.

The absence of such features, and such uniformity, suggests that Indian student varieties of English at Carlisle Institute, 1880–1881, were *codes-under-construction*, codes that students were creating, as individuals and as a group, on the basis of the knowledge of language they had acquired in their home/tribal communities, were learning from their teachers, and were learning from each other. This, of course, was not the school's plan for English language development, but it was certainly a reasonable alternative if, as I have argued here, the students arrived at the schools with minimal familiarity with English (if that) and found themselves thrust into an tightly controlled environment where they were expected to be English proficient and where use of other language options elicited immediate negative sanctions.

Student-to-student conversations help explain the variations in English usage that Schuchardt's data display. Remember that students attending these schools came from many different language backgrounds and that, in many tribal speech communities, rules of discourse obligated speakers to acknowledge their own tribal background, and those of their speech partners, when they participated in conversations with outsiders. Using ancestral language discourse for this purpose at Carlisle Institute or other boarding school settings would prompt swift retaliation from school authorities since Indian language conversations were not allowed at these schools. These restrictions forced students to build indicators of tribal background and contrast into their English discourse.

According to Malancon and Malancon's research (1977), tribally centered variability was an equally prominent theme in the Indian English used by students attending Haskell Institute (Lawrence, Kansas) in 1915. The Malancons' analysis centered around a collection of essay examinations and other written materials prepared by Indian students in their junior and senior years at the Haskell Institute (now Haskell College) in Lawrence.[9] The Malancons identified the most frequently recurring grammatical features in these texts (see table 5.1), many of which continue to be highly visible in Indian English grammars. But they also noticed that these features were not distributed uniformly within their corpus. However, they began to see greater regularities in this distribution once they plotted the distribution of those features against the students' tribal/language backgrounds.

Table 5.2 summarizes their findings on this point. Note that individual features show up at quite different frequencies in different codes—feature 1, *subject-verb misagreement*, ranges from 7% (Sioux) to 27% (Cherokee, Choctaw), while feature 3, *internal/deletion* of pronoun or relative, ranges from 2% (Cherokee) to 31% (Sioux).

Note also that varieties that use some features at comparable frequencies do not necessarily use other features the same way. Feature 5, *lexical variation*, was the most frequently employed for Crow, Chippewa, and Choctaw students, for example, but there was very little similarity in the other features that had high frequencies of occurrence in these codes—features 1, 2, 4, 7, 8 for Crow, 6, 7, 10, 12 for Chippewa; and 1, 8, 11, 12 for Choctaw.

There are several ways to explain the tribally centered diversity displayed in table 5.2. First, it is possible that students came to Haskell already fluent in

TABLE 5.1 GRAMMATICAL FEATURES, HASKELL INDIAN ENGLISH, 1915

1. Subject-verb word misagreement:
   The **birds does** a great deal of harm. (Sac and Fox)
2. Tense mixing/variant use of tenses:
   People *dug* hole in the ground and **have** it for house. (Potawatomi)
3. Internal deletion of pronoun or relative:
   Free water is not useful *[ ]* soaks the plants. (Sioux)
4. Addition/deletion of determiner:
   It keeps our teeth in **a** good condition. (Crow)
5. Lexical variation:
   They make a **bird law** not to harm the birds. (Sac and Fox)
6. Preposition variation:
   Columbus sighted land; it was **on** the Bahama Isles. (Wichita)
7. Deletion of past tense marker:
   The seeds I have **mention** are . . . (Arapaho)
8. Spelling errors:
   If not, **they** wouldn't be anything to feed them. (Sioux)
9. Syntactic variation:
   Every sentence capital letter must be used. (Creek)
10. Copula deletion:
    He can do anything he wants to, providing it *[ ]* not against the law.
    (Chippewa)
11. Deletion of plural/unnecessary plural:
    People have better health*s*. (Potawatomi)
12. Deletion of auxiliary:
    The race horse *[ ]* used for riding. (Potawatomi)

Source: Malancon and Malancon (1977: 147–49). Note: the Malancons used Leechman and Hall's (1955) typology of features of American Indian "pidgin English" as the blueprint for this classification. Criticism of these labels (e.g., Wolfram 1984: 35) should rightfully be directed at Leechman and Hall.

Indian English—which had become established in their home/tribal community by 1915—and that the English they had learned at home was ancestral language–centered, then as today, and that they used these varieties of English to meet the obligations to speak English that the boarding school environment imposed on them.

Second, it is possible that Indian students who attended Haskell Institute came to the boarding school unfamiliar with English and used their proficiency in ancestral language grammar and discourse as a basis for developing a site-specific, functional English fluency—much as Indian students at Carlisle Institute had done some thirty-five years before.

It is also possible, depending on the students' tribal background and home community, that both of these explanations might have applied to groups of Indians students attending Haskell Institute in 1915.

TABLE 5.2   DISTRIBUTION OF GRAMMATICAL FEATURES BY TRIBE

Tribe	Grammatical Feature											
	1	2	3	4	5	6	7	8	9	10	11	12
Creek	14%		19%	19%	14%		5%		10%	5%		14%
Crow	17%	12%		12%	41%		6%	12%				
Arapaho	17%	5%		8%	27%	23%	10%	5%	5%			
Chippewa					32%	17%	17%			17%		17%
Sioux	7%	12%	31%	10%	12%	7%	7%		7%		7%	
Sac and Fox	16%	8%	5%	6%	22%	14%	10%	4%	5%	4%	2%	4%
Pueblo	12%		17%	12%	34%	5%	5%		5%	5%		5%
Potawatomi	24%	9%	3%	18%	11%	3%	23%			3%	3%	3%
Cherokee	27%	4%	2%		29%	8%	4%	4%	11%	4%		
Wichita	8%	15%	8%	8%	8%	8%	17%	8%	20%			
Choctaw	27%				40%				7%		13%	13%

Source: Malancon and Malancon (1977: 151). Grammatical features are encoded by the number assigned to them in Table 5.1. The percentages indicate the frequency with which the features occurred in the written essays of students from each tribe, compared to the number of times the features could have occurred in those essays. For example, 14% of the Creek students' written English sentences contained constructions with "subject-verb misagreement," compared to 17% of the Crow students' sentences and 7% of the Sioux students' sentences. Cases where a percentage value is not provided indicate features not attested in the written English of students from that tribe.

Finally, we need to remember that the students represented in the Malancons' corpus were juniors and seniors and had presumably been subjected to Haskell's English-only institutional restrictions for some time. So whether they came to Haskell already speaking Indian English or acquired their Indian English skills as part of their adjustment to boarding school life, the Malancons' data suggest that the English language instruction provided at this site did not eliminate the students' proficiency in nonstandard, tribally centered English. If anything, the multitribal nature of the school environment probably *heightened* development and retention of these contrasts.

INTO THE TWENTIETH CENTURY

I have focused in some detail on the conditions of English language learning in the federally operated boarding schools because, as I interpret the historical data, boarding school experience played a pivotal role in redefining the patterns of English fluency in Indian country. Importantly, under this arrangement, English was no longer a language known and used by individuals, as had been the case for so many of the tribes in previous years. Boarding school education made English proficiency accessible to whole segments of the tribal speech community; and student recollections of the rigors of English-only boarding school policies gave them reasons to transmit English skills to other community members who were likely to be sent to those schools.

Significantly, the English that Indian students learned in boarding school settings and brought home to their tribal speech communities was not necessarily the English that their teachers wanted them to acquire. As I have explained, classroom instruction was only one of the sources for English language development available to Indian students attending these schools and—judged by the evidence in student writing samples—standard English grammar was only one element influencing their definitions of English proficiency.

To understand the history of English in Indian country after the beginning of the boarding school era, we have to understand why the tribes retained fluency in these "nonstandard" English codes. I consider this question in some detail in chapter 6. Here, as a prelude to that discussion, I want to examine some of the events that furthered the spread of English in Indian country and intensified the likelihood of tribal contacts with English-speaking non-Indians.

Important in this regard was the passage of the Dawes Act of 1887, which legitimized non-Indian access to lands formerly set aside exclusively for use by the tribes. Reservations and other areas of trust land became "checkerboarded" under the provisions of this act, as federal agents assigned individual Indian families their own parcels of land (ignoring, in the process, the landholding interests of larger kin-based or other corporate social groups) and non-Indian settlers staked their claim on the unassigned lands. What began as non-Indian homesteading soon included the construction of roadways to connect those homesteads, then the emergence of settled communities of non-Indians, and then other evidence of non-Indian expansion. In the process, areas that had been exclusively Indian in composition and language were now being transformed into increasingly English-oriented social domains. Congress made substantial revisions in the Dawes Act in 1906 and endorsed efforts to restore to (some of) the tribes lands alienated through that policy. Even so, the checkerboard Indian and non-Indian residence patterns and the growth of on-reservation opportunities for non-Indian-controlled English discourse that accompanied those residence patterns remain familiar states of affairs throughout Indian country today.

Changes in federal Indian policy proposed by the Meriam report (Meriam et al. 1928) also affected the "presence" of English in many Indian speech communities. The authors of this report proposed that tribes, not the federal government, should be the primary actors in any attempt to "resolve" what they termed "the problem of Indian administration" and that effective Indian education had to be the foundation for such problem-solving. They found the federal boarding schools were disruptive to family and community life and worked contrary to the best interests of the tribes. They proposed to replace that policy with a shift toward locally based education by setting up a system of on-reservation day-schools, making use of public schools where possible and relying on boarding schools only when distances between home and school sites made daily commuting impractical.

The Meriam Report's recommendations became part of Federal Indian policy in the 1930s; by 1934 nonresidential, community-based education programs—operated by federal authorities or through contracts with public schools located adjacent to Indian lands—had become the primary channel for delivering instructional services to the tribes. These day-schools did much to minimize the discontinuities between school and tribal community that had become commonplace during the boarding school era (see comments in Szasz, 1974). At the same time, even though some of these schools offered literacy training in ancestral languages (Navajo, Hopi, Lakota), the curriculum of the day-schools remained largely non-Indian oriented, and locating these schools in or near Indian communities added substantially to the English language "presence" in those settings.

After the end of World War II, and in response to growing non-Indian desire to terminate services to any of the tribes now able to take charge of their affairs, the federal government mounted an aggressive campaign—the Employment Assistance Program—to give vocational and technical training to Indian young people and adults, to find jobs for the trainees in off-reservation, urban settings, and to assist them in their relocation and transition into the non-Indian labor force.

This policy was not disruptive when jobs could be found in areas adjacent to Indian communities; families could remain at home while wage-earners commuted to and from their job-site on a daily or weekly basis. But when participation in this program obligated trainees to move (with or without other members of the family) to unfamiliar, off-reservation surroundings, the consequences for tribal cohesion were considerably more serious. Both sets of circumstances imposed job-related needs for functional English fluency; the English skills that trainees had not learned in the home community quickly had to be acquired in off-reservation, urban/employment settings—often, according to personal narratives I have collected at Isleta and Northern Ute, from other Indian workers also employed in the same facilities.

Mindful of this problem, the Commission on the Rights, Liberties and Responsibilities of the American Indian placed great emphasis on improving educational opportunities for Indians at all age-levels, during its review of federal efforts to provide economic and social services to the tribes (cf. Brophy and Aberle 1966). The commission's suggestions for educational improvement were consistent with the philosophy of termination underlying all federal policy during this period: move Indian students from Indian schools into public school settings as soon as they are prepared to do well in those non-Indian settings (Brophy and Aberle 1966: 156 ff.). Federally operated day-schools and boarding schools should prepare Indian students to make the transition into the public school settings; federal programs should take primary responsibility for Indian education only when public school alternatives are not available.

The commission's report did not contain explicit recommendations regarding English language instruction; given its commitment to mainstreaming Indian students, explicit statements to that end were not required.

Indian students had been attending public schools for some years prior to the preparation of the commission's recommendations, and the Johnson-O'Malley program provided federal funds to those schools, to help defray the special costs (e.g., salaries for teacher aides, instructional materials, supplies) they incurred when educating these students. But the commission's recommendations called for public schools to intensify their efforts in Indian education—which became especially important as the federal government began to shift responsibilities for Indian services to state and local agencies and to take other steps to terminate its involvement in Indian affairs.

In the 1970s, when federal commitments to tribal self-determination replaced the "termination" policies of previous years, public schools continued to be important foci for delivering educational services to the tribes—and to contribute to the spread of English in those settings. New legislation—particularly the Indian Education Act (P.L. 92-318) and the Indian Self-Determination and Educational Assistance Act (P.L. 93-638)—gave Indian parents and community members more control over the education of their children. To exercise that control, parents and community members had to master non-Indian styles of English discourse, since the arena of control included school board meetings, one-on-one conferences with school principals, conference sessions with BIA officials, and other domains where non-Indian English was the code-of-choice.

Indian students began to master new forms of English discourse as a result of public school education, as well. Public schools brought Indian students into close contact with non-Indian students their own age. This gave Indian students the chance to watch how non-Indian classmates interacted with non-Indian teachers and school authorities and with each other—and it introduced them to task-oriented language skills that they had not been able to observe directly when attending Indian-only day- or boarding schools.

Whether these encounters encouraged Indian students to acquire non-Indian student usage is difficult to assess. Even at grade school levels, Indian students are certainly aware of differences between Indian and non-Indian English grammars and discourse and use special phrases (e.g., Northern Ute students say "he's talking like a cowboy," Lakota students say "she's using the big man's English") to tease their classmates who move too far away from student perceptions of Indian English norms. But, non-Indian-oriented English fluency being so closely tied to school success, public school settings forced Indian students to make such comparisons between English codes. The shifts in student English skills and changes in student ancestral language proficiency reported in chapter 1 are some of the by-products of those comparisons.

CHAPTER 6

FUNCTIONS OF INDIAN ENGLISH

A complex sequence of events connects the English codes introduced to the tribes on the Atlantic coast at the beginning of the colonial period with the English codes spoken throughout Indian country at the end of the twentieth century. What started as a non-Indian-controlled mechanism of trade, exploration, political negotiation, and conquest developed into a set of tribally focused alternatives to standard English, regional non-Indian English, and (in some cases) ancestral language discourse. Having described some of the conditions that brought about the historical development of these English codes, I now want to explore these codes' functions. What are speakers of Indian English saying—and doing—when they use Indian English, rather than some other language variety, as their code-of-choice in a given speech domain? How do these messages differ when Indian English is the only Indian language option they control or when it is their only variety of English?

BACKGROUND: ENGLISH AS THE LANGUAGE OF THE METROPOLIS

Before I can answer these questions, I need to recognize that—tribal efforts toward cultural maintenance, self-determination, and sovereignty notwithstanding—daily life in Indian country is heavily regulated by concentrations of economic, social, and intellectual power located outside of community boundaries and beyond the scope of tribal control. Jorgensen (1970: 84ff.) uses the term *metropolis* to refer to these concentrations of power and uses *satellite* to identify entities that become sources of labor, goods, and services for the metropolis and fall under its influence in other ways. Under this formulation, Indian reservations, rural communities, and urban Indian enclaves can be considered satellites to some larger metropolis. And since the institutions that control these satellites, as well as the personnel who operate and manage those institutions, are often usually based in cities or connected to agencies with urban ties, it is common to see references to the metropolis (the economic/political phenomenon) linked with references to the most prominent urban area within a given region.

There is at least one such urban area connected to every on-reservation and rural Indian community,[1] and urban institutions can influence every aspect of daily life within those communities. At Northern Ute, as I explained in chapter 1, people regularly make use of the shopping, entertainment, and health-care facilities in the Salt Lake City area (though they have to make a 300-mile round-trip to do this) and often move back and forth between reservation and city when seeking opportunities for education or employment.

Not all tribal communities are close enough to urban areas to allow for frequent travel; even when distances are small, geographic barriers, weather patterns, absence of transportation, and other factors can make travel from home to city a difficult task. Hence the importance—from the point of view of the metropolis-satellite model—of the smaller, predominantly non-Indian communities that have grown up on or near Indian lands.[2]

Non-Indian communities provide a range of commercial services—grocery stores, drugstores, hardware, clothing and other specialty shops, car and truck repair—that may compete with services available through Indian-owned businesses on Indian lands. And while the reception given Indian customers may not always be cordial in these non-Indian business settings, tribal members can usually find ways to justify doing business in these communities. Their stores usually offer a greater variety of goods and services, compared to those available in Indian-operated businesses closer to home. Frequently prices are lower. And in some cases—such as movie theaters, packaged consumables, franchised fast-food facilities—non-Indian communities offer services that may not be available in Indian settings at all.

Indian-owned businesses are placed at considerable disadvantage under such conditions of competition; to combat the appeal of local-level, non-Indian enterprise, Indian business owners may adjust their inventories to reflect merchandise or services provided by their competitors, purchase advertising time on non-Indian-controlled media sources, or refocus their activities to accommodate the interests of non-Indian customers as well as Indian ones. And to broaden their chances for success, they may move their place of business out of an exclusively Indian setting and into one of the surrounding non-Indian communities.

Not all non-Indian businesses are in competition with Indian-owned enterprises. Sometimes, if they did not provide services, several areas of commercial activity would not be available to Indian communities at all. Non-Indian-controlled regional banks provide loans to cover startup costs, and non-Indian insurance agencies sell policies that protect individual investments. Indian wholesalers provide needed merchandise and other support services essential to daily operations of Indian businesses, and non-Indians from the surrounding communities may become employees in these firms.

The metropolitan functions imposed through local, non-Indian communities are not limited to the domains of economic opportunity and exchange. If public schools provide educational services to Indian students, the school authorities that operate those facilities are based in these non-Indian communities, which gives them direct control over curriculum, staff hiring, and school finance. Even in instances where Indian schools are administered by the Bureau of Indian Affairs or by tribal governments, the curriculum of these schools must meet country and state educational standards and members of the school staff are as likely to come from non-Indian settlements as Indian ones.

Similarly, tribally or federally operated clinics may provide health-care services within Indian community settings, but clinic staff—who may not be members of the local Indian community—may refer Indian patients to non-Indian-controlled, regional medical facilities when out-patient services cannot address their medical needs.

Responsibility for law-and-order functions in many tribal communities are shared by tribal and non-Indian authorities, though questions of jurisdiction often grow out of those divisions, requiring continuous dialogue between representatives of both parties. While the political sovereignty of the tribes has long been recognized through treaty agreements and affirmed through various components of federal Indian law, tribal governments still have to address the concerns of local and regional non-Indian governments, and program development may not be able to proceed without promises of support and cooperation from those governments.

Complicating all such local-level negotiations are the more inclusive dialogues that connect the federally recognized tribes to the Bureau of Indian Affairs and the financial and policy-related arrangements that link all of the tribes to other agencies and programs throughout the federal system. All of these federal entities maintain offices "on or near" Indian settlements; their representatives establish connections with local, regional, and state-level agencies and their oversight authority can help or hinder tribal efforts to negotiate their own agreements in that regard. Recent changes in federal law have given interested tribes new mechanisms for cutting through traditional administrative complexities so they can increase their own opportunities for self-government; some argue, however, that the regulations and procedures which enable tribes to pursue "self-determination" in these terms simply replace traditional forms of metropolitan control with other, more subtle mechanisms to that end.

To date, the metropolis-satellite model has been used to describe the limitations imposed on economic and political life in Indian country. It seems to me that the relationships between the metropolis and its satellites have implications for language learning and language usage in American Indian and Alaska Native communities and that language choices themselves play critical roles in the construction and maintenance of these relationships.

Such is especially the case when, as is true throughout Indian country, the language traditions of the metropolis and its satellites are not identical. Inequalities in power and privilege guarantee that the language of the metropolis—not some neutral code or *lingua franca*, as would have been the agreed-upon strategy at earlier points in tribal history (see chapter 5)—will represent the interests of the metropolis to its satellites in these cases. Hence, even in tribal communities where interests in ancestral language literacy, maintenance, and renewal run high, English remains the language of advertising, radio, television, and other audio/video programming, newspapers and maga-zines, school textbooks and other instructional materials, public health an-nouncements, labels for canned goods and other commercial products, restaurant menus, applications for driver's permits and hunting/fishing licenses, credit card receipts, and checking accounts. And judging from the number of loan words and loan translations that can show up in ancestral language discourse, English continues to address these functions, even when the language of the metropolis is not the code-of-choice in particular settings.

Consider the conversation in example 6.1 (adapted from Grobsmith 1979) in these terms. This conversation took place in a general store on the Rosebud (Sioux) Indian reservation in South Dakota. The speakers, two Lakota women, are examining samples of yard goods used in the preparation of "Indian shawls" (part of the "traditional" attire worn by Lakota women on ceremonial and other special occasions) while they discuss their own plans to produce shawls.

Grobsmith (1979: 359) comments as follows on this conversation:

> It is apparent from this brief excerpt that while the flow of the conversation is in Lakota, English terms are interjected when the women refer to certain concepts such as "regular size," "one and three-fourths yards," "wide," "forty dollars," "be ready by fifteenth," and other words to describe concepts related to amount, size, money, and specific dates.

Judging by comments elsewhere in Grobsmith's article, it is not unusual to find Lakota speakers using English references in otherwise exclusively Lakota-oriented

EXAMPLE 6.1

A LAKOTA CONVERSATION

Sp 1: Now there's one thing, too, this *le* [is] regular size.

Sp 2: *Hah^n* [Yes].

Sp 1: *Naku^nniyek 'e'as henu oyakihi kte . . . le . . . le.*
[It's a nice adult size; you could wear it, too . . . this . . . this.]

Sp 2: One and three-fourths yard *le* [is] this.

Sp 1: *O na e'e letkiya* [And this way it's really] wide. *Lila*[very] wide *ca* [and so] I'll have to cut this.

(later in the discussion)

Sp 2: It figured out to forty dollars.

Sp 1: And so *Hoca i^nska* . . . if you are going to pay half of it, *iyuha yakaezu hanta 'as*, it'll all be ready by fifteenth.

Source: Adapted from Grobsmith (1979: 359). Lakota statements are given in italics, and their English translations in brackets.

speech settings. In fact, the presence of English "loan words" is one of the features that distinguishes what Rosebud people term *ikceya woglaka* ("to talk ordinary," informal or "fast" speech) from *yat'i^nsya woglaka* ("to talk firm" or formal speech).

Ikceya woglaka is the language of ordinary discourse on the Rosebud reservation. As Grobsmith (1979: 356) explains:

> One hears fast speech used at home, at schools, at the stores, during business interactions, at pow-wows, and during any and all casual conversations on the reservations. Even one who knows the formal style of speaking will rely on fast speech for everyday conversation and reserve the formal style of speaking for ritual or oratorical contexts.

Grobsmith (1979: 356) describes the more formal Lakota variety (*yat'i^nsya woglaka*) as "a slow, formal style of speaking, generally limited in use to the elderly or those having public political or religious status." The syntax of this code is considerably more complex than that found in *ikceya woglaka*, and so are its descriptive references, metaphors, and appeals to inference. For example, *Woyukca ki he nata ekta imakuagiye* "An idea is hanging outside my head" is an elaborated and metaphoric presentation of the notion expressed as *Woyukca wa bluha* "I have an idea" in informal speech. Similarly, the formal statement *Hona naku^n ce'api wa imakuagiye* "I am carrying a cry that is hanging outside of my heart" corresponds to the statement in informal speech *Naku^n watohasna wac'e* "Sometimes I cry."

Given these contrasts, we can understand why loan words are not appropriate for *yat'i^nsya woglaka* usage, whatever the issues under discussion. As Rosebud people explained to Grobsmith, "it is considered improper to use shortcuts in formal speech" (1979: 359). However, English loan words and other shortcuts are entirely appropriate when (as in example 6.1) *ikceya woglaka* is the speakers' code-of-choice, given the rapid, to-the-point presentations of meanings characteristically associated with that code.

But noting that the presence of loan words in example 6.1 is consistent with the speakers' choice of code does not explain why these speakers used loan words, rather than Lakota-based constructions, to express "concepts related to amount, size, money, and specific dates" relevant to this example. Certainly, Lakota language tradition contains words and phrases that can express these concepts, and the participants in this conversation, being fluent speakers of their ancestral language, must have been aware of them.

It is possible, of course, that their avoidance of Lakota vocabulary in these statements was an arbitrary act, intended to introduce linguistic variety into a conversation between friends and nothing more. But their avoidance of those terms could also suggest that, at those points in the dialogue, the speakers decided that ancestral language vocabulary did not provide the appropriate frame of reference for the ideas they wanted to express. That is, shawls may be "traditional" attire for Rosebud Indian women, but comparing fabric samples in a general store and arranging to purchase a designated length of the desired selection through time-payment plan are activities closely tied to the influence of the metropolis and should be described as such—even if the description takes place within a Lakota language conversation.

This is exactly what the Lakota women were doing when they made their selective use of English during the discussion of yard goods and shawls and what other American Indians and Alaska Natives are doing when they include loan words and other English expressions in ancestral language discourse. Use of such terms shows how deeply rooted in Indian country the influence of the metropolis has become. Such usage also shows why it is important for individuals in Indian country, whatever their language loyalties and preferences, to develop some level of proficiency in English.

Importantly, as I have argued in each chapter of this book, the English that people learn in Indian country may be similar to the English used and valued by the metropolis and its institutions, but it is not always identical to that English variety. Even in situations where the benefits of fluency in the metropolitan code cannot be denied—for example, when tribal representatives negotiate with local, state, and federal authorities for improvements in employment, education, health care, and other social services or demand support for tribal efforts to retain or recover access to traditional resources—speakers will treat Indian English as their code-of-choice when making particular statements, if not for the discourse as a whole.

Such choices suggest that, from the speakers' point of view, the significance of English in Indian country is not determined entirely by its connections to the metropolis. English serves other functions—tribally centered functions—in American Indian and Alaska Native speech communities; some of these complement the approaches to discourse valued by the metropolis, while others conflict with those approaches or have nothing to do with the metropolis' interests in English at all.

ANCESTRAL LANGUAGE FUNCTIONS OF INDIAN ENGLISH

Metropolitan vs. tribal dimensions of Indian English fluency are clearly displayed in Pye's (1985) description of language learning and language socialization among the Chilcotin. The Chilcotin people live on six reserves in central British Columbia. Their ancestral language is a member of the Athabaskan language family and was the primary language of the tribe until the 1960s, when paved roads made Williams Lake and other nearby non-Indian towns more accessible to tribal members and also made the natural resources of the reserves more accessible to non-Indian sports enthusiasts and ranchers. Shortly thereafter, schooling programs on each reserve brought Chilcotin community members, particularly young people, into even closer contact with English and with English speakers.

All of these changes made community members aware of the importance of English language skills, and the access to other forms of opportunity they could provide. Pye (1985: 7) writes:

> Chilcotin parents are extremely concerned for their children's future, and view the English language as an important means of ensuring success. The local school teachers constantly reinforce this theme by telling parents that their children need more work on their English language skills.

Most parents, who grew up speaking only Chilcotin, remember the problems they faced when English was the only language permitted in the classroom; they endorse teachers' efforts to maintain an English-only school setting and do what they can to create a similar environment for language learning within the home.

English does more than represent the interests of the metropolis in this setting, however. In earlier times, Chilcotin family discourse was structured quite tightly along generational lines: "Traditional talk belonged to the domain of the parents. Children were expected to be silent and observant" (Pye 1985: 4). Chilcotin parents continue to organize Chilcotin language–based interaction with their children and other young people from their community in terms of these rules. Detailed conversations in Chilcotin between parents and children are quite rare. If parents speak Chilcotin to their children at all, they do so in short, direct statements that are given once and not repeated. Not surprisingly, this system leads to delays in the children's fluency in their ancestral language and contributes to the "silent, observant" behavior that Chilcotin parents traditionally expect from the young people of their tribe.

So with the introduction of English have come new approaches to "Indian" communication into the Chilcotin speech community. The close association between English and the school, an institution designed specifically for the young people of the tribe, makes English an especially appropriate code to use with children and adds a component to the tribe's language inventory that did not exist, as such—a culturally sanctioned form of "baby talk"—in earlier times.

Pye found that parents make full use of this code and that parents and children jointly participate as equal partners in daily conversation. In fact, Chilcotin adults under age 50 told Pye that they were more comfortable speaking English to their children than they were speaking Chilcotin. Parents noted that the "production delay" traditionally associated with the development of Chilcotin fluency did not show up when children began learning English and concluded from this evidence that English must be an easier language than Chilcotin for their children to learn.

Teachers were not so optimistic about the young people's fluency in this community-centered English code. They explained to Pye (1985: 9–10): "children who speak the dialect are not doing noticeably better in school than their [older] brothers and sisters who speak Chilcotin," students for whom the school, rather than the home and community, was the primary focus for English language development.

Part of the difficulty here may be due to the grammatical detail of these codes. As Pye (1985: 9) notes, Chilcotin children:

> have not switched directly to a standard dialect of English. Instead they are learning a dialect which seems to have retained some of the phonological and syntactic features of Chilcotin. For example, they frequently devoice word-final consonants such as allomorphs of the plural and auxiliary -*s*. They will also use resumptive pronouns, producing such sentences as: *I throw it in the water, rock* or *I stole somebody's gun, R's gun.*

In other words, the variety of English that has "taken over the role of baby talk in the Chilcotin culture" (Pye 1985: 5) is quite different from the language of the metropolis and language used by those who represent its interests within this community. Here, as in comparable situations in Indian country, such difference works to the disadvantage of the Indian child.

Moreover, Pye observes, by using Chilcotin English, rather than Chilcotin, as the language of socialization for Chilcotin children, parents are diminishing what already are limited opportunities for the children to have active encounters with their ancestral language. Already, he reports (1985: 9), some children were beginning to show a lack of interest in speaking Chilcotin and were less than enthusiastic when others in their age group spoke that language in their presence:

> One of [Pye's] two year old subjects had a five year old sister who teased her every time her mother tried to get her to speak Chilcotin. The older sister resents her mother giving special attention to her sister, but also communicated the feeling of most children (and their parents) that Chilcotin is not worth speaking.

Indian English serves multiple functions within the Chilcotin speech community. It has replaced Chilcotin as the language of socialization and, not being grounded in the rules of ancestral language discourse, has created new channels for communication for children, parents, and other adult members of the tribe. Chilcotin people value these opportunities for community-centered language exchange and provide further incentives for young people to treat Chilcotin English as their "preferred" linguistic code—even in settings like the school, where language usage would otherwise be regulated by the interests of the metropolis.

Isleta Pueblo

At Isleta pueblo (New Mexico), Indian English has also begun to be associated with child socialization and other functions formerly addressed through ancestral language discourse. Here, however, the cultural and linguistic issues that define the context of socialization are different from those found at Chilcotin, and the social implications of Indian English fluency in this setting are quite distinct as well.

Children at Isleta grow up as first-language speakers of Isletan English. They may also learn Isletan Tiwa as a first language, depending on the age and language background of the child's primary caregiver during their early years. Children who regularly spend time with their grandparents (because their parents work away from the home during the day, because of adoption, or for other reasons) become fluent in Isletan Tiwa, and for them Isletan English is very much a second language. Children who spend time in day-care centers, or who stay with neighbor families or in the homes of their parents' age mates are much less likely to be ancestral language speakers, though they often acquired enough vocabulary and grammatical skills to be able to understand that language when others speak in their presence.

The on-reservation day-school, operated by the Bureau of Indian Affairs, provides instruction for students from kindergarten through grade six. Traditionally, teachers at the day-school have been mostly non-Indian in background and first-language speakers of non-Indian English. Teacher aides, in contrast, were members of the pueblo, and many of them used the ancestral language to clarify points of instruction or for other purposes when talking with Isleta students. Even so, English is the "official" language of instruction at this school, and school authorities constantly stress—to students, parents, and visitors alike— the importance of English language proficiency.

In contrast, student proficiency (or lack of proficiency) in Isletan Tiwa remains largely unaddressed in the school's curriculum. And the consequences of this arrangement have not been surprising: student English skills move closer to the school's definition of "appropriate" English usage as their grade-level and years in school increase, and student Isletan Tiwa skills begin to decline.

Home language preferences, which mirror assumptions about language and the metropolis voiced by parents at Chilcotin, may also contribute to this outcome. Some parents are convinced that fluency in Isletan Tiwa will hinder their children's school achievement. Consequently, while there are families where Isletan Tiwa is the language for conversations between parents and children, there are more families where parents use Isletan Tiwa when speaking to each other and to other Isleta adults but use English—usually Isletan English—when speaking to their children.

Domestic discourse involves a lot of code-switching, especially when persons of different age-levels are participating in the same conversation. It also conflicts with the pueblo's rules of verbal etiquette, which designate the ancestral language as the appropriate code when non-Indians are in earshot of the conversation. So Isleta parents have to make deliberate, conscious decisions to use English instead of Isletan Tiwa when speaking with their children; the frequency with which parents make those decisions—and violate ancestral language norms—shows how closely they associate English fluency with successful participation in the school and other metropolitan domains.

Fluency in (Isletan) English remains the predominant theme throughout childhood and adolescence, and this pattern may extend into adulthood. The pattern changes only when—after high school, college, completion of military service, or brief relocation to another part of the country—tribal members decide to establish permanent residence at Isleta and become active participants in the daily life of the pueblo. At that point, speaking Isletan Tiwa becomes a mandatory language skill and people who are not fluent in this language have to acquire (or reestablish) this skill as rapidly as possible.

At issue in this requirement are some features of social organization that make Isleta a pueblo rather than a place of residence for an aggregate of Indians. At Isleta, the officials who have charge of the secular components of community life—the governor, the lieutenant governor, the council, and so on—are elected by the adult members of the pueblo, not appointed by the pueblo's religious leadership. The pueblo's constitution, ratified by the pueblo membership in 1947 and amended several times since then, identifies these officials (using their English not their Tiwa names), lists their responsibilities, and establishes procedures for elections and for the orderly transitions of power between rival candidates. The constitution also allows all heads of households and other adult members of the community to attend weekly meetings of the council, to observe the discussions of issues critical to pueblo life that go on in the council sessions, and to participate in those discussions when they wish to do so. Informal, one-on-one politicking is equally important to this system. All of these exchanges are carried out in Isletan Tiwa, since Tiwa—not English—is the appropriate code for *adult* conversation at this pueblo.

To be a candidate for formal office under this system, or to become a key player in the system's informal domain, a person must be willing to make a public commitment to the principles of community life that make Isleta a *pueblo* community. These include giving community members a helping hand in times of need or hardship, offering sound advice and wise judgment when others seek out opinions, and meeting responsibilities in agriculture (for reasons explained in chapter 1), in ceremonies, and in other religious/spiritual activities that occur throughout the year. Fluency in Isletan Tiwa is necessary for all of these activities; in effect, it is the language through which adults express their public commitment to community life and its traditions.

Young adults learn Isletan Tiwa—or relearn it, depending on family language history—through several means. Community members encourage them to use whatever Tiwa they know as the basis for everyday conversations when talking with elders and with each other. Community members also remind young adults to use Tiwa, rather than English, in the presence of outsiders. Religious leaders assign activities for young adults to perform during ceremonial occasions, which include verbal responses as well as physical labor. Young adults, on their part, draw on their recollections of Tiwa grammar and discourse if they spoke it during their childhood years, on the observations they have made as they watched and listened to adults speaking the language at home and in public places, and on the verbal skills they can acquire from their age-mates as they practice speaking Tiwa to each other. Certainly, the ancestral language skills implicit in their Isletan English grammar contribute to the (re)learning process. And it is also at this time that young people receive formal introduction to areas of language skill that they will not encounter through everyday discourse settings—the meaning and rules of usage associated with ceremonial vocabulary, for example. Outsiders classify such efforts as part of the pueblo's "initiation"; pueblo members, when speaking in Isletan English—particularly to outsiders—cryptically refer to this experience as "learning the secrets."

Thus, similar to the case at Chilcotin, Indian English functions as a kind of baby language within the Isleta speech community, and parental use of this language option reflects a formal, conscious commitment to encourage their children's acquisition of English skills. At Chilcotin, younger members of the community are beginning to devalue fluency in the ancestral language in favor of fluency in English. At Isleta, in contrast, the significance of ancestral language fluency for pueblo life continues to be widely recognized in its own right by all age-levels in this community. The functions assigned to Indian English may be similar in both cases, but the usage has quite different consequences at each site.

A final point: Pye does not discuss Chilcotin parents' attitudes toward impending ancestral language loss. Isleta parents, for their part, are certainly aware that this at-home emphasis on (Indian) English fluency has detrimental effects on the children's ancestral language skills. I have talked about these issues with Isletan adults each time I have worked or visited at the pueblo, from 1968 to 1991; consistently in these conversations, Isleta parents tell me (as one parent observed recently): "The children's English skills are fine, it's their Indian that needs attention."

But even as parents and community leaders raised these concerns, most remained adamantly opposed to any plan to offer bilingual instruction in the pueblo day-school or off-reservation junior and senior high schools. Apparently, while Isleta people are aware of the young people's language needs, they do not consider non-Indian approaches to language instruction to be the appropriate mechanisms for responding to them. This suggests a high degree of community confidence in the opportunities for language (re)learning extended to young people once they are ready to assume responsibilities, as adults, within the pueblo.

Northern Ute

Indian English is also integral to child socialization on the Northern Ute reservation and it serves other ancestral language functions in this setting.

Fluency in Ute English has also prompted some adjustments in on-reservation discourse that are quite different from those described for Chilcotin and Isleta.

The Northern Ute Tribe's Division of Education estimates that only 40% of the Ute adults on this reservation, and only 25% of the Ute children, are "adequate or better" speakers of the ancestral language. Unlike the case on other reservations, ancestral language fluency does not pattern consistently along generational lines here. So while there are families where all members are fluent speakers of Ute, regardless of age-level, it is more common to find families using English rather than Ute as the language of child-rearing and other domestic tasks.

The English in question is heavily influenced by features of Ute language tradition, but it is English, all the same. And under these circumstances, Ute children are much more likely to become first-language speakers of this English variety rather than Ute. The English-oriented instruction in the on-reservation public schools reinforces the need for student proficiency in English, as does the unavoidable daily interaction with non-Indian residents of this "checkerboard" reservation.

Ute parents fully support the school's efforts to strengthen student English fluency, though they have also supported attempts to add ancestral language instruction to the school curriculum when funds have been available for that purpose. According to Division of Education assessment of these issues, parents agree that the proper place for Ute language instruction is the home and that individual Utes have to take responsibility for language teaching—and for language learning. These are difficult tasks to address, when Ute English has become the basis for daily conversation within the home.

Understandably, under such conditions, Ute English has also become a basis for daily conversation outside of the home—in settings where the ancestral language has been the preferred mode of discourse in previous years and where the ancestral language is still the language of choice for some speakers.

In some cases, having both languages in the same setting helps Ute people separate the traditional "core" of an event from the more mundane, secondary activities that also occur in that context. For example, persons conducting a sweat lodge ceremony use Ute or other Indian languages when offering prayers and making other statements necessary to the ritual, but shift to English when reminding restless children to pay attention to the ceremony or when explaining the meaning of certain activities to first-time participants.

The presence of both languages in the same speech setting can have more complicated effects on social interaction. For example, twice each year, the tribal charter requires tribal government to convene a meeting of the Northern Ute General Council, so that the tribal membership-at-large can review and sanction actions taken on their behalf by their elected officials and provide advice regarding issues that are still under discussion. Tribal officials use English to organize the agenda of the meeting and to manage the discussion throughout the evening. However, tribal members often make presentations from the floor in Ute, instead of English, and tribal officials respond to those comments in Ute, prompting other Ute speakers to respond in kind.

The resulting exchanges can be lengthy, and persons who are concerned about tribal affairs but are not fluent speakers of the ancestral language find it difficult to maintain interest in the council meeting agenda under these circumstances. Absence of translation services, or of synopsis of the dialogue once the discussion comes to an end, makes the experience even more frustrating—to the point that some adults use the language "barrier" to explain the low turnout at the General Council meetings.

Tribal officials realize that they may be alienating segments of the tribal membership when they conduct General Council business in Ute. At the same time, they know they may alienate Ute-speaking tribal members if they allow English to predominate at these sessions. Some of these officials, seeking to clarify their position on these themes, include ancestral language proficiency when they list their qualifications for re-election on their campaign posters (which are worded, by the way, in English) or during pre-election debates.

To use Ute English in (what were formerly) ancestral language domains, speakers have to comply with some of the rules of discourse associated with the ancestral language tradition. That tradition places great value on speaker-centered, individualized discourse, and the grammar of Northern Ute provides any number of linguistic options to help speakers meet this expectation. For example, pairs of vocabulary words let speakers distinguish "traditional" and "modern" attitudes toward a given topic; rules of pronunciation help speakers specify their band membership; tense/aspect markers underscore the degree of confidence with which speakers present their statements. By choosing carefully between these options, Ute speakers can construct highly individualized meanings and references. This allows them to demonstrate their willingness to comply with tribally defined rules of interpersonal behavior and affirms their commitment to traditional cultural practice in other domains.

English grammar provides many fewer markers for indicating speaker point of view, and Ute English speakers find that they have to address these expectations through other means. Adult Ute English speakers, for example, may add -*inah* ([I'+na^h]) or -*neh* ([nE']) to the end of an English phrase or clause, as a way of eliciting listener support and confirmation for their statements and asserting that they consider their comments to be worthy of support.

Ute adults can include -*inah* and -*neh* in standard English sentences, though it is more likely that they use these markers as part of Ute English constructions. They are particularly likely to do so if they are talking Ute English with someone who is older and is a speaker of Ute or if they are talking with non-Indians—particularly when the topic under discussion is of great interest to Ute people and Ute adults want to underscore the importance of a statement to their non-Indian listeners.

Ute adults may use a second strategy for coding speaker point of view into (Ute) English discourse. At issue here is an almost exact replication of the verbal style used by Tonto (the "faithful companion" of the Lone Ranger) and other stereotyped Indian characters from the early days of radio and television. Speaking English in such terms involves, among other things, a slower speed of presentation than would normally occur in this setting, insertion of *-um, -uh,* and other "dummy" syllables into phrase and clause sequences, and deletion of articles, noun endings, and verb final tense/aspect suffixes—none of which show up in Ute English under ordinary circumstances.

The deletion is not applied systematically or globally; varying the forms of surface constructions throughout the exchange is part of the "fun" of talking in this English style, or so my friends tell me. This strategy seems especially well suited for conversations with non-Indians, particularly those who are not fully oriented to the subtleties of reservation life and may not understand the satire of Indian/non-Indian relationships implicit in this usage. Importantly, such statements would be directed at fellow Utes only in a joking situation; and talking in these terms to an older member of the tribe, for any purpose other than comic relief, constitutes an inappropriate and highly disrespectful form of discourse.[3]

The Lumbee and the Brackettville Seminole

According to the Chilcotin, Isleta, and Northern Ute examples, English—more specifically, Indian English—can be closely associated with the metropolis in Indian country, yet be linked with *some* of the social and symbolic functions that the speech community traditionally assigned to ancestral language discourse. There are situations where Indian English, its connections to the language of the metropolis notwithstanding, now assumes *all* ancestral language functions for its speakers, and I conclude this section with the two examples of such arrangements for which we have documentation.

The first example is the Lumbee of south-central North Carolina. Earliest descriptions in the colonial records note that the Lumbee were similar to the Algonquian and Siouan tribes living in the Tidewater area of Virginia and North Carolina in every way but one. Unlike their neighbors, the Lumbee were speakers of English at the time of contact. There was no evidence of Indian language usage within their speech community, nor was there evidence of any association with a language tradition other than English (Blu 1980: 36–44; and see especially p. 37).

Even though they were English speakers, the Lumbee were adamant in their expression of their Indianness; as time passed, their location in what outsiders viewed as undesirable, uninhabitable land left them relatively free to maintain their traditions and their identity (Brewer and Reising 1982: 34) —something Lumbee people continue to do today.

The anthropologist Elsie Clews Parsons conducted folklore research in Lumbee country in 1918, though she identified the Lumbee as "*Cherokee of Robeson County*," a usage still popular among some non-Indians in that area of the Carolinas. In the published account of her findings (Parsons 1919), she noted almost no instances of "Indian vocabulary" (her term) in their oral English. Karen Blu (1980: 247, n.7) reported the same finding during her ethnographic field research some sixty years later:

> Whether linguists would classify the Indian mode of speech as a separate dialect, I am not qualified to say. There have been no technical studies of the matter, but I can say by the time I left Robeson County, after seventeen months of field work, I could hear differences between most Indians and non-Indian speakers, which helped me identify Indians. And Indians themselves can often identify the precise area of the county from which another Indian comes simply from his speech.

The "Indian mode of speech" that Blu mentions here is, of course, English-based, and the linguistic features of this English variety have now been examined by Brewer and Reising (1982) as part of a reanalysis of data from the Lumbee area gathered for the *Linguistic Atlas of the Middle and Southern Atlantic States*. Their analysis has identified several features that, when compared to the English of other groups in this area, prove to be unique to Lumbee English usage.

Among these features are two kinds of vocabulary items, some of which were common to English at an earlier time but are no longer used productively outside of the Lumbee community—for example, *token*, "a noise or sign provided by a spirit to indicate that death or evil is imminent" (Brewer and Reising 1982: 37). There are also vocabulary items in Lumbee English that have never been reported for speakers of English outside of the Lumbee community, such as *juvimber* (pronounced with the primary stress on the first vowel), the Lumbee English term for a homemade slingshot.

There is one detail of pronunciation uniquely associated with Lumbee English. Brewer and Reising (1982: 40) label this feature "the Tidewater diphthong, the use of centralized [əI] rather than /ai/" before voiceless consonants (***night, light***) voiced consonants (***five, spider***), and in open syllables. Some non-Lumbee from surrounding area also use this "Tidewater diphthong" in their English, but it occurs only before voiceless consonants, and not in other environments.

Importantly, [əI] does not have a uniform occurrence across Lumbee country. For example, Lumbee residents of Prospect, North Carolina, considered by other Lumbee to "have the most unusual or old-fashioned language, that is, most distinct from other Lumbee communities and from standard English" (Brewer and Reising 1982: 42), use [əI] 38.6% of the time in the voiceless environment and 81.8% in the voiced environment. Lumbee from Pembroke, North Carolina, use [əI] 14.0% of the time in the voiceless environment and 18.2% in the voiced one. These contrasts suggest that [əI] usage allows Lumbee people to specify their home/reference community and other facts about their association with Lumbee culture when they talk English—the same way that Northern Ute, Lakota, and other western tribes people indicate band membership and community of residence through features of ancestral language grammar. And, as suggested by the statements already cited, Lumbee people are very much aware of the social messages Lumbee English contains.

Brewer and Reising also report that Lumbee men use [əI] in voiced environments (the usage that shows greatest contrast to other forms of English in the Tidewater region) much more frequently than do Lumbee women. Whether Lumbee people are aware of this sex-related patterning, and what significance they assign to it, cannot be determined from Brewer and Reising's data.

The lexical items unique to Lumbee English also carry social messages in this speech community. These items highlight Lumbee/non-Indian differences, particularly in conversations with outsiders. For example, some Lumbee use *token* "as a 'test item,' calling upon non-Lumbee for a definition, an invariable result of which is laughter, much to the puzzlement of the non-Lumbee. Few non-Lumbee can define the word to Lumbee satisfaction" (Brewer and Reising 1982: 34).

My second example comes from the Seminole communities of Brackettville and Del Rio, Texas. Members of these communities are, to varying degree, Indian and Afro-Indian in background. Their ancestors fled to Mexico from Oklahoma and Arkansas during the middle of the nineteenth century to avoid enslavement by Creek and non-Indian slaveholders. They met up with members of other Indian tribes who had migrated to Mexico as well as persons of Mexican descent and began to identify themselves with the label "Mexican Seminoles."

In 1870 members of this group returned to the United States to help the U.S. Army in its campaigns against the Apache and the Comanche. In exchange for these services, they received salary and free land on which to build permanent homes for their families. They were assigned to Fort Clark, Texas, near the site of present-day Brackettville and Del Rio, moved their families to that area, and have considered it their home ever since.

The linguistic diversity within the Brackettville Seminole community provides a direct reflection of the community's past. Adults in this community are speakers of the regional variety of "standard English," Spanish, and the distinctive, English-related variety that community members call *Seminole*.[4] Fluency in Seminole among the community's young people is somewhat less extensive, though the local Seminole cultural organization, which, according to Haynes (1977: 288), "is vigorously involving young and old Seminoles in reviving the cultural practices of the most vibrant days of their history," is creating opportunities for learning and using Seminole and doing other things to strengthen community pride in this unique language tradition.

Hancock (1977) notes that linguistic features in Brackettville Seminole resemble features found in varieties of English used by slaves and freedpersons in the Southern States before and immediately after the Civil War. If so, then Seminole also shares linguistic features with Afro-Caribbean creole and with other language varieties associated with African- and Portuguese-based creole traditions. Hancock's (1977: 1) research finds particular parallels between Seminole and Gullah, the Black English variety spoken on the Sea Islands off the coast of Georgia:

> It is now possible to confirm that with very few differing characteristics, the language as spoken in Brackettville . . . today represents an offshoot of Georgia Gullah, and is in some respects more conservative or archaic than the modern Atlantic coast dialects of that language.

Haynes, after several weeks of fieldwork in Brackettville in 1975, reached largely similar conclusions. However, she found numerous instances where the surface form of Seminole sentences contrast with those found in Black English vernacular as a whole, but shows that these contrasts reflect differences in the speakers' use of similar grammatical rules, not differences in rule detail. Importantly, she is also unwilling to assume that the Black English tradition is the only source contributing to Seminole grammar and discourse. She cites the influence of vocabulary and syntactic features from Mexican Spanish, particularly words from the rural northern areas of the Republic, and wonders whether influences from the Indian languages spoken in those areas may also be present as well.

However its historical background is described, Seminole is distinct from the other language traditions used in the Brackettville and Del Rio areas—and it is considered such by its speakers. Haynes (1977: 290) notes:

> Seminoles easily distinguished Seminole from English and Spanish as a separate language, and one reflecting their cosmopolitan history and ethnic characteristics. One Seminole who had travelled widely in the US Army suggested that Seminole and "Geechee" were related in that they had European features in common (as opposed to English features, only) as a consequence of the roving history of the Seminoles in the Southern USA. No Seminoles called their language behavior either a creole, Black English or Indian English: they spoke *Seminole talk*, *Seminole*, or *Seminole language*.

Not surprisingly under these circumstances, speakers regularly shift between Seminole, other varieties of English, and other language traditions, as appropriate to the social message implicit in the setting, topic, or audience. Church activities, for example, involved spontaneous prayers in English, but singing in Seminole. Bar conversations were conducted in English, Spanish, or Seminole, depending upon the age of the participants and the topic under discussion. Seminole is categorically *not* used only in three situations: talking on the telephone with a non-Seminole, describing personal experiences with non-Seminoles to Seminole friends, and describing experiences outside of the Brackettville area—(non-Indian) English is the preferred language choice in these cases. Otherwise, intercode variation was the expected speech pattern for members of this community, and code-switching was an appropriate and highly valuable linguistic skill.

A person can be a member of the Brackettville Seminole community and not be a speaker (or admit to being a speaker) of Seminole. Haynes (1977: 289) notes that two members of the community with "mainstream aspirations" wondered why she wanted "to hear that ugly talk," and that others recently returned to Brackettville from New Mexico "claimed an inability to speak the 'Seminole language,' apparently feeling that their proficiency in a more Hispanic version [*sic*] would contribute to their differentiation in the Brackettville society." In most cases, especially for individuals and families who closely associate with other areas of Brackettville Seminole tradition, Seminole is a viable, valuable language option that serves many of the community-specific, community-focused functions associated with ancestral language discourse in other tribal/community settings.

INDIAN ENGLISH AS A LOCAL LANGUAGE "STANDARD"

Speakers of Indian English use these English codes to meet speaking tasks and obligations associated with their ancestral language tradition. But they also use Indian English in settings where ancestral language traditions are not so important to effective discourse. Here the social messages associated with these codes are defined quite differently; often they suggest the idea that Indian English is the "correct" way for Indian people to talk English—especially in front of outsiders.

Colorado River Tribes

Penfield-Jasper (1982) writes extensively on this point in her descriptions of Indian English on the Colorado River reservation (southwestern Arizona). There are Mohave, Chemehuevi, Navajo, and Hopi residents on this reservation and these identities remain strong even as residents work together, as members of the Colorado River Tribes, to address water rights, non-Indian land claims, educational services, and other issues of common concern.

Indian children attend school in the predominantly non-Indian, on-reservation town of Parker, Arizona. Non-Indian children from Parker are in the majority in these classrooms, especially at the junior and senior high school grade-levels. The teachers and school authorities are primarily non-Indian; the school curriculum pays little attention to Indian student backgrounds and interests.

Parker is also the business center for the reservation, and Indian adults encounter the same pervasive non-Indian presence in the stores, restaurants, offices, and other commercial facilities that their children find in the classroom.

In other settings where distinctions between ethnic and political groups are so visibly displayed, language loyalties quickly become important markers of group differences. Yet when Penfield-Jasper worked with Mohave students and families in the Parker community, she found that only 10% of the Mohave under age 20 were speakers of their ancestral language, and the remaining 90% were monolingual speakers of English. Her analysis of their English uncovered a long list of syntactic, semantic, and pragmatic features that closely paralleled characteristics of Mohave grammar. English pronunciation was the one area of Mohave student English least influenced by ancestral language detail. Even so, once Penfield-Jasper became familiar with the Indian English discourse used on this reservation, she found she could accurately judge whether an Indian student was Mohave or came from some other tribal background, simply on the basis of English usage.

She also learned, through discussions with schoolteachers and business people from the Parker area, that non-Indians could also make accurate judgments once they became familiar with local English norms. And, she learned, Mohave students themselves recognize the distinctive qualities of their English. They make judgments about their fellow students' behavior and regulate those students' access to "in-group" activities on the basis of English grammar and usage. Not surprisingly, "other Indian and non-Indian students who aspire to membership in Mohave peer groups will try to learn certain aspects of the [Mohave student] dialect in order to become more accepted" (1982: 25).

Imitating the English of non-Indians, or Indians from other tribes, is one of the favorite forms of comic play for Mohave young people, and if they hear another Mohave using non-Mohave grammatical constructions, that person becomes the focus of their teasing and ridicule. Mohave adults make similar assessments of each other's English and may also participate in the teasing and ridicule.

Apparently, Mohave English tradition includes criteria for evaluating the "appropriateness" of *any person's* English discourse, and speakers of Mohave English are familiar enough with those criteria to recognize the social and cultural messages they contain. These are not the criteria that guide non-Indian definitions of "appropriate" English—and the differences in point of view here have serious implications for Mohave students' school experience.

Mohave students know that going to school means interacting with non-Indians on a regular basis. They have heard stories about schools and about teachers from their older brothers and sisters. They have heard their parents talking about education. They may have visited classrooms when their parents attended parent-teacher workshops. And, given the Mohave community's practice of censuring inappropriate English usage and the comical imitations of non-Mohave English that regularly occur throughout the community, it is likely that students come to school realizing that (non-Indian) teachers talk English differently from Mohave people and are able to identify some of the features that make teacher English so distinct.

It seems unlikely, given Penfield-Jasper's comments about language attitudes in this community, that Mohave students consider *their own* English to be deficient in any way. Mohave students are first-language speakers of Mohave English, and the criteria that support their expectations about classroom English discourse have been guiding their participation in community-centered English discourse for some time.

Schoolteachers use entirely different criteria to assess the English language skills in their classrooms. As Penfield-Jasper discovered through her interviewing, these teachers believe that ancestral language interference creates the problems that Indian students have with English; when they discover that most Mohave students do not speak their ancestral language, teachers conclude that these students will not experience any barriers to standard English proficiency. Penfield-Jasper(1982: 29–30) continues:

> When the teacher hears the Mohave children speak, [these] expectations are reinforced. They have little accent and are warm, open children; again, no language problem is expected. After seeing their classroom work, teachers usually notice that Indian children have problems with some grammatical structures, but only occasionally. They may notice that they are sometimes slower readers and may have trouble with simple language tasks. The problems are attributed to almost anything from poor nutrition to too much television, but not to dialect difference.

Notice that by citing nonlinguistic factors (e.g., poor nutrition, too much television) to account for the presence of nonstandard constructions in Mohave students' English, teachers are treating Mohave student English skills as conditions over which the school has no control. Such references shift the responsibility for school-effective language instruction to parents and other members of the home community; because teachers are not in a position to change parental attitudes, teachers come away with very little incentive to promote student language change.

The students, on their part, are not looking for teachers to provide them with such incentives. They know that the teachers' English is different from the English codes valued in their home community and that under ordinary circumstances community members would make jokes about teacher English and about the persons who talk English in such terms. When teachers attempt to correct Mohave students when they make "mistakes" in grammar or discourse, or to offer explanations for appropriate usage, Mohave students hear the irrelevance of the comments, measured against local language rules, and react accordingly. Classroom commands like "Repeat after me!" or "Listen when I say . . ." express similar messages and raise additional questions about the teacher's suitability to be a role model for language learning in this setting.

Isleta Pueblo

Isleta pueblo is another Indian speech community that has developed criteria for "appropriate" English skill that differ substantially from those used by non-Indians in their area. Earlier in this chapter, I noted how one Isleta adult recently told me that her children's ancestral language skills need development, but that their English skills were fine. I have heard this comment, worded in various ways, for more than twenty years of work at this site. Throughout this period, I have heard somewhat different assessments from (largely non-Indian) teachers at the on-reservation day-school and members of tribal government who supervise employment and job-placement services for this community. From their point of view, Isleta students' proficiency in English is far from satisfactory, and much work needs to be done to improve their spoken and written English skills.

Given the importance of Isletan English to child socialization and other areas of community life at this pueblo, I can understand why Isleta parents do not share the school's perspective on student English language needs. The parents' assessment takes into account the language skills that students need to have as members of their pueblo, not the language skills that may be important in non-Indian domains. They look to the schools to address language needs relevant to those domains—which is why they oppose school-based attempts to supply ancestral language instruction, even as they continue to raise concerns over unmet ancestral language needs. Under this system—and very much unlike the conditions that Penfield-Jasper describes for the Mohave—differences between home/school English usage need not become an obstacle to student English development, because Isleta notions of "appropriate English" do not apply to situations (or persons) not already associated with community life.

Isleta parents are aware, of course, that people from different tribes speak English in different ways. In fact, most American Indians and Alaska Natives recognize such differences and refer to them when the social situation makes it appropriate to offer such comments.

There was a meeting in the early 1970s between officials of the Mississippi Choctaw Tribe and officials from the Choctaw tribe of Oklahoma. The agenda was filled with serious matters and the officials and their assistants were conducting themselves with all of the dignity appropriate to the occasion. The atmosphere in the room was tense, and the presence of representatives from the Bureau of Indian Affairs and other federal agencies did little to relieve tension.

The meeting began with opening remarks from a member of the Oklahoma Choctaw Tribe, since they were the sponsors of this conference. Because non-Indians were present, he spoke in English—Oklahoma Choctaw English. As he finished speaking, one of the Mississippi Choctaw leaned across the table and said—in Mississippi Choctaw English—quietly enough for everyone in the room to hear: "Hey, are you sure that you guys are red-skins, and not red-necks?" The people at the conference table dissolved into laughter and then got down to business, the somberness of the occasion now replaced by an atmosphere much more compatible with Choctaw social style.[5]

The speaker's statement is a splendid example of Choctaw Indian humor, and that alone had a lot to do with the change in atmosphere at the meeting. But his explicit reference to "red-necks who try to be red-skins" also contributed to this change. The Oklahoma Choctaw, like all of Oklahoma's tribes, have had to contend with such impersonations (and their consequences) since the days of the Indian removal; and Mississippi Choctaw, longtime residents of rural Mississippi, have had to contend with similar intrusions from their non-Indian neighbors. In other words, the speaker's statement appealed to the common interests of the conference participants and reminded them of the importance of working together in the conference setting.

But the explicit message could have such an impact only if the listeners understood the implicit message it contains: "pretend Indians" reveal their non-Indian background as soon as they begin to talk. To appreciate that message, listeners must understand that Mississippi Choctaw people speak English differently from Oklahoma Choctaw people, that both groups speak English differently from non-Indians, and that neither group would want its members to talk like non-Indians in public settings. Once again, the social implications of "appropriate" speech contribute heavily to the effectiveness of Indian English discourse.

COMMUNITY-BASED INDIAN ENGLISH DIVERSITY

Now I want to examine situations where Indian English is not the only variety of English used within a tribal speech community or (as is often the case in Indian country) where different segments of the tribal community have their own Indian English codes. Indian English grammar and discourse still distinguish tribal members from outsiders in such cases, but they also reinforce contrasts in social organization and cultural practice relevant to life within the tribe.

Rosebud Sioux

This is certainly one of the functions of the English-related "communication alternatives" (her term, 1979: 355) which Grobsmith found on the Rosebud (Sioux) reservation. English, the language of the metropolis, is influential in this setting; and for some speakers, non-Indian-based "standard" English has become the preferred code for daily conversation. More commonly, English language choices cluster around three varieties of nonstandard English, each of which is used by a particular segment of the Rosebud speech community and, Grobsmith finds, by members of that segment alone.

Speakers of the first variety of Rosebud English are the elderly, full-blood members of the tribe. They are also fluent speakers of their ancestral language and, as far as possible, orient their personal life around Lakota traditions. Accordingly, their use of English reflects Lakota grammar and discourse.

Speakers of the second variety of Rosebud English include the Rosebud adults and older children who have lived away from the reservation for some period (e.g., while working, attending school, or serving in the military) but have returned to Rosebud. Their English conforms to standard language syntax, Grobsmith (1979: 360) notes, "but their pronunciation is still heavily influenced by Lakota phonology."

Speakers of the third variety of Rosebud English are younger Indians who, in Grobsmith's (1979: 360) description, are

> generally well educated or are currently in school, are usually mixed blood and may have alternated residence between reservation and urban areas. Their nonstandard English variety is associated with the speech of non-Indians of lower socio-economic groups in urban areas, rural farm workers and ranchers, and with groups having limited exposure to formal education.

Little influence from Lakota phonology shows up in this English variety. In fact, Grobsmith notes, this variety is virtually indistinguishable from the English of the non-Indians who live in areas adjacent to the reservation.

Reviewing these categories,[6] Grobsmith sees a difference between the rules governing ancestral language variation and variation in English on this reservation. Compared to Rosebud Lakota usage, Rosebud English "is not nearly so contextual, but rather is determined by which variety of English the Lakota speaker knows. One does not switch between standard English and a non-standard variety [e.g., the way some Lakota speakers switch between *yat'i^n sya woglaka* and *ikcaya woglaka*], one speaks what one knows" (1979: 359, with my addition).

I am not convinced that the principles governing language choice-making in these cases are as distinct or unrelated as Grobsmith claims.

First of all, the speakers associated with these varieties of Rosebud English parallel the speakers associated with ancestral language variation on this reservation. That is, by Grobsmith's report, those who use the first English variety tend to be proficient users of both the formal and informal Lakota language styles—*yat'i^n sya woglaka* and *ikcaya woglaka*—discussed in an earlier section of this chapter. Speakers of the second variety, if they speak Lakota, speak *ikcaya woglaka* alone. Speakers of the third variety are uniformly monolingual in English and do not speak any Lakota at all.

Second, again according to Grobsmith's comments, what Rosebud people know about English is largely a reflex of their age, relative social seniority, on/off-reservation residence pattern, and other details of life experience—the same factors that influence speakers' knowledge of Lakota and their use of that knowledge in ancestral language discourse settings. Hence, Grobsmith finds older Lakota speakers switching from *ikcaya woglaka* to *yat'i^{n}sya woglaka* on ceremonial and oratorical occasions or to draw attention to some culturally relevant feature in a Lakota conversation; otherwise, they use the socially more neutral *ikcaya woglaka*, the same Lakota variety that other Lakota speakers use on all occasions.

Why don't the other speakers of Lakota use the "formal" language on "formal" occasions? The reason cannot be unfamiliarity with the code, since people hear Lakota elders speaking *yat'i^{n}sya woglaka* on ceremonial occasions and during other special speech events. They recognize the distinctiveness of its oratorical devices, expressive references, and sentence/paragraph structures, even if they do not make use of those features in their own Lakota discourse. But they also know that these are the Lakota language skills appropriate for older, more experienced members of the Lakota community—skills that, with appropriate life experience and validation in other areas, they may someday acquire. Until then, *ikcaya woglaka* is the appropriate form for their Lakota discourse.

So while young people report having "considerable difficulty in understanding this variety" (Grobsmith 1979: 356), this comment says more about these speakers' position within tribal structure than it does about their level of ancestral language skill. William Powers (1986: 11) has made the same point when discussing "sacred language" usage at nearby Pine Ridge (Sioux) reservation:

> When questioning native speakers about the differences between sacred and secular language, the Oglala assert that sacred language is simply not understood. They claim that the words are unknown, strange and even humorous. They believe that sacred language can be understood only by *wicasa wakan* "sacred men": it is the language they use to talk to each other, pray and sing.

However, "lack of understanding" does not prevent Pine Ridge people from commenting on the meanings of specific words and phrases in this sacred code (Powers 1986: 11–12):

> If one . . . questions native speakers about specific lexical items and grammatical features that are acknowledged to be the essential components of sacred language,

many Lakota speakers are quite capable of interpreting the parts, despite their admitted incomprehension of the whole.

Under this system—and, I submit, at Rosebud as well—context-related code-switching is a relevant ancestral language skill for only a small segment of the tribal community. Otherwise, Lakota language-related choice-making is governed by social status and life experience—the same principle that applies to choice-making in on-reservation discourse in Rosebud English. Not only does "one speak what one knows" at Rosebud, as Grobsmith observes, but one speaks what one is ***supposed*** to know, as determined by one's place in the social organization of the on-reservation tribal community.

Isleta Pueblo

Somewhat different conditions surround English-related choice-making at Isleta pueblo (New Mexico). Because the pueblo is so closely connected to nearby Albuquerque, Isleta adults are likely to have firsthand knowledge of non-Indian as well as Indian-based English codes and to alternate between metropolitan and Isletan English varieties when they talk with other community members as well as outsiders.

The details of these alternations can best be described as shifts between positions along a continuum of "speech styles," with the language of the metropolis at one end of the continuum and a highly ancestral language–influenced variety of Isletan English at the other. English language variation for older members of the pueblo, who may be more fluent in Spanish than in English, involves only the ancestral language–related codes.

Greater movement along this continuum, with English usage showing varying degrees of overlap with Isletan Tiwa grammar and discourse, is especially evident in the English of young Isleta adults, especially those who are attending college or vocational schools, serving in the armed forces, or otherwise personally influenced by non-Indian language norms. Acquiring (or regaining) ancestral language fluency, once they establish residence at the pueblo, broadens the language options available within any speech event. Elementary and secondary school students also show varying degrees of Tiwa influence in their English codes, even if they are not speakers of their ancestral language. Only for the youngest members of the pueblo does ancestral language fluency ever restrict speaker opportunities for English-based choice-making, and this occurs only in homes where Isletan Tiwa, rather than Isletan English, is the language of choice for conversations with children.

influence in their English codes, even if they are not speakers of their ancestral language. Only for the youngest members of the pueblo does ancestral language fluency ever restrict speaker opportunities for English-based choice-making, and this occurs only in homes where Isletan Tiwa, rather than Isletan English, is the language of choice for conversations with children.

Unlike at Rosebud, where each segment of the reservation community uses its own English style, there is a fluid, constantly shifting quality to Indian English discourse at Isleta pueblo, and the constraints that ordinarily govern code-switching in such cases (e.g., context, topic, and participant background) take on special significance within this pueblo setting.

One such constraint prohibits persons from the pueblo from using *any* code resembling the language of the metropolis when discussing matters of personal concern with other members of the pueblo; this constraint takes on greater force if the discussion is taking place within an on-reservation setting, and greater force still if the person initiating the conversation is younger (by age or social status) than the respondent.

Isleta people who ignore this constraint can expect to be teased and, if they continue to use metropolitan language in this setting, to be openly criticized for "putting on airs," "pretending to be better than they really are," "acting like an *apple* [i.e., red on the outside, white on the inside]," or "talking like a tomahawk." (The last two refer to images frequently cited in "Red Power" circles during the 1970s.) Such remarks do not reflect negatively on the speaker's skills in non-Indian English discourse; in fact, as I have already explained, most community members want to be proficient speakers of the language of the metropolis and want the same for family and friends. The language of the metropolis is valuable because it gives access to opportunity in externally controlled speaking domains. English discourse *within* pueblo settings needs to follow pueblo-based rules of speaking, not conform to expectations established within the non-Indian world.

Distinctions between outsider and insider discourse have been part of the language tradition of this speech community for some time. Comments in the Spanish colonial documents and later sources suggest that Isleta people learned as many languages as their commercial, kinship, and other ties to persons outside of their home community might require. Pidgin/creole languages, like *linguae francae*, were not acceptable language options under this framework; because they are designed to be structurally "neutral" and equally accessible to all participants, those codes obscure the very distinctions that the insider/outsider dichotomy seeks to maintain.

How much proficiency Isletan speakers might develop in any of these "outsider" languages depended on many factors. Particularly important in this communication with outsiders and remained such until the beginning of the twentieth century, when pueblo members began to associate this function with English.

There are occasions when Isleta speakers will relax their adherence to insider/outsider language distinctions. Language choices can be quite free-ranging when all participants in the conversation are from Isleta, are of similar age, and share other points of personal background. If all speakers are from Isleta, but from different age-levels, the language preferences of the older speaker(s) determine the scope of code-switching, and the younger speaker(s) adapt their language choices accordingly.

But topic of discourse can intensify the adherence to the insider/outsider distinction. Certain topics require speakers to introduce an Isletan point of view into the discussion, even if the language of the metropolis is the code-of-choice in that setting and the co-participants in the discussion are outsiders. In fact, the more Isleta-oriented such discussions become, the more likely it is that speakers will construct their English comments in terms of ancestral language models. When English conversations involve only persons from the pueblo, English discourse, already Isleta-oriented as required under the insider/outsider constraint, becomes even more vividly grounded in Isletan Tiwa grammar.

This is what makes the collection of letters that Joe Lente, the artist of the *Isleta Paintings* (Parsons 1962), sent to Elsie Clews Parsons, the anthropologist who wrote the first monograph on Indian life at Isleta pueblo (Parsons 1932), such an important resource for Indian English research. Parsons worked at Isleta in the 1920s; her contact with Isleta people had been limited, and the issues discussed in her monograph reflected that limitation. Evidently Lente, an adult member of the pueblo and someone richly familiar with ceremonial practice and other features of traditional Isleta life, found a copy of the monograph, read it, and decided that some sections of the text were not sufficiently detailed. So he contacted Parsons by letter and offered to prepare a series of watercolor drawings depicting daily life in the pueblo, which Parsons could include in future publications on pueblo life. Parsons saw Lente's offer as a chance to gain an insider's perspective on the pueblo, and she agreed to send him a small payment to cover his fees and expenses each time he sent her a completed painting.

Lente worked on this project over a five-year period (1936–1941), producing more than 140 watercolors. He sent them to Parsons in small groups, including with each set a handwritten letter commenting on the scenes that the drawings displayed. He also used the letters to reply to some of the questions Parsons had raised, by return letter, about earlier submissions. Parsons reviewed the materials then sent Lente his fee along with her next set of follow-up questions.

Lente sent his last set of paintings to Parsons in 1941, and communication between the two of them ended abruptly. Shortly thereafter, Parsons began assembling this material for publication. She prepared a few paragraphs to explain the ethnographic details depicted in each of the paintings, drawing heavily on the comments that Lente himself had made about each picture. After Parsons's death, Esther Goldfrank (a close friend of Parsons, who herself had worked at Isleta in 1924) completed the editorial task. The resulting volume appeared in print as *Isleta Paintings* (Parsons 1962). Several years later Goldfrank assembled a collection of Lente's letters to Parsons for a companion publication (Goldfrank 1967).

Ten years after the publication of this collection, John Wayne carried out a detailed analysis of Lente's use of English in the letters he wrote to Parsons (Wayne 1977). Wayne was interested in how speaker knowledge of different linguistic traditions contributed to proficiency in Indian English. He felt that a careful analysis of written Indian English texts could provide useful insights in this regard, particularly if the writer could use a range of (Indian as well as non-Indian) English models to guide the construction of those texts.

The letters in Goldfrank's collection were well suited for this task.[7] Lente spoke Isletan Tiwa and Isletan English, and he used both of these codes when he wrote to Parsons. And because he had to respond to her questions, her standard English texts provided additional guidance for the task.

According to Wayne's analysis, Lente organized his letters in terms of a three-part scheme that only partially resembles western-styled professional/personal correspondence. Part I contained his greetings and other introductory remarks. Wayne found an openness and sincere tone in Lente's comments, suggesting that Lente was writing to someone he considered to be a friend and confidant. In some letters, Lente also used part I to answer Parsons's questions about pictures he had previously sent to her; when those comments occurred in this section, their tone was also personal and cordial.

In part II of each letter, Lente inventoried the paintings he had enclosed and commented on particular activities or events depicted there. In most letters, this was also the section where he replied to Parsons's questions. Unlike the personal tone established in part I, part II was the "business" portion of the letter, and Lente's written English in this section marked the shift in topic and register in various ways (see below).

In part III, Lente returned to the more personalized style found in the opening paragraphs. In this section, he offered other comments about his artwork, about the likely consequences if Isleta people discovered what he was doing, about life in general at the pueblo, and so on. Frequently, Lente presented as much ethnographic information here as in part II; however, he did not

EXAMPLE 6.2
LENTE LETTER 1

---

no 1

Isleta New Mex
May 16th 1939.

Dear friend
   I had received your letter on time and
I was glad I made a to Zuni and
are dancing for the rain. I am enclosing
5 drawing
No 1 Cornchief giving meal to medicine man at
medicine man private room and medicine man is
ready to recived it from woman for sweath
baths at river.
No 2 Medicine man, the medicine chief helper
getting the stone Red hot ready when Medicine
Chief return with women early in the morning
before sun rise. You have all this in book what
kind of stone they use [she a, hau]
No 3 Medicine chief carrying woman to river
to gave a sweat baths. the woman holding on
the top of the father. worning her on nay to
have her good thought because our mother
old fire lady is mean Might Burn your life out
[page ends]

no 2.-

No 4 They are in side the oven the have a hole in
the middle and the red hot rock are place in it
The Medicine Chief starting to pore water over it to make
steamheat the water is fix with roots medicine water
with power. They sing 4 songs before you get
out on last song you feel crying for the
heat you getting water Just run on your
body dry your mouth on 4 you will run
out Crying and jump right over water
They do this near river so they will cool of quick.
You have all this on history you will
find it. No5
The Hunter brought his Deer at his home the
2 war captains came an visiting and prayers at
Dead deer. as they dress them and beads. you
have that on history I think on 338 somewhere

Think this will be all for this time
so I will wait for an answer on 26 Friday
          over.
[page ends]
    Mr. Joe B. Lente
      Gen Del
   Albuquerque new Mex.

Source: Goldfrank (1967: 93–95).

EXAMPLE 6.3
LENTE LETTER 2

Isleta New Mex
Aug 20 36

Elsie Clews Parsons
Dept of Anthropology
Columbia University
New York City
NY
Dear Friend
Will drop you a few lines how is Mrs
Parsons now day. I hope fine also I am well
and still trying to make living all this work
I am doing is very secret no person never see
this things but the people Join in Society
no person will do this. becaue they are afraid
they have great believed in it and say if they
ever tell they will die or go in ppor health
I am not I am ready to die anytime but I'll
have little good time with this little money what
I get. No person will ever now what I am doing
I know most every secret of Ind. I can sing
any clan songs. Well did you received some
drawing I send by air mail about month
ago I want hear. and let me know soon as
possible. I had drawn a large pitcure

[page ends]

about sick woman Curing and walking
her around the altar and snake. you have
story about this in history. and Clan
dancing with scalp of Navajo and
how they dress and making medicine
for weak heart people.

Well I guess this will be all
I will send you drawing as soon
as I hear from you I'll send them
at Albuq station and you send
me mail at Isleta.
so good by

I am Your Friend

Joe B Lente

Isleta

New Mex

Source: Goldfrank (1967: 34–35).

EXAMPLE 6.4

LENTE LETTER 3

Isleta New Mex
Oct 9th 1940

Dear Friend

    I had your mail 18th of Sept and
was glad to git it amigo. I am sure gaving
you some wonderful work of the things that
you never expect that you learn. Now I will
gave you time. I will wait for this mail on
1 of Nov. and if its not enough I will
gave you one month to ans. Next time.

          No 1 pitcure

    Marriage ceremonial of Laguna for the
law or prest the lady or girl when girl find a love
a boy or man she wants the girl go over to boy
parent house then she will sit at the boy house
sit there all day then the parents ask her if
she is will or want to marry their boy the
the boy father ask her if she want take a
boy as husband and will to live together
as long as their ife last the the boy
mother ask the girl if she really want
take her son before our Mother Corn and
wash her head with my son in our oldwoman
yaca in bog bowl to get together as same family
then the girl answer I will. I will take your
son as husband before our mother corn an old woman

[end of page]

yaca. then when girl promise every to
respect and promise ever that as she is
will to do work and be as same family,
Then they call a boy aunt and come to house
boy home and one ear of corn it has to be
black pollan then aunt roast ear of corn in
fire place the when roasted the aunt take
the corn from fire then pray all direction
then in pray call Mother Corn and place
in middle of Room in basket and call
the girl and boy to eat that corn then
as they eat the medicine man or this
old close relation to pray for them as they
eat corn.

[Detailed discussions of three more pictures follow, concluding with the comment: See how much I know?]

Dear amigo I am afraid I have to stop
soon as I am tell you too much which
you don't know and what some people dont
know. even if they are Indian.
This is all secret of Kichina Ceremonal even the
people of this village don't know how this
bear kichina are as he come in midnight
only when people go to sleep they dont
dance this outside plaza no more because
there to much cars white people even in night
so the dont bring this no more
                    Good by
                Respectfull Your Amigo
                      Joe B Lente
                        as usual.

Source: Goldfrank (1967: 148–51).

comment on any of his pictures in this section, and the linguistic features that characterized his writing in part II did not appear in this section of the text.

Example 6.2 contains one of Lente's letters, written during the fourth year of the correspondence. The display duplicates the layout, spelling, and punctuation of the original text (Goldfrank 1967: 93–95). The introductory comments run for five lines and include the greeting (*Dear friend*) and other personal remarks, and conclude with the phrase *I am enclosing 5 drawing*. Lente frequently used this phrase to mark the transition into part II, the comments on the enclosed paintings; note the change in the placement of the text on the page, the length of the paragraphs, sentence syntax, and other details. Part III details are minimal in this case: a formulaic statement of conclusion and a reminder that Lente expects Parsons to reply at a specified time—*I will wait for an answer on 26 Friday*, ending the letter with the same reference used to begin it.

Example 6.2 is quite different from the first letter Lente sent to Parsons (see example 6.3) and also different from the letters Lente wrote during the final days of their correspondence (see example 6.4).[8] Wayne noticed these changes and was not surprised by them. He assumed that, as Lente read more of Parsons's distinctively metropolitan prose, and became more experienced in responding to her questions, he would also become more adept at framing his written English in standard English terms. Hence, Wayne hypothesized, the number of standard English grammatical constructions and related features of standard English written usage should increase, letter by letter, throughout the five-year correspondence period, while the number of Isletan English constructions should decline.

Wayne decided to test this claim about Lente's "linguistic acculturation" by determining the frequency of constructions with Isletan English vs. standard English subject-verb agreement in each of Lente's letters,[9] constructing the ratio of frequencies from each letter, then tracing the changes in those ratios across all of the correspondence. His calculations showed the expected increase in standard usage and a decline in Isletan English usage, but only in the portions of the letters presenting Lente's personal, one-on-one exchanges with Parsons (usually parts I and III). Part II, where Lente described the content of the paintings and discussed the significance of the depicted event within the pueblo's social and ceremonial life, showed no shift in the direction of standard English concord. In fact, according to Wayne's analysis, part II of these texts shows only minimal indication of Lente's newly acquired mastery of written standard English; if any shift in frequency occurred over time in this section, it was toward an increased frequency of Isletan English usage.

This is an understandable patterning, given what has already been said about the rules of speaking that govern English-related code-switching at this pueblo: standard English was Parsons's "native language" and this obligated Lente to employ a standard English-based code when communicating with her. At the same time, as Wayne explains, "Parsons was an outsider. [Part II] dealt with information pertaining to Pueblo religion, a subject that would never be discussed with non-Isletas or outsiders" (Wayne 1977: 209). Retaining a highly noticeable, heavily Isletan Tiwa–influenced syntactic features like nonstandard subject-verb concord in those sections, even while he was actively incorporating standard English subject-verb concern in the remaining sections of his letters, became an effective—and culturally quite appropriate—means of underscoring the specialized, restricted nature of the information he was discussing there. The English form of the commentary, and the violations of standard English grammar that it contained, made certain that the "special status" of this information was not to be overlooked by an uninformed outsider.

Oklahoma Cherokee

Marble City, a rural community in eastern Oklahoma, offers additional examples of (Indian) English diversity and its social consequences (Guyette 1981). Half of the residents of Marble City are members of the Oklahoma Cherokee Tribe; the remainder are non-Indians who control the community's business, financial, and educational resources. Cherokee access to those structures is limited, and the segmentation of interests within the Cherokee community makes it difficult for local leaders to organize alternatives to that arrangement.

One cause of this segmentation is diversity in religious/ceremonial affiliation. In earlier times Cherokee people shared a common belief system and common spiritual practices. Today some Marble City Cherokee are Methodists, some support the more traditional Stomp Dance activities, while others claim to have no single religious "preference." Another source is the recent breakdown in neighbor-to-neighbor interaction, a support network that maintained Cherokee kinship categories and reinforced the cross-cutting social ties that integrated members of different kin groups into a larger community whole.

Cherokee language use at Marble City patterns along the lines established by these social segments. For some members of the local Cherokee community, particularly for those who maintain traditional social practices, Cherokee language fluency is still "flourishing in at least one domain." Often this domain is associated with membership in the Nighthawk Keetoowah, one of the Stomp Dance societies. For others, Cherokee fluency is falling into what Guyette terms an "obsolescing state" (1981: 219).

Guyette's fieldwork explored the cultural and social factors promoting Cherokee language obsolescence in Marble City. One important issue in that respect was the low regard with which Marble City's residents (Indian as well as non-Indian) held public expressions of Cherokee identity. Guyette found that some Cherokee people could offset the negative effects of such attitudes through their affiliation with the Nighthawk Keetoowah and other identity-affirming Cherokee institutions. Others have simply decreased their use of Cherokee language as a primary means of public communication and instead—particularly in conversations with their children—have replaced it with a "model of English heavily influenced by Cherokee phonology and syntax" (Guyette 1981: 224).

In some ways, the emergence of a Cherokee-based English variety in this setting is consistent with the functions of Indian English discussed in this chapter. However, speaking Cherokee English in this setting does not allow speakers to extend ancestral language functions into non-Indian speech settings, nor does it help speakers align themselves more closely with the concerns of the metropolis. Granted, it gives Cherokee people an alternative to non-Indian English discourse—but look at the consequences of using that alternative within this social setting.

By favoring this Cherokee-based English variety, parents are allowing Marble City attitudes about Indian-language proficiency to influence the shape of their own verbal repertoire; by doing so, parents intensify the already marginalized position that they hold within this community. Fluency in this

English variety is also affecting the verbal repertoire of Cherokee children, who do not become fluent speakers of Cherokee under this arrangement, but do not become proficient speakers of the local or regional English "standard" either. Guyette (1981: 224) explains:

> [The parents'] nonstandard variety of English . . . seems structurally incomplete in the case of at least some speakers, . . . [resulting in] a difficult communicative situation for parents. The frequency of linguistic interaction is decreased between parents and children in some cases due to the difficulties in communication. Parents, embarrassed at their Cherokee identity, tend to withdraw from children and neighbors. Or, as the situation is described by parents themselves, they are "ashamed."

I have no way of knowing how often Indian English proficiency makes Indian parents, in this or any speech community, feel "ashamed." I include Guyette's example in this section because it illustrates yet another set of issues contributing to English-related code-switching and code pluralism in Indian country.

INDIAN ENGLISH IN THE CLASSROOM

My purpose in part IV is to discuss some of the "language problems" confronting speakers of Indian English in classroom settings and to determine how fluency in Indian English contributes to those "problems." These issues were central to my work in schools and communities on the Northern Ute reservation during the period 1979–1989, and I draw extensively on data from those studies in the following chapters.

To begin this discussion, I use information from the speech community profile (chapter I) and other sources to describe the social context of schooling on the Northern Ute reservation. Next I discuss the language backgrounds of Northern Ute students, and identify features of grammar and discourse which make Ute student English distinct from other English varieties used by students and teachers at the on-reservation schools.

These features color Ute students' decisions about correct and incorrect spellings for English words, and they also make it easier for Ute students to answer certain types of content questions on worksheets, examinations, or standardized tests, and more difficult for them to answer questions in other formats. Examples of Ute student performance on spelling exercises and test-taking tasks lead into a more detailed analysis of text-related inferencing, story-(re)telling, and essay-writing—and the ways in which these students' Ute English skills influence their performance in those domains.

CHAPTER 7

CONTEXTS OF SCHOOLING ON THE NORTHERN UTE RESERVATION

Since I intend to focus on the relationships between language skills and educational experience on the Northern Ute reservation, I need to make some additional observations about life on this reservation and the influence of Ute language and culture on school experience there. Most importantly, as I explained in chapter 1, while the reservation boundary remains undisturbed and areas of the reservation remain firmly under the control of Ute families and communities, non-Indians have also gained access to land within that boundary, and non-Indian communities have developed there as well.

Northern Ute people are in no sense isolated from their non-Indian neighbors. Because there is no single commercial or social center on this reservation, Utes regularly travel to one location to buy groceries, another to wash clothes at a commercial laundry, a third to visit relatives or friends, a fourth to enjoy a film, go dancing, or pursue other amusement, a fifth to attend religious services, and so on. Travel to Vernal (20 miles east of the reservation) or Salt Lake City (150 miles to the west) can be just as likely under this arrangement as travel to Roosevelt, Neola, or Duchesne. Such movement keeps Ute people in touch with other members of the tribe living outside of their home community and makes one-on-one interaction with non-Indians an almost unavoidable dimension of daily life.

What is true for tribal members is also true for tribal government. Whether the issue is highway maintenance, affordable housing, irrigation and water management, employment services, or schooling (see below), federal, state, and county authorities as well as the various offices within Northern Ute tribal government may claim to have sole authority for decision-making or (depending on the issue) they may make it a point to defer responsibility for action to some other agency. Problem-solving at Northern Ute has to mediate between the interests of a range of Indian and non-Indian agencies. It is not always easy to achieve such consensus, or to maintain it—particularly when the tribe's right to establish goals and priorities is itself one of the issues under discussion.

THE SCHOOL SITES

Schooling at Northern Ute became heavily contested in this fashion in the early 1950s, when the federal government closed the on-reservation boarding school at White Rocks and transferred the Ute students to public schools located on or adjacent to reservation lands. In Utah the counties function as school districts and operate the public schools; since the Ute reservation falls within two counties, the federal government had to convince two school systems to provide educational services. Previously, these schools had served a predominantly non-Indian clientele; under this new arrangement, these schools now had to contend with a larger and culturally more heterogeneous student population, which required renovation and/or construction of school facilities, expansion of student transportation services, hiring of new staff, and other adjustments. The counties negotiated for federal funding to help them meet these costs. In addition, the federal government agreed to provide funds for the construction of a new high school that Utes and non-Indian students could both attend, which, as Jorgensen explains it (1964: 305–6), "would give Utes and Basin Whites similar educations and prepare each for mutually compatible lives in the Uintah Basin." While the school has a Roosevelt (Duchesne County) mailing address, the building straddles the Uintah/Duchesne county line, so that students from both counties could have access to the facility. Appropriately, the school was named Union High School, and it continues to provide services to secondary school Ute and non-Indian students living on the west side of Uintah County and the eastern side of Duchesne County.

The county governments made no effort to consolidate elementary-level school services, however. Instead, Ute students were expected to attend the public school closest to their home/community. A network of community-based elementary schools already served non-Indian students living within the reservation boundary in Duchesne County, and these schools took responsibility for educating Ute students from the same area.

Conditions in Uintah County were somewhat more complex. Since Ute students had previously attended federally operated schools, and the majority of non-Indian families lived in the east side of the county and away from the reservation, school authorities had not found it necessary to operate public schools inside reservation boundaries. Non-Indian students living in that area were bused to schools in Vernal, the county seat, some 30 miles east of the Uintah-Duchesne county line.

With the closing of the federal schools, Uintah County was faced with an increased demand for elementary school services, but no schools to provide them. For a while, Ute students were bused to schools in Vernal, but parents raised concerns about the travel time (especially during the winter months, when the roads can be heavily snowpacked) and other issues; the multicultural flavor of Vernal's classrooms also proved problematic for some teachers. In the 1960s Uintah County school authorities opened Todd School at an isolated site on the west side of the county and assigned K–8th grade Ute students from that area to that school. The school was not, however, located near these students' home communities. Non-Indian K–8th grade students living on the west side of the county were also expected to attend Todd School; however, arrangements were made to accommodate the students in Vernal if parents preferred this option, as some did.

In the 1970s the county school board approved funds for the construction of a new "middle school" (West Junior High) on land adjacent to the elementary school. They assigned students in grades 7–9 to this school and reclassified Todd School as an elementary school for students in grades K–6. Continuing growth in the student population led to the construction of a second elementary school on the western side of the county in the fall of 1983. This school was placed in the predominantly non-Indian community of Lapointe, approximately twenty miles northeast of Fort Duchesne and ten miles east of Todd School.

In 1979, when I began my studies of Ute student classroom-language skills at Todd School, the school served a total of 700 students, 45% non-Indian and 55% Indian (almost all of Northern Ute tribal background). After Lapointe School opened (fall 1985), the school population was reduced to 500, and the ratio of non-Indians to non-Indians shifted to approximately 50/50.

These statistics suggest that more Ute students than non-Indian students moved from Todd Elementary School to Lapointe Elementary School. This finding surprised me. When the plan to open Lapointe School was first announced, Ute parents told me that they wanted their children to remain at Todd. Lapointe was a non-Indian settlement, almost all of whose residents were members of the Mormon church, and they feared that the school curriculum would reflect the educational and cultural priorities of that constituency. As discussion of this issue continued—during Parents' Committee meetings at Todd School, at the on-reservation laundromat, at the K-Mart in Salt Lake City, and at other locales—some Ute parents decided that, even with its explicitly non-Indian orientation, Lapointe was the preferred school site for their children: "See, with all the *mirkanoocew* [white people] there, the county won't cut back funds for Lapointe School the way they do for Todd," one tribal official explained. Even so, as it turned out, her children did not attend Lapointe School. They told their mother that they wanted to be with their friends, who were staying at Todd; her own preference to the contrary, she decided to respect their wishes.

THE CLASSROOMS

The administrators in the Uintah and Duchesne county schools have always been non-Indian in ethnic background. And until recently, the same has been true for the classroom teachers and the academic tutors/counselors, the custodial staff, and the lunchroom personnel. In 1979 Todd School had five classroom teachers and two instructional aides who were of Indian background. The Wykoopah (Ute/English bilingual education) program brought a team of six Utes onto the staff of Todd School (and later Lapointe School) during 1980–1986. Funding for the program came from the U.S. Office of Bilingual Education and Minority Language Affairs, with a small matching allocation from county funds. When the grant period ended, the county was unwilling to meet the total operating costs for the program or to retain its staff, and the Indian presence within the Todd School staff declined substantially.

Instructional aides have never been assigned to these school's classrooms. Before the opening of Lapointe School, this meant that each teacher worked with approximately 35 to 40 students, of Indian and non-Indian backgrounds, throughout the school day. Maintaining order in the classroom became a primary theme in all teacher-student interaction, and I think this explains why teachers at all grade levels relied on seat-work, rather than teacher-centered presentations or class discussion, as their primary focus for in-class instruction. That is, each lesson plan centered around a set of activity sheets, workbook problems, or other exercises that the students were expected to complete individually and on their own initiative while working at their desks.

Typically, each lesson began with the teacher offering opening remarks to orient the students to the task; usually the teacher worked through one or two of the problems or exercises to be certain that students understood what the task required. Then the teacher reminded the students how much time they had to complete the task (usually five to ten minutes for the lower grades, and fifteen to twenty minutes for grades 4–6), and told them to begin. If students found they needed additional help with the task, it was their responsibility to seek assistance from the teacher, who was seated at her or his desk (grading papers, preparing for activities later in the day, or completing paperwork) or monitoring the class from some other central location. Seeking assistance meant that students had to leave their seat and come to the teacher, so at any point during the lesson several students could be clustering around the work station, vying for teacher attention.

The teacher did not allow students to talk to their fellow students while work was in progress. Of course, some students always tried to have such conversations, either when they finished the exercise or once they became bored with the task; if the teacher noticed the students talking, he or she gave the students a verbal reprimand and reminded the whole class to "do their own work."

When the period for the seat-work activity ended, the teacher collected the students' activity sheets or other papers. The teacher might also spend a few minutes reviewing the assignment and working a few problems with the class. Usually students were not given the opportunity to correct their worksheets in class, however. The teacher reviewed the worksheets, assigned a grade based on the number of problems completed as well as number of correct answers (criteria for grading varied considerably between teachers, I discovered), then filed the worksheets in the students' folders.

Classroom learning under this arrangement was heavily teacher-controlled, as it is in most elementary school settings. Note, however, that the learning process itself was student centered and largely student regulated— something that has far-reaching effects on Ute students' classroom experiences, as I will explain below.

The opening of Lapointe School lowered the number of students enrolled at Todd—but it also lowered the number of teachers working there, since some of them were transferred (or chose to relocate) to the new school. So the student-teacher ratio at Todd School still remained high (one teacher for twenty-five to thirty students) and seat work remained the focus for classroom instruction (and classroom management) at all grade-levels throughout the years I worked at that site.

Here, according to my field notes, is the scenario during a "typical" classroom day at Todd School during this period. Students arrived at the school as early as 7:30 A.M. They come by county school bus, by car, or on foot. The principal and office staff were also on-site at 7:30. Faculty were in their classrooms before 8:00 A.M. Students began assembling in the classrooms at 8:15 A.M. (though in cold weather they waited in the halls and entered the classrooms when the teacher arrived). The school day "officially" began at 8:30 A.M. with the Pledge of Allegiance to the flag and the teacher's reading of the day's announcements.

While the allocation of time varied by grade-level and instructor, topics for instruction during the morning hours were consistent across grade levels and included (often in this order): language arts, reading, spelling, and mathematics;

social studies and natural science were topics for the afternoon. Instruction in each subject area followed the seat-work format just described: a few minutes of teacher commentary, a longer period of student-centered, student-managed problem-solving, a few minutes of summary and review, and the end-of-the lesson collection of papers and a shift to the next content-area and the seat work planned for that day.

Students who completed their seat work ahead of time could, with teacher permission, read a library book, work with the classroom computer, or pursue some other activity of personal interest. Students who did not complete those assignments either remained in the classroom during recess or were told to complete the work at home that evening. Some teachers monitored these homework assignments quite carefully; others did not, given the new classroom management tasks facing them on the following day.

Classes ended at 2:15 P.M., and by 2:30 P.M., students were on their way home. Faculty worked in their classrooms until 3:30 P.M. then left the campus. The school principal and office staff usually worked until 4:00 P.M. or later in the day.

There were two major breaks in this routine: the mid-morning recess (approximately 10:00 A.M. for fifteen minutes), and lunchtime (including a second recess period). Lunch was served in the school cafeteria between 11:15 A.M. and continued until 12:30 or 12:45 P.M. Each classroom was assigned a 20-minute period for lunch; but because students from Todd and West used the same facilities, the lunchroom was always crowded and noisy, and students told me they preferred to eat quickly and go out onto the playground.

Teachers were assigned lunchroom duty or playground duty on a rotating basis each month, to make certain that students were supervised during the times they were away from the classroom. If the teachers were not on duty, they ate lunch in the staff lounge, visited with their colleagues, then returned to their classroom to prepare for the afternoon. Only rarely did teachers eat lunch with their students.

Students in each classroom were scheduled to make one trip to the school library each week, for story-telling activities, to watch a video or film, or to check out and return library books. The school librarian supervised this activity; the teacher remained in the classroom. With teacher permission, students could also go to the library during their "free time," before classes began or at the end of the day.

Students eligible to receive academic tutorial/counseling services faced additional breaks in their classroom routine. They worked in one-hour sessions with the tutors/counselors, reviewing topics in reading, language arts, and mathematics connected to the issues they were discussing in the regular classroom.

Eligibility for these services depended on the requirements of the sponsoring program: students of Ute or other Indian background received tutorial assistance under the Johnson-O'Malley program (Bureau of Indian Affairs) and Part A of the Indian Education Act (U.S. Department of Education); "under-achieving" students (defined by standardized test scores) who came from low-income family backgrounds received assistance under the Chapter I (U.S. Department of Education) and Resource (Utah State Department of Public Instruction) programs. Frequently, as many as one-third of the students in a classroom would be working with tutors/counselors from one or more of these programs and, depending on eligibility requirements, some students could be scheduled to leave their classroom two or three times each day to receive the instructional support services to which they were entitled.

THE POLITICS OF THE SCHOOL CURRICULUM

The course of study for each grade level was determined in several ways. State guidelines established the basic expectations, and county decisions focused those priorities somewhat more tightly. Within that framework, each school had leeway to make final decisions on curriculum questions. This included textbook selection, use of tightly sequenced, skills-oriented instructional "packages" like the Open Court reading system (see discussion later in this chapter), integration of drama, computer, literacy training, and other "enrichment opportunities" into the classroom day, and so on. Changes in state-level educational policies in the 1980s, prompted by the U.S. Department of Education's national assessments of the problems facing America's schools, set tighter expectations regarding achievement gains for students at each grade level and linked teacher merit pay increases to student performance on achievement tests. Even then, however, state policy assumed that individual schools would develop their own strategies for meeting these goals and did not attempt to impose a single set of instructional practices to those ends.

The autonomy enjoyed by each individual school under this arrangement has to be balanced against the control over educational practice retained by the school superintendent and the school board in each county. These authorities have oversight responsibility for public education in Utah and exercise that authority regularly, particularly in areas of school finance. They coordinate the distribution of income from property tax revenue and from other county- and state-level sources to the individual schools. They receive funds from federal programs and re-grant those funds to the individual schools according to county-determined criteria. Their decision in this regard reflects an educational agenda whose provisions do not take into account the concerns voiced by school principals, teachers, parents, or (in this case) tribal government. Importantly, in the case of Uintah County schools, the school board does not question the right of the Northern Ute Tribe and its Division of Education to set priorities relevant to the education of Ute students; but the school board does not accept the tribe's assertion that such priorities should apply to educational programs that the tribe does not administer or fund directly.

There are no mechanisms through which Northern Ute tribal government can influence school board decision-making, other than informal, one-on-one conversation. No member of the Northern Ute Tribe has ever been elected to the school board in either Uintah or Duchesne County. Individual tribal members may attend board meetings and speak on particular issues when time allows, but the school board does not make itself accountable to tribal government for any of its actions.

The county's position in this regard is consistent with what tribal members know about schooling from their own life experience. And it is also consistent with the conditions they find when they visit their children's schools. The institution is not Ute-friendly, parents explained during the interviewing for the Math Avoidance Study (Leap et al. 1982: 170–81). (Non-Indian) teachers and school staff know very little about Ute language or cultural traditions; the curriculum says nothing about Ute people, Ute history, or Ute achievements; the large-group classroom format hinders Ute students from speaking up in class; restrictions on cigarette smoking and food consumption make it difficult for parents to socialize comfortably, even if they find staff members willing to listen to their concerns or to develop ways of responding to them.

CLASSROOM LANGUAGE(S)

Language issues in Ute student education reflect the school systems' non-Indian commitments and intensify the distance between tribe and classroom at these sites. Even during the time when the Wykoopah program was providing ancestral language instruction to Ute students on a regular basis, English was still the language of schooling on this reservation. Textbooks and other instructional materials were printed in (standard) English, as were the students' worksheets, their examinations, and their report cards. Grading itself was an English language activity—teachers use "letter grades" (*A, B, C*, and so on), rather than Ute-oriented symbols to indicate the relative worth of a student's performance on any task. And communication between school, home, and community is also English-based: this is the language teachers use when writing notes to parents in English and conducting conferences with parents when they visit the school. This is also the language of business for the monthly meetings of the school's Parent-Teacher Association.

The English in question here is the language of the metropolis, and all of the messages of conformity, hierarchy, and power displayed by that code in political and economic domains are reproduced within English-based classroom interaction. Importantly, there are differences between the "standards" for language use reflected by language of the metropolis and the English regularly spoken by Ute students (e.g., Ute student English) and by their non-Indian class-/age-mates (e.g. student Basin English). There are also differences between the language of the metropolis and the varieties of English spoken by teachers and school authorities, particularly those who have lived in the Uintah Basin for some time (adult Basin English) and those who have moved to northeastern Utah from Oklahoma, Ohio, or other areas of the country where people also maintain distinctive English styles.

Because they are in positions of authority within the classroom, teachers' ways of speaking English carry authority—even if the rules of grammar and discourse do not always replicate those of the metropolitan code. In fact, from my observations of language dynamics at Todd School, *all* varieties of teacher English at this school share certain assumptions about "appropriate classroom usage" by which teachers evaluate their students' classroom performance and overall enthusiasm for learning. These include:

o maintaining *silence* when another person is speaking to indicate listener respect and attentiveness; maintaining silence when someone invites you to speak, however, suggests shyness, undeveloped social skills, or unfamiliarity with the topic under discussion;

o *question-asking* as a means of soliciting information. Questions are speaker-centered constructions, use of which need not assume that listeners will be able to provide appropriate responses; there may be times when speakers ask questions because they know the listener cannot respond.

o *continuity of discourse*, to ensure that all comments in a given discussion build directly on the point of view outlined in the initial speaker's remarks.

o *turn-taking* options guided by the speakers' social status and position within the existing power hierarchy of the conversation.

The classroom discourse guided by these assumptions is heavily teacher-centered and teacher-controlled; in some ways, it parallels the *initiation-reply-*

evaluation sequences (Mehan 1985) found in teacher/student uses of language in many American schools and is not unique to this on-reservation setting.

My classroom observations at these schools suggest that non-Indian students organize classroom discourse in terms of similar assumptions. Certainly, according to their comments during interview sessions and in informal conversations, they know that "talking out of turn" or other violations of these expectations will produce negative reactions from their teachers and, quite likely, will be topics for discussion during parent-teacher conferences. While Ute students participate as actively as their non-Indian classmates in classroom discourse, their use of English in those settings reflects different assumptions about "appropriate" classroom discourse. These include:

- o maintaining *silence* when another person is speaking indicates listener respect and attentiveness. Maintaining silence when a Ute student is invited to speak, however, is a way for the student to request more information about the task or for other adjustments in the social setting—not an unwillingness or inability to respond.
- o *question-asking* as a means of acknowledging the information controlled by others. Questions are listener-centered constructions. Speakers ask questions only when they are certain that the listener has sufficient background to be able to provide an answer; being asked a question imposes an obligation on the listener to respond.
- o *continuity of discourse* depends on listener's use of inference. Speakers are not obligated to connect their comments to the preceding speaker's remarks; if anything, speakers are expected to make distinctive contributions to the dialogue.
- o *turn-taking* options assure that all persons who wish to speak will have the opportunity to do so; social status and power grow out of conversations, and do not automatically exist in advance of those exchanges.

Classroom discourse constructed in terms of these assumptions leads to teacher/student exchanges like that in example 7.1,[1] where the teacher expects the student to produce "the right answer" and constantly adjusts the conversation to that end, while the student is responding to the teacher's questioning in entirely different terms.

Dispite the teacher's comment in line 6, it is not clear whether the student understood the principles of multiplication and division that are at issue in this exchange. He gave a correct answer (line 5, repeated on line 11) only when

EXAMPLE 7.1   THIRD GRADE MATHEMATICS LESSON ON NINE TIMES NINE
(WINTER 1981)

---

1 Teacher: What is nine times nine?
2 Student: Ninety.
3 Teacher: No, that is too big. We know that nine times nine is
4   eighty-one. What is nine times nine?
5 Student: Eighty-one.
6 Teacher: Eighty-one. You know that nine times nine is eighty-
7   one. Can you get a nine out of here [motions to the 90
8   ⁃ on the board]?
9 Student: Yes.
10 Teacher: OK, if we take nine out of here, what do we have ?
11 Student: Eighty one.
12 Teacher: What about eighty-three divided by nine ?
13 Student (without hesitation): Ten.

---

modeling the teacher's comment; otherwise, his answers were not satisfactory to the teacher, as her comments indicate (lines 3, 14).

I have observed and tape-recorded many such exchanges while conducting classroom observations at Todd School. Consistently, I found that non-Indian students faced with such situations either admitted that they did not understand the task and asked the teacher for assistance or made no reply to her questions and sat in silence until she shifted her attention to another student. Ute students, I found, use neither of these options: silence and admission of ignorance go against the assumptions guiding their participation in such discourse. Instead, they do their best to cooperate with the task imposed on them by the teacher's questions, even if, as shown in example 7.1, they have to come up with their own approaches to problem-solving in order to have something to say.

The dialogue in example 7.2, a transcript of the opening portion of a third-grade mathematics lesson, shows how Ute student assumptions about classroom discourse guide their participation in a larger teacher-student exchange. The teacher was introducing a unit on money and the mathematics associated with using money in daily life. The issues she raised during the discussion anticipated tasks the students were about to face on that day's mathematics worksheet. The conversation is teacher-controlled; she initiates requests for student commentary, she evaluates their responses, and most of the "talk" in the transcript is "teacher talk." But even within those restrictions, the Ute students' (students 1, 2, 7, and 9) reliance on Ute English rules of discourse makes their participation in the dialogue quite distinct from that of their non-Indian classmates, and on more than one occasion (see lines 8, 19, and 70, for example), it elicits less than favorable responses from the teacher, as well.[2]

EXAMPLE 7.2 THIRD GRADE MATHEMATICS
LESSON ON MONEY (WINTER, 1981)

---

1 Teacher: Get out your mathematics books. After you get your
2   books, you will turn to page thirty-six. [pause]. OK, now
3   that you are on page thirty-six, who can tell me what these
4   pictures are inside the black box? What are those things?
5   What do we call it?
6 Students in chorus: Money.
7 Teacher: Money. What is another name for money?
8 Student 1 (Ute): Penny, nickel.
9 Students in chorus: Coins.
10 Teacher: Who can tell me what those pictures are inside
11   that . . . what kinds of coins are they?
12 Students in chorus: Pennies, nickels, dimes, quarters.
13 Teacher: OK, let's look at the first one. What color is
14   the first one on that page?
15 Students in chorus: Brown.
16 Teacher: What was that first coin, [student 2]?
17 Student 2 (Ute): Brown.
18 Teacher: What kind of coin is it?
19 Student 2 (Ute): Brown.
20 Teacher: I know [a little annoyed]. How much is it worth?
21   [student 3]?
22 Student 3 (non-Indian): One cent.
23 Teacher: What can you buy for one cent?
24 Student 3 (non-Indian): A piece of bubble gum. I don't know. A
25   piece of bubble gum.
26 Teacher: Bubble gum, sometimes. Now it has gone up to how many
27   cents? Bubble gums are how many?
28 Students in chorus: Five cents, ten cents.
29 Teacher: OK, now you see those colored round things up on the
30   board. Let's pretend they're like money. [Student 2], how much
31   is this here?
32 Student 2 (Ute): Twenty-five.
33 Teacher: Twenty-five *cents*. [Student 4], how much is this?
34 Student 4 (non-Indian): [silence].
35 Students in chorus: [laughter, which increases as student 4's
36   silence continues.]
37 Teacher: Shhhhhhh.
38 Student 4 (non-Indian): [silence].
39 Teacher: Well, what about the yellow one, [Student 5]?
40 Student 5 (non-Indian): Five.
41 Teacher: Five cents. What about the pink one, [Student 6]?
42 Student 6 (non-Indian): Ten cents.
43 Teacher: OK, let's write the names right below the coins here
44   [does so, with student help]. OK, let's do some adding with

45   the coins here. If we had one quarter and added one nickel
46   to it, what would you have?
47 Student chorus: [a variety of answers, given all at once].
48 Teacher: OK, if we had one penny—
49 Student 7 (Ute): Thirty-one.
50 Teacher: OK, one penny and one dime, how much would we have?
51 Student chorus: [a variety of answers].
52 Teacher: [Student 3], [Student 3], if we had one cent and we added ten
53   cents to it how much would we have?
54 Student 3 (non-Indian): Eleven.
55 Teacher: Eleven what?
56 Student 3 (non-Indian): Cents.
57 Teacher: OK, here is a hard one for . . . [Student 8]. If we had one
58   quarter, one dime, and one penny, how much would we have,
59   [name]? If we had one quarter, one dime, and one penny, how
60   much would we have, [Student 8]?
61 Student 8 (non-Indian): [silence].
62 Teacher: [Student 8] [annoyed tone]!! Here we have twenty-five,
63   add ten, how much is that ?
64 Student chorus: Thirty-five.
65 Teacher: Add one more.
66 Student chorus: Thirty-six.
67 Teacher: OK, [Student 4], if you had one dime, one nickel, and
68   one penny, how much would you have? How much, [Student 4]?
69 Student 4 (non-Indian): [silence].
70 Student 2 (Ute): I know how to do that.
71 Teacher: Shhhhhh.
72 Student 4 (non-Indian): [goes to board, starts to write].
73 Teacher: What is that ? [reads the numbers 10, 5, 1] OK, so
74   that is how many—
75 Student 4 (non-Indian): Fifteen.
76 Teacher: And you added one penny, that would make it—
77 Student 4 (non-Indian): Sixteen.
78 Teacher: Good. OK, [Student 9]. If you had one quarter, two
79   nickels, and one dime, how much would you have?
80 Student 9 (Ute): [silence].
81 Teacher: Two quarters, so that would be how much? Twenty-five
82   and twenty-five is how much?
83 Student 9 (Ute): Fifty.
84 Teacher: And two of these?
85 Student 9 (Ute): Sixty.
86 Teacher: Sixty what?
87 Student 9 (Ute): Monies.
89 Teacher: OK, let's look at the problems on page 36. Number
90   one: "what are the values in cents" [and she continues with
91   the instructions specific to the seatwork assignment.].

SPELLING AS A CLASSROOM DISCOURSE

Differences between Ute student and teacher assumptions about "appropriate discourse" are not limited to student-teacher verbal exchange. These
differences show up in Ute students' use of English when carrying out the
seat-work activities that make up the core of their classroom day; they affect the
Ute students' performance on those activities and the evaluations of their
performance that teachers give.

Spelling is one such classroom activity, and in the remainder of this
chapter I focus on the characteristics of Ute student English spelling as found
on spelling tests, in assigned compositions, and in writing activities of their own
choosing, showing how Ute students' assumptions about "appropriate speech"
and other features of their English grammar and discourse contribute to
performance on these tasks.

Spelling occupied a central place in the English language curriculum at
Todd School throughout the research period. Teachers saw close ties between
their students' ability to spell words correctly and their mastery of word
recognition, word attack, and other reading strategies. And they saw linkages
between spelling and the development of written language skills, so that some
teachers used the frequency of correctly or incorrectly spelled words as a rough
indicator of the student's overall performance-level on a particular writing task.

The format for spelling instruction varied little across grade-levels or
individual classrooms. On Monday teachers gave their students a list of words
(usually ten to fifteen in number) for which they were going to be responsible
that week and assigned them a set of tasks (creating sentences, dictionary
activities) to help the students become familiar with the spellings. On
Wednesday students took a practice exam; the teachers read each word and the
student wrote the word on the answer sheet. Students who did well on this exam
were usually not required to take a second test on Friday; those whose
Wednesday performance was less satisfactory used the second test to improve
their weekly grade. Whatever their grades on these exercises, students were
expected to have mastered the assigned spellings, and to be able to use the words
correctly in written English contexts, by the end of the week. Cumulative
spelling tests (drawing on words from several weeks' assignments) along with
careful evaluation of students' use of spelling in their writing assignments
allowed teachers to monitor students' retention of this information over longer
periods.

I decided to pay attention to the Ute English dimensions of Ute student
English spelling for two reasons. First, whenever I talked about language arts
needs with teachers and Ute parents, both groups insisted that spelling posed

particular problems for elementary school Ute students and that the school's efforts at spelling instruction were not creating improvements in these conditions. Consistently, teachers told me, Ute students in their classroom scored much less successfully than their non-Indian classmates on the Wednesday and Friday spelling tests. Required participation in preliminary "practice tests" and other remedial exercises had little effect on this pattern. Even when teachers and/or parents coached Ute students individually, in preparation for these tests, the outcomes still tended to be disappointing. And while spelling skills at the first and second grade levels were certainly not strong, teachers felt that spelling skills of most Ute students actually declined the longer they stayed in school; this was one reason why, as grade level increased, so did the number of Ute students assigned to the schools' tutorial/counseling programs.

Some teachers, and many of the parents, associated the persistence of Ute students' spelling problems with the school's use of the Headway (or, as the teachers referred to it, the Open Court) reading curriculum (Carus et al. 1982). Open Court assigns a specific letter or letter-combination and a descriptive label to each of the contrastive sounds in oral English (*m* is "the ice cream sound" since children say *m-m-m-m* when they get their ice cream). Once students learn to associate letters, labels, and sounds, they are able to "sound out" unfamiliar words in their reading assignments, expand their sight-vocabulary, and make sense out of irregularly spelled word sequences (the "exceptions" to the sound-symbol relationships that they have now mastered) whenever they encounter them.

The problem was, or so some teachers and parents thought, that Ute students were using their Open Court–based word-attack skills to help them write, as well as read, unfamiliar (or unremembered) word sequences. From my assessment, even if Ute students were transferring skills across language arts domains, other factors were also influencing their spelling. For one thing, Open Court was a recent addition to the language arts curriculum, yet Ute students had problems with spelling at all grade-levels, and spelling had been an issue in Ute student education for quite some time. Moreover, when I began to examine samples of Ute student written English, many of the spelling errors I found had nothing to do with the sound-symbol relationships taught through the Open Court program.

To approach this issue more systematically, I began to obtain copies of the weekly spelling tests of a sample of Ute students enrolled in one of the second grade classes at Todd School as of January 1983; I continued collecting spelling tests from these students as they completed second grade (June 1983), moved through third grade (September 1983–June 1984), and completed half of their fourth grade year (September–December, 1984). I located the misspelled words that showed up in these tests and began sorting these words into categories based on the similarities and differences in the "errors" they contained.

By the fall of 1984, I was able to use these categories to establish four general types of Ute student spelling errors, in terms of which individual Ute students' spelling skills could be assessed. (Ute student spelling precedes standard spelling in each example.)

1. Alterations in letter sequences.

siad	said
recieve	receive
biger	bigger
grabed	grabbed
* mountian	mountain

Errors in this category include reversals of standard English letter sequences (siad) as well as the deletion of one item in a pair of repeated letters (biger). Errors of this type also show up in the written English of the Ute students' non-Indian classmates; but even if there is nothing "uniquely Ute" about these errors, they still have to be addressed by the school's language arts curriculum.

2. Word substitutions:

their	there
through	threw
seen	some
are	or

English homonyms condition some of the spelling patterns in this category; general similarities in word-shape contribute to other patterns. Note that the outcome of these substitutions does not necessarily retain the meaning expressed by the target word; this can be especially problematic when students are constructing written essays.

3. Adjustments in syllable structure, including:

3a. Replacement of complex vowel spellings with single vowel(s):

bet	beat
ske	sky
guss	guess
staet	stayed

3b. Deletion of vowel nuclei:

Canda	Canada

swimg	swimming
srcl	circle

3c. Deletion of *l* or *n*:

seif	self
tayo	tail
turd	turned
mats	mountains
aimal	animal

3d. Addition of extra vowels or consonants into syllable structure:

tripete	tripped
acna	ached

Frequently, errors of this type produce a distinctively nonstandard spelling, which may make the intended word unrecognizable to persons not familiar with Ute students' English spelling "style."

4. "Invented" spellings:

tuff	tough
cusohs	cousins
becuse	because
minets	minutes
nise	nice

As was the case for items in category 1, items in this category also show up in the English of the Ute students' non-Indian classmates, though the details of the invented spelling are not necessarily the same in all cases.[3]

Given this typology, my next task was to calculate the frequency of occurrence for each of the categories within the corpus. I decided to do this for individual sets of spelling tests, then to average frequencies by category across each school semester. Table 7.1 presents the results of these calculations (stated in percentages) for the fourth grade Ute student spelling tests.

TABLE 7.1   MEAN FREQUENCY OF UTE STUDENT SPELLING ERRORS
BY TYPE IN SPELLING TESTS (FALL SEMESTER, 1984)

3b.	Deletion of V or VC sequences	29%
4.	Invented spellings	29%
3c.	Deletion of *l* or *n*	13%
3a.	Replacement of long V by short V	10%
3d.	Addition of V or VC sequences	10%
2.	Word substitutions	5%
1.	Alterations in letter sequences	4%

According to the data in table 7.1, Ute students made type 3 errors more frequently than any other type during this semester; 62% of their spelling errors fell within that segment of the typology. Invented spellings (type 4) ranked second in frequency, accounting for 29% of the errors. Word substitutions (type 2 errors) due to homonyms or other factors ranked third at 5%, and alterations in letter sequences (type 1 errors) ranked fourth at 4%.

The ranking of these frequencies gave me a basis for evaluating the effects that the Open Court reading system might be having on Ute student spelling skills. Invented spellings (type 4), vowel replacements (type 3a), word substitutions (type 2), and sequence alterations (type 1) are the most likely products of Open Court's emphasis on sound-symbol relationships. However, even if all of the errors in these types could be traced to Open Court influence, that would account for only 48% of the Ute students' errors on these spelling tests, leaving a substantial 52% of their errors to be explained through other means.

An equally plausible influence on Ute students' spelling skills is the sound pattern of the students' (spoken) Ute English, particularly the (ancestral language–based) rules that govern syllable structure in this English code. Speakers of Ute English frequently rework standard English consonant and vowel patterns into highly regular, C-V-C-V sequences (see discussion in chapter 4). Speakers do this by adding vowel or vowel-consonant sequences, or deleting those elements, from the standard English word form. Resonants [l, r, m, and n] have the status of vowels *or* consonants under these rules; and when resonants function as vowels, vowel segments adjacent to the resonant within the syllable may be eliminated, especially when the vowel segments are other than [u, o and ə].

Ute English pronunciation patterns account for all of the spelling errors listed in table 7.1 not directly associated with the Open Court sound-symbol rules; for example, deletion of V or VC sequences (29%), deletion of *l* and *n* (13%), and addition of V or VC sequences (10%). And it is possible that Ute English syllable structure rules may be involved in the replacement of more complex vowel sequences with single vowel segments (e.g, *bet* in place of *beat*), the invented spellings, and other of the (presumably) Open Court–related errors, as well.

Ute English rules of discourse may also be influencing Ute student performance on these spelling tests. Spoken Ute English places high value on personalized discourse, and each speaker of this English variety is expected to construct statements noticeably distinctive from the statements provided by other participants in the speech event. Appropriately, how speakers address this goal varies from one speaker to the next. Some rely on vocabulary choices, some draw on certain metaphors or other recurring phrases, others make use of unexpected combinations in word order and sentence form. What results, as far as spoken Ute English is concerned, is a highly decentralized use of shared grammatical skills in every Ute English discourse setting.

During my review of the Ute students' spelling tests and in other examples of written English, I found ample evidence of personalized discourse in Ute students' English spelling. Particularly telling here is the *diversity* in spellings that individual Ute students give to the target words in each week's assignment.

Table 7.2 shows what this diversity can entail, by comparing the performance of five Ute fourth grade students on one of the fall 1984 spelling tests. Student A's performance identifies the target words for this task. (This student's spelling, by the way, consistently followed standard English rules on all of the spelling tests I reviewed. She is a fluent speaker of her ancestral language. I have observed her speaking Ute on the playground and in out-of-school social settings; rarely, however, did she use Ute in the classroom.)

TABLE 7.2   Sample Spelling Tests: Fourth Grade Ute Students
(Fall Semester, 1984)

		Student		
A	B	C	D	E
1. blanks	plays	blank	backs	blanke
2. neighbor	nadr	naber	nibsir	nader
3. anchor	acr	aner	ackr	ankor
4. belong	blog	belong	beleog	belong
5. hold	hold	hold	hod	hold
6. candle	cando	candle	cadl	ckandle
7. chorus	crus	coruse	cort	chors
8. shouted	shated	souted	stdd	shoted
9. circle	cucl	sircle	srcl	srcl
10. Christmas	cismis	Chsmus	Comas	chritier
11. make	mack	make	make	make
12. ache	ack	acna	acke	ache

All of the types of spelling errors identified in table 7.2 show up in these students' spellings, as do instances where spelling conforms to standard English models.[4] In no case, however, did all of the these students come up with the same spelling for any of the target words. And in only two cases did as many as four of the students agree in their choice of spellings.

As it turns out, personalized discourse is not only relevant to Ute students' English spelling, it affects their English-related language choice-making in other areas of classroom discourse—and it is one of the major tenets defining appropriate behavior in traditional and contemporary social domains for Ute people as a whole.

Elsewhere (Leap 1987: 182), I have used the term *self-dependence* to describe this component of Ute interpersonal behavior; characteristics of *self-dependence*, as they apply to Ute students in classroom settings, include the following:

> Ute students ... find it appropriate to follow their own initiatives inside and outside of the classroom, to take personal responsibility for the consequences of their actions, to expect that other people will also pursue their own initiatives in terms of their own sense of responsibility, and to assume that other people will extend the same respect for personal autonomy to them.

I constructed this description based on classroom observations, comments from Ute students during interviews, and information gathered through a set of values clarification activities used during a study of Ute student math avoidance patterns (Leap et al. 1982: 188–228). Other scholars working at Northern Ute have also identified these themes and described their importance for life on this reservation. Allan Tindall (1975: 18, 13; cited in Cuch 1987: 69), for example, contrasts Ute and non-Indian approaches to pick-up basketball: "Ute games are structures of individual performances, while [non-Indian] games are strategic organizations of group effort. [The Utes] play basketball according to a premise of individuality, not of mutuality or control over other men."

Joseph Jorgensen (1964: 501, cited in Cuch 1987: 69; emphasis added) explains the Ute resistance to Christian missionization in similar terms:

> The emphasis that the Utes have long placed upon the role of the individual in seeking visions and the faith which they credit to various individuals who claim to have supernatural powers may have discouraged them to accept the claims of the prophets (Christianity) or those stumping for *the truth of one religion over all other religions.*

Y. L. Witherspoon (1961: 125, cited in Cuch 1987: 69) puts the matter quite simply: "Since the child is seen as an individual, he is early given the right to make his own decisions and to act upon them." Forrest Cuch, former director of the Northern Ute Tribe's Education Division, summarizes all of these comments with his phrase *social independence.*

It may seem unrealistic to expect that (non-Indian) teachers will accept Ute student spelling errors as expressions of the students' social independence or by-products of culturally sanctioned expressions of personal initiative. It is clear that spelling tests provide Ute students with opportunities to use English in distinctly nonstandard ways and that Ute students find nothing inappropriate or irregular in doing so. Attributing Ute student performance on spelling tests to interference from the Open Court reading curriculum entirely overlooks the connections between these students' spelling "errors" and other components of their English skills.

CHAPTER 8

DRAWING INFERENCES WHEN READING

Reading, like spelling, is a language skill that is central to elementary school education in all of America's public schools. Reading instruction begins at the kindergarten and first grade levels when teachers train students to recognize relationships between sound and letters, to develop word-recognition and word-attack skills, and to begin acquiring their inventory of words known "by sight." Classroom activities oriented toward these goals include oral and written exercises assigned to the class as a whole, reading and discussion in small groups (often containing students of similar ability levels), and individualized tasks involving teacher-student pairs. Student use of the library and reading materials available in the home augments the skills development obtained through these classroom activities.

Reading instruction in all of these forms continues throughout the elementary school years. The importance of reading is also underscored throughout this period. The school curriculum treats the "textbook" (and the "written word" generally) as the primary source for information that students must master in order to "do well" in the classroom. Reading figures prominently in the standardized tests and other activities that monitor student academic gains throughout the year, and reading is central to the school's efforts (e.g., the report card, the teacher's note) to advise parents about their children's progress or shortcomings each term.

Elementary schoolteachers on the Ute reservation have always treated reading as a classroom priority in exactly the sense just described. During the period I worked in these schools, teachers were enthusiastic about trying new approaches and techniques if they seem likely to improve student reading skills. Teachers accepted the Open Court reading program for this reason, even though the Open Court curriculum required most teachers to make substantial changes in their techniques of reading instruction. As they explained with enthusiasm, they found Open Court instruction did much to improve Ute students' ability to recognize sound-letter correspondences, identify new words, and make sense out of the content of unfamiliar reading passages.

My classroom observations and work with individual students supported the teachers' assessments. Certainly, some Ute students may not have fully mastered the reading skills expected for their grade level, and others try to avoid situations where reading is a necessary language skill. But most Ute students, if asked to do so, could read materials in their textbooks and talk about some of the main points presented in the texts. And some Ute students became enthusiastic readers, particularly during their earliest years in elementary school.

At the same time, according to teacher reports—and from comments students made during classroom observations and interviews—reading is not a skill that Ute students appear to value. Enthusiastic readers explained that they enjoy reading because it is an activity that they can do by themselves, not because reading is useful in the classroom. Other Ute students report that reading is "dull"; if they need to acquire new information, they prefer to "watch somebody do it and then try it yourself."

Certainly, even with the extensive presence of the language of the metropolis and its speakers on this reservation, reading has only a limited significance in the students' lives outside of the school.

o There are reading materials in the Ute students' homes. These include the tribe's newspaper (published monthly), the area's newspapers (one published in Vernal, the other in Roosevelt), supermarket sensationalist tabloids, and nationally focused sports, fashion, and "celebrity" news/entertainment magazines. All of these publications convey their intended messages through illustrations, photographs, and diagrams and rely on the accompanying written statements to amplify the information presented through visual means. The information supplied by watching television and using other media sources provides a general knowledge base against which these visual cues and associations can be interpreted. In other words, readers do not need extensive word-print "literacy" in order to enjoy, or to learn from, these items.

o To keep in touch with relatives and friends, Ute people use the telephone or travel the necessary distance so they can converse directly. Ute people rarely write letters and do not expect to receive letters from their friends. They do enjoy receiving postcards—again, a medium in which the written message is only one component of the total text.

o Personnel in tribal offices and other on-reservation business settings maintain written records of meetings, conversations, and other transactions, but Ute people are much more likely to remember, and act on, the person-to-person spoken-language exchanges and the verbal commitments they contain. Likewise, the spoken word, not the on-paper text, sets the ground rules against which Ute people are likely to evaluate each other's behavior.

o While some Utes have attempted to create writing systems for their ancestral language, none of those systems has ever been endorsed by the tribal membership as a whole, and (except for those Utes associated with the Wykoopah program) most Ute adults are suspicious of attempts to develop ancestral language literacy on this reservation— which makes them suspicious of literacy in any form or for any purpose.

So, how well *do* Ute students read? Standardized test scores offered mixed perspectives on this issue, since Ute students usually scored at or above grade level on some reading-related tasks, but below grade level on other tasks. Teacher assessments of Ute student reading skills varied widely, depending on which students were the focus of the discussion. In the main, teachers told me, Ute students at all grade levels have problems with reading comprehension; most teachers added they could not understand why Ute students would have such problems now that Open Court instruction had improved their word-attack strategies and broadened their sight-vocabulary.

I was tempted to conclude, given the teachers' comments about Ute student technical skills, that student disinterest in reading and the low priority given to reading in the out-of-school setting were the likely sources of their comprehension problems. But then I started sitting in on reading group activities in third, fourth, and sixth grade classrooms. I listened while Ute and non-Indian students read aloud—to the teacher, in small, structured groups, and to their friends. And I observed teachers and students working together to resolve particular areas of reading difficulty. I found through these experiences that there were other sources influencing Ute student reading comprehension.

To explore those influences in greater detail, I scheduled a series of reading skills–oriented interview/discussion sessions with individual third and fourth grade students and with pairs of students during the spring of 1983. During these 30-minute sessions, students read selections from one or two reading passages, using materials I had selected to conform with their grade-level and overall reading ability. Then we talked about the content of the passage and the information they had learned by reading it.

TABLE 8.1
<small>READING ERRORS DUE TO UTE ENGLISH–BASED
ALTERNATIONS IN SYLLABLE STRUCTURE</small>

Student	*bewitched*	*prepared*	*crawled*	*suddenly*
1	bewich-tId	pourd	craw-led	su-den-et-liy
2.		prep-pard		
3.	blew-icht	prom-pard	craw-lend	
4.	be-wic-ed	pe-ri-pard	craw-led	s -dent-liy

I interviewed a total of twenty Ute students, ten from each grade, and I also interviewed sixteen non-Indian students, ten third graders and six fourth graders. I audio-taped the students' reading and the discussions that followed. After transcribing those tapes, I compared the students' reading with the original texts, to identify segments in the narratives where the students gave alternative readings to the text-form. Then I reviewed their description of the main events in the story and other details of the story-line, as presented to me during the follow-up discussion, to determine where alternative readings of text-form coincided with alternative interpretations of text-content.

I learned several things about Ute student reading skills from this analysis.

First, the Ute students' oral reading contained errors of various types, some of which (as shown in table 8.1) could be associated with certain rules from Ute English pronunciation—in this case, the addition of vowels and consonants and other rearrangement in syllable structures. More frequently, however, Ute student reading errors resembled those made by their non-Indian classmates— errors that any elementary school students, regardless of language or cultural background, were likely to make when reading these texts.

Second, Ute students' discussions of the content of reading passages were somewhat different from those of their non-Indian classmates. Rather than attempting to present a chronological summary of the story as a whole, or to describe what (to a non-Indian adult listener) would be the *main* events in the story-line, Ute students consistently oriented their comments around specific events or themes, some of which they discussed in considerable detail, even though by doing so they left other segments of the text without comment. Once they made their comments on those themes, Ute students moved the discussion in other directions, focusing on issues that (from my point of view) were not always connected to the passage under discussion.

Table 8.2 lists the text-segments in one of the stories I used in this exercise (a modern-day version of *Tom Thumb*) and indicates which of the segments were

TABLE 8.2

FOUR UTE STUDENT VERSIONS OF *TOM THUMB*

Text segments	Ute Students			
	1	2	3	4
Merlin walks down the road.	x		x	
Merlin goes to a farmhouse.		x	x	
Merlin is hungry.		x	x	
Farmer and wife invite him in to eat and rest.		x	x	
Farmer and wife are sad because they have no children.	x	x		x
Merlin says their wish will be granted.		x		
Tom Thumb is born.	x	x		
The Fairy Queen visits.				
She names Tom, gives him clothes.				x
Wife makes a pudding.		x		
Tom watches, and falls in.	x	x	x	x
Tom starts kicking.				
Mother gets frightened, throws out the batter.	x	x		x
Tinker picks it up.	x			
Tom makes noise.	x			
Tinker throws it away.	x			
Tom escapes, runs home, gets a bath, goes to bed.	x	x	x	x
Mother takes Tom to milk a cow.	x			
Mother ties Tom to a thistle.				
Cow sees Tom's hat.				
Cow tries to eat Tom.		x	x	
Mother screams.		x		
Cow is frightened, drops Tom.		x	x	
Tom helps drive cattle.				
Raven picks up Tom.		x	x	
Raven drops Tom in ocean.		x	x	
Fish swallows Tom.		x	x	x
Fish gets caught, cut open, and Tom jumps out.		x	x	x
Tom goes to see the king.	x	x		x

mentioned when four of the Ute students in my sample presented their versions of this story during the follow-up interview. Notice how each student represented in this table made a selective use of the events in the original narrative; in a fashion similar to the Ute students' performance on spelling tests (chapter 7), note also how each student's version of the story individualizes the content of the original text, sometimes including many of the events from one segment of the story, but other times mentioning only one (or none) of the events from another segment.

In other words, while the Ute students were certainly willing to cooperate with the retelling task, they did not feel obligated to account for the whole of the text in order to be task-cooperative. Accounting for the whole narrative *was* the goal that the non-Indian students tried to address (with varying degrees of success) during the follow-up portions of their interviews.

Third, the Ute students' performance during their oral reading rarely predicted their performance during the follow-up discussion. That is, students may have pondered every word in the reading passage in cautious and measured tones, interrupted their reading with long periods of silence as they worked through the passage, or seemed to be in great discomfort when complying with this task; but they were just as likely to give satisfactory responses to content questions as were those who read rapidly and without pausing to decipher individual words. And there were also instances where Ute students who read the passage without interruption and with appropriate expression turned out to be unable to discuss text-content in any detail, even though they made clear through their comments that they were quite willing to cooperate.

Fourth, miscue patterns aside, Ute students relied heavily on inferencing strategies rather than verbatim content-recall to orient their discussions of text-content. They did this by piecing together clues and hints from various sections, by linking comments in the text with information they derived from outside sources, and by relying on other types of creative, content-making strategies. The target passage was an important source of reference here, but it was not the only source the students used for this purpose—in many cases, it appeared to me to be the source they consulted least frequently.

Example 8.1 shows the opening of the follow-up discussion to the *Tom Thumb* story given by student 4 from table 8.2, a third grade Ute female who speaks her ancestral language and lives in a home where her parents, brothers, and sisters frequently speak Ute instead of English. The interviewer in this case was a Ute woman who worked for the Wykoopah project and agreed to help me with the interviewing for this study.

Following the agenda we set for the interviews, my assistant began by asking student 4 to describe what happened at the beginning of the *Tom Thumb* story (lines 1–2). Student 4 did not answer the question directly; instead, she referred to segments of the opening events (*He was walking . . . he fell . . . Merlin . . . in a hole . . .*) and became more specific in her replies only when the interviewer's questions became more focused. Note, moreover, that while her comment begins with information drawn from the opening of the text, (Merlin

EXAMPLE 8.1
Tom Thumb Retold by Ute Student 4

1	Interviewer:	Let's answer some questions. What happened first
2		in the story? The first thing that happened, do you remem-
3		ber?
4	Student 4:	He was walkin'.
5	Interviewer:	Who was walkin'? You know who it was?
6	Student 4:	[shakes head "no"]
7	Interviewer:	What did he do when he was walking?
8	Student 4:	He fell.
9	Interviewer:	Who fell? Tom? Or Merlin?
10	Student 4:	Merlin?
11	Interviewer:	He fell. How come he fell?
12	Student 4:	In a hole.
13	Interviewer:	In a hole? Huh ? What happened first in the
14		story? You remember? What happened to the farmer and his
15		wife?
16	Student 4:	They were sad. They didn't have no children.
17	Interviewer:	OK, then what happened?
18	Student 4:	Tom left.
19	Interviewer:	Who is Tom?
20	Student 4:	Not Tom.
21	Interviewer:	Did they get a whole bunch of children? One or a
22		whole bunch of children?
23	Student 4:	One.
24	Interviewer:	What was his name?
25	Student 4:	Tom.
[dialogue continues]		

was walking down a road in the reading passage) most of her replies build directly on the information supplied by the interviewer's questions, which makes it difficult to determine how much information she gleaned from the reading passage.

The student uses the same strategy to respond to the investigator's question (lines 14–15) about the farmer and his wife. Again, her opening comment (line 16)—*They were sad. They didn't have no children*—is drawn directly from the original narrative, as is her reply to the next question (line 18): *Tom left*. The investigator is not happy with the two isolated comments and wants the student to provide more detail. Once again, the student shifts from text-content to follow the guidance supplied by the investigator's questions. And once again, the question-answer sequence makes it difficult to judge whether her response to the investigator's question (line 24) reflects her own knowledge or a reinterpretation of the comment she made, then withdrew, in response to an earlier question (lines 17–20).

Student 4's use of question-centered inference in this discussion draws directly on a discourse strategy that is widely attested in Ute student (and adult) English: speak directly to the content-clues supplied by the person asking you a question. By using this strategy, student 4 was able to respond to all of the investigator's questions; but from a teacher's point of view, using this strategy did not produce a satisfactory performance on this task.

I came away from this analysis convinced that I needed to learn more about the inference strategies Ute students used when reading, and more about their reasons for favoring inference over more literal interpretations of text content. Use of such strategies, I suspected, was contributing to the Ute students' "problems" in reading comprehension—and might be contributing, in some sense, to their disinterest in reading, as well.

As I have already explained, I soon connected the students' use of inferencing to rules governing their question-asking and question-answering in other classroom settings, rules that are closely aligned to the treatment of question constructions in Ute English (and Ute language tradition) as a whole. (I say more about these rules in chapter 9). But I suspected from my analysis of the interview transcripts that other issues were involved here; to explore them, I needed a data-gathering strategy more structured than the one I had just employed—a strategy that would give Ute students ample opportunities to make use of their inferencing skills and give me the chance to identify connections between inferencing and reading comprehension.

Cloze testing, I decided, could be a helpful data-gathering strategy in this regard; that is, I could ask Ute students to read and answer content questions about a passage where every *n*th word has been deleted from the original text. These deletions produce a reading passage filled with "holes" (see example 8.2) and obligate the reader to focus the reading process around the restoration of

EXAMPLE 8.2
Sample Format For a Cloze Test Passage

The lands   the poles are too cold   most people.
Find the South   on the population map. No   lives on
the continent of   . But a few scientists stay   to
study the weather. Now   the North Pole and the   Circle.
Only a few people   in the Arctic. Those few   live there
cannot farm and   food. The ground is frozen,   they must
live by hunting   and fishing. The animals and fish   catch
are not enough to   many people. So not many   live in
the Arctic.

deleted meanings and/or reconstruction of text-message in spite of the "holes." Readers with strong inferencing skills (and Ute students, I suspected, were in that category) should be able to read such passages and make sense out of text-meaning with little difficulty. And if their approach to inference led them to interpret text meaning differently than intended by the original passage, it should be easy to trace the connections between text-details that led the readers to those conclusions.

Moreover, given that the Ute students' non-Indian classmates come from different linguistic and cultural backgrounds, it seemed likely that the non-Indian students' use of inferencing, and the conclusions about text-message which they derived through such means, would differ as well. Involving non-Indian students in the cloze test activity would help me identify more precisely Ute and non-Indian student contrasts in reading comprehension and other areas of text management.

As my source for the text of the cloze tests, I used a set of reading-related, seat-work activity sheets, selected from school-approved, supplemental language arts workbooks. Each worksheet contained a three- or four-paragraph reading passage (usually with no more than 100 words) along with six or eight content-oriented follow-up questions in varied formats (e.g., multiple choice, true-false, fill-in-the-blank, short-answer completion). I made the necessary adjustments in the reading passage, deleting every sixth word, to create the cloze text format. I did not alter the form or the content of the follow-up questions.

Students in the third and fourth grade classes during the 1983–1984 academic year participated in the first phase of this project. The third graders continued to participate during the fall semester of their fourth grade year (1984–1985), allowing me to determine if familiarity with the cloze text format over time might influence their performance on this task. (Importantly, I found no evidence that it did.) Because there were two classrooms at each grade-level, with Ute and non-Indian students in each classroom, I was able to make a four-way "test group"/"control group" comparison of the students' response patterns (see table 8.3) each time one of the worksheets was assigned.

I expected from my preliminary observations to find the following themes structuring the similarities and differences in student performance on these tasks:

1. Because of their adeptness at inferencing, Ute students would answer cloze-test-related content questions with greater accuracy than would non-Indian students reading the same passage; and
2. Because the cloze test format encourages readers to use inferencing skills, Ute students assigned cloze test reading passages would answer

TABLE 8.3
FOUR-WAY COMPARISONS USED IN CLOZE TEST ANALYSIS

	Class 1 (reading cloze text)	Class 2 (reading unaltered text)
Ute students		
Non-Indian students		

text-related content questions with greater accuracy than would Ute students reading passages in the original, unaltered forms.

As it turned out, the student performance patterned somewhat differently than I expected. Statistics from the third grade students' cloze test activity (October 1983—see table 8.4) illustrate some of the characteristics of that pattern.

1. Ute students reading the cloze test and Ute students reading the unaltered text answered content questions with comparable accuracy. The average number of correct responses was identical for each group; while there were different values for the standard deviations, the differences were never large enough to indicate statistically significant contrasts between the response patterns.

This suggested, consistent with my expectations, that the Ute students assigned the cloze tests did not find them any more difficult to work with than did Ute students assigned unaltered reading passages. At the same time, and

TABLE 8.4
COMPARISONS OF THIRD GRADE UTE AND
NON-INDIAN STUDENT CLOZE TEST RESPONSES

	Class 1 (cloze text)	Class 2 (unaltered text)
Ute students		
no. respondents	10	16
av. # correct	3.5	3.5
stand. dev.	+0.36	+1.1
Non-Indian		
no. respondents	18	16
av. # correct	3.0	4.0
stand. dev.	+0.78	+0.8

contrary to those expectations, Ute students assigned the cloze tests did not show greater mastery of text content compared to those working with the unaltered passage. Instead, it appears, text-format had no effect on the Ute students' success in using inference (or other strategies) to extract information from these passages.

2. Non-Indian students reading the cloze test answered fewer content questions correctly than did the non-Indian students who read the unaltered text. The average scores for these groups showed greater contrast than do scores for any pairing of the groups that participated in this task. Apparently, altering text form presented real difficulties to students of non-Indian backgrounds; unlike the situation for their Ute classmates, the techniques that the non-Indian students used to reconstruct text-meaning were quite dependent on text-format for their success.

3. Ute students assigned the cloze text answered the content questions with a greater degree of accuracy than did the non-Indian classmates assigned the same text. But non-Indian students assigned the unaltered version of the same text answered content questions with a greater degree of accuracy than did their Ute classmates.

In other words, instead of the neat, Ute vs. non-Indian contrasts implied by my original expectations, student performance on the cloze test exercises patterned in the terms suggested in table 8.5. I administered cloze test reading exercises twelve additional times during the period October 1983–December 1984. In each instance, difference in text form was closely linked with accuracy of the non-Indian students' performance on the content questions, but proved to have no statistically significant effects on the Ute students' success in answering those questions.

While at first this pattern surprised me, it soon began to make sense, given what I now knew about the reading instruction provided to students at this school. Teachers continually stressed to students that a written text is a linear sequence of words, phrases, and clauses, each of which must be read and

TABLE 8.5
RELATIVE SUCCESS OF RESPONSES TO CONTENT QUESTIONS

Highest
average scores

                  Non-Indian students, unaltered texts
                  Ute students, altered texts and
                  Ute students, unaltered texts
                  Non-Indian students, altered texts

Lowest
average scores

interpreted strictly in terms of the order and arrangement on the printed page. If a student encountered an unfamiliar text segment in a reading group or during other oral reading exercises, the teacher asked the student to pause to apply one or more word-attack strategies ("sound it out," "look at word shape," "try to guess what word might come next") until the student could make sense out of the segment (or the teacher supplied the correct answer); only then did the teacher give permission for the student to continue reading, segment by segment, in the same linear fashion used before.

Cloze test passages, given their "holes" in text format, interrupt the linear reading process, and these interruptions can become problematic for persons accustomed to interpreting texts in such a tightly structured fashion. This, I think, is why the non-Indian students reading these texts had the greatest difficulty answering the content questions and why the non-Indian students reading the unaltered texts performed so much more effectively on those tasks.

The fact that the Ute students' task performance did not show such variation suggests that their use of inferencing was not limited to word-by-word, linear text interpretation. In fact, as I looked more closely at Ute vs. non-Indian students' responses to particular cloze test content questions, and reviewed their performance on other reading tasks, it began to seem likely that Ute students were drawing on information from all segments of the passage when they read, rather than working strictly in terms of information immediately adjacent to the individual word or phrase.

Let me describe two of the data-sets where the Ute students' *text-inclusive inference strategies* were vividly displayed.

THE ANTARCTICA CLOZE TEST

During the spring of 1984 I asked students in two third grade classes to read a brief passage about the continent of Antarctica and to answer content questions based on that passage. One paragraph from the unaltered version of that passage (the cloze test version can be found in example 8.2) read as follows:

> The lands around the poles are too cold for most people. Find the South Pole on the population map. No one lives on the continent of Antarctica. But a few scientists stay to study the weather. Now find the North Pole and the Arctic Circle. Only a few people live in the Arctic. Those few who live there cannot farm and grow food. The ground is frozen. Instead they must live by hunting and fishing. The animals and fish they catch are not enough to feed many people. So not many people live in the Arctic.

Consistent with the general trend for the cloze test experiments (see table 8.5), non-Indian fourth graders reading the unaltered text gave the highest number of correct answers for the content questions on the worksheet, while non-Indian fourth graders reading the cloze text gave the fewest such responses. As before, Ute students' success in answering content questions was unaffected by the text-form.

Student responses to one of the worksheet questions (question 2) departed quite dramatically from that pattern, however. The question was: *What is another name for the continent of Antarctica?* The replies patterned along the lines shown in table 8.6. That is, only three of the fifty-six students participating in this activity answered this question correctly; all three of them were Ute students and all three had read the cloze test form of the passage. None of the Ute students who read the unaltered text answered this question correctly. In other words, in this case, form of text did appear to make a difference in the Ute students' responses to the question.

As expected, none of the non-Indian students reading the cloze text

TABLE 8.6
RESPONSES TO ANTARCTICA QUESTION

| | Cloze text | | | | Unaltered text | | | |
	Ute		non-Indian		Ute		non-Indian	
South Pole	3	(15%)	0	(0%)	0	(0%)	0	(0%)
North Pole	5	(25%)	4	(57%)	3	(37%)	13	(62%)
Other responses	12	(60%)	3	(43%)	5	(62%)	8	(38%)
Total # responses	20		7		8		21	

answered this question correctly, but neither did any of the non-Indian students who read the unaltered text—the group that gave the highest number of correct responses in other settings and thus could have been expected to have the greatest success in answering this question.

The response pattern becomes especially intriguing, given the way in which the cloze text format displayed the information relevant to question 2. The central concept in this question—*Antarctica*—never appears in the altered text; this is one of the words deleted from the passage when the cloze text was formed. So to answer this question correctly, the students reading the cloze text had to recognize that *Antarctica* was the central concept in the question; note that the term did not appear in the text; restore the term to its appropriate position within the text; and trace its connections in text reference to the phrase *South Pole*. At that point, they could answer the question correctly.

Considered in these terms, students assigned the unaltered version of the passage should have found question 2 to be a much less complicated question to answer. As before, they had to recognize that *Antarctica* was the central concept in the question. But because the unaltered text contained no missing elements, the relationship between these items was already accessible. So steps 2 and 3 in the inference chain could be bypassed; and step 4 should not have been problematic at all.

As it turned out, working with the unaltered text proved to give no particular advantage in the question-answering process for either Ute students or their non-Indian classmates. More than half of the non-Indian students associated *Antarctica* with the North Pole; more than half of the Ute students made other associations, some text-related, others outside its frame of reference.

So why did the only correct responses come from the Ute students working with the cloze test version of the passage? The answer, I submit, lies in the similarities between the internal organization of this text and some basic properties of Ute English grammar.

The key word in question 2 (*Antarctica*) occurs in the passage after its semantic partner (*South Pole*) has been introduced. Hence readers had to make the connection between these two items, as required under step 4 of the inference chain, through a back-to-front, or right-to-left, assessment of text content. Right-to-left syntactic constructions are common occurrences in Ute English syntax, as they are in Ute language tradition, and persons who participate regularly in Ute English conversations are accustomed to retrieving meaning from sentences and paragraphs constructed in these terms.

This put Ute students in an advantageous position to answer question 2—provided they were willing to shift away from the classroom-based, left-to-right processing of text meaning and use Ute English grammatical rules as their guide to text interpretation. The cloze test format already obligates readers to make creative and innovative assessments of text content, and I was not surprised to find that the only students who answered question 2 correctly were Ute students working with this version of the text. Perhaps, had the successful analysis of text meaning not required such an abrupt shift to nonstandard grammatical rules, more Ute students would have responded to this question correctly.

SLIM GREEN

As part of my on-site research during the fall of 1984 (see discussion of this project in the following chapter), I asked students in one of the fourth grade classrooms to read and discuss a story about a small green garden snake named "Slim Green." The story describes his adventures one warm spring morning, while he is searching for food and a comfortable place to sleep.

One passage of that story reads as follows:

> Slim Green was careful not to go too near the swamp. A big bullfrog lived
> there and sometimes he ate little snakes. So did Marsh Hawk who had a nest in
> the swamp near the meadow. Marsh Hawk was a big brown bird with long wings
> and sharp, curved talons. Marsh Hawk often flew over the meadow looking for
> just such things as little snakes to eat. Slim tried to hide whenever Marsh Hawk
> was near.
>
>   (Harris and Harris 1955: 7–8)

Four of the twelve Ute students and all eight of the non-Indian students
participating in this task read and discussed this portion of the story without
modifying text detail. But the remaining eight Ute students used the third person
feminine pronoun (*she*) when referring to the "big brown bird" during the
follow-up discussion. In three cases, Ute students actually identified the bird as
Marsha Hawk when they read this portion of the story out loud.

Of course, no damage is done to the narrative content if the students
specify the bird's gender in this fashion. The text is not explicit, either way, on
this issue, though there are details in the passage just cited that could be used to
infer female gender, should the reader be interested in doing so:

- The sentence that introduces Marsh Hawk to the reader immediately
  associates the bird with its nest. Nesting habits are more closely
  associated with females than with males, especially in the higher
  elevations in the American West. What Ute students know about hawks,
  they have learned from observations in such settings.
- The text notes that Marsh Hawk is a "big brown bird." In northeastern
  Utah, female hawks tend to be larger and less brightly colored than are
  male hawks.
- The text notes that Marsh Hawk "often flew over the meadow looking
  for [food]," an activity that is also more closely associated with females
  rather than males. This is particularly the case when the nest is filled
  with newborn birds.

It could be argued that Ute students who constructed a gender inference out of these
details were simply taking information from the text on face value and, in the
process, were showing how skilled they were at drawing associations between such
facts. Presumably, however, there were equally skilled readers among the non-
Indian students participating in this exercise, yet none of them added a gender
designation when they read or discussed this paragraph. Hence there must have been

factors other than careful reading that led Ute students to formalize gender inferences in this fashion.

Three such factors were relevant here, by my analysis, and any one or more of them could prompt any Ute student to assign female gender to this character.

First, gender is an important element in any discussion of animal life at Northern Ute. Folktales and other traditional narratives specify gender for animal characters and story-tellers refer to characters by gender-based titles as well as names (e.g., Old Lady Chicken Hawk, Old Man Coyote). By introducing gender-reference and gender marking into this text, these Ute students were bringing the *Slim Green* story in closer alignment with the style and the form of the other animal narratives with which they were familiar.

Second, making these additions also allowed Ute students to establish their own ownership over the narrative. Narrative ownership is a common practice in Ute English story-telling contexts (see discussion of this point in the next chapter). Ute English speakers are inclined to use this convention when several speakers tell the same story and each wants the narrative to be distinctive. But they also make use of it when the story in question comes from a nontraditional source, and Ute English speakers want to anchor it more firmly within a Ute-centered narrative domain. My research sessions presented such a situation to these students, and it was entirely appropriate under Ute English rules of discourse for them to revise the text accordingly.

Third, there is a rule in Ute English sound structure that obligates the speaker to place an additional vowel segment (usually a [ɨ]) in word-final position, so that consonant clusters that do not occur elsewhere in word structures of this English variety will not occur across word boundaries. This rule closely parallels one of the constraints governing syllable structure patterns in the Ute language tradition. It shows up most frequently in the Ute English of persons who learned their English directly from Ute speakers or who are native speakers of Ute themselves, though other speakers of Ute English also use this rule from time to time.

The [-s#h-] sequence in the phrase *Marsh Hawk* is one of these clusters. The sequence could not be deleted, since it occurs in the name of an important character in the story. And some students complied with the requirement of the text and pronounced the [-s#h-] sequence when they encountered it, thereby violating a rule of Ute English phonology and, perhaps, setting the stage for violations of other such rules elsewhere during their reading.

Other students paused silently after reading *Marsh* then read *Hawk*, then continued with their reading or inserted a verbal pause marker—*Marsh m-m-m-m Hawk*—between the two consonants in the sequence. Each of these strategies prevented the formation of the inappropriate consonant cluster; both

involved conventions of pause marking and hedging that occur in many varieties
of oral English conversations but are not ordinarily found as such in Ute English
discourse.

Still other students inserted the additional vowel, in the sense required
under Ute English (and Ute language) rules of pronunciation. For them, avoiding
the [-s#h-] sequence involved a replacement of standard English expectations
about appropriate sound combinations with more restrictive, Ute/Ute English–
based expectations. In the process, these students constructed a sequence—
[*mar+šɨ+hawk*]—now marked directly for female gender, thereby reinforcing
the gender inference applied to this portion of the text because of its animal motif
and/or the speakers' commitments to narrative ownership.

There is nothing in the story-line of this portion of the *Slim Green* narrative
that requires assignment of female gender status to *Marsh Hawk*, and the
non-Indian students who worked with this passage saw no reason to comment
on this theme. But eight of the twelve Ute students did see reasons to do
so—prompted by an approach to text interpretation that treats the whole text,
not just linear sequences of single words and phrases, as a database for
inferencing.

CONCLUSIONS

Given these insights, and the other observations noted throughout this
chapter, I can now understand why teachers at Todd School consider reading
comprehension to be a problematic issue for Ute students and why Ute students'
performance on reading tests is not always as satisfactory as the teachers or Ute
parents might desire.

As a group, I found the Ute students at Todd School to be quite creative
in their management of information retrieved from written texts. They could
isolate individual events from the story-line, identify the importance of those
events, and elaborate at length on their details, sometimes overlooking other
events that, from an outsider's point of view, were just as significant to the
meaning and message of the text.

Moreover, their interpretations of specific events or segments within that
text were not limited strictly to the information contained within single words
or phrases or presented in their surrounding environment. Instead, Ute students
used the *whole* text as their database, adding to that base assessments of
discourse style, speaker situation, and other features of text performance and
other aspects of language and culture knowledge not explicitly tied to text detail
at all.

In other words, judging by the information collected through my research, these Ute students, as a group, had more than enough skills to be able to participate actively and (from their own perspective) successfully in classroom-based reading activities. At the same time, their reading skills are not always consistent with those that are addressed and valued by the school's language arts curriculum. It is *those* differences, and not any deficiency in their knowledge of English, that produce the problems in reading comprehension that these students face in the elementary school classroom.

CHAPTER 9

QUESTION-ANSWERING AS STORY-TELLING

In this chapter, I want to take a closer look at a feature of Ute student classroom English mentioned in the last chapter—a pattern of question-answering that shows the student's familiarity with the topic under discussion, but does not develop that topic along the lines intended by the question. Hence the following exchange during the orientation discussion on money (example 7.2 in chapter 7):

13 Teacher: OK, let's look at the first one. What color is
14   the first one on that page?
15 Students in chorus: Brown.
16 Teacher: What was the first coin, [student 2]?
17 Student 2 (Ute): Brown.
18 Teacher: What kind of coin is it?
19 Student 2 (Ute): Brown.
20 Teacher: I know [a little annoyed]. How much is it worth?
    [student 3]?
21 Student 3 (non-Indian): One cent.

Student 2's responses (lines 17, 19) to the teacher's questions (lines 16, 18) were consistent with the terms of the discussion, but did not supply the information the teacher intended the students to supply.

Another Ute student used a variant of this response pattern when he answered teacher requests to solve certain multiplication and division problems numbers by giving numbers divisible by ten (example 7.1):

1 Teacher: What is nine times nine?
2 Student: Ninety.

and later in that discussion:

12 Teacher: What is eighty-three divided by nine?
13 Student: Ten.

Ute students answered questions in this fashion during their science and social studies classes, as well as during mathematics lessons. But they made extensive use of such replies when answering teacher questions about reading assignments. They did the same thing with me, during the one-on-one interviews associated with my reading research. Often their replies made it difficult to determine whether they understood the passage I asked them to read or whether they were using information acquired separately from the reading process to answer my questions.

Such was the case throughout the *Slim Green* interviews (the source for the *Marsh Hawk* example discussed in chapter 8), with Ute and non-Indian fourth grade students during the fall of 1984. My purpose in that project was to gain information on Ute student use of inferencing while reading. I built this exercise around a section of the *Slim Green* narrative (Harris and Harris 1955) at the suggestion of the school librarian, who told me that Ute students in the upper elementary grades found adventure stories with animal characters very appealing.

I interviewed twenty Ute and twelve non-Indian students from one of the fourth grade classes during this project. (Scheduling problems prevented me from interviewing the remaining four non-Indian students in this class.) I worked with each student individually. The interview setting was a small room used to store portable computer equipment and as the classroom for the school's gifted and talented program. Each interview ran for thirty to forty minutes. I began by describing the purpose of the interview and asking questions about student residence and family background. Then I gave each student a copy of the first two chapters of the book (nine pages, 1,030 words), invited them to read the text silently, then asked them to read it out loud. Next I asked each student to answer some content questions that probed how well the student had internalized the story-line, whether the student could recognize critical details of the narrative, and how easily the student could construct inferences about story-content based on textual clues.

As I always did during my student interviewing, I tape-recorded the session for later analysis. As in other segments of the reading research, Ute students were highly cooperative with the terms of the task and in most cases their responses showed that they had gained more than a casual understanding of story-content while reading the text. (The non-Indian students were also cooperative, though some made clear through their abbreviated commentary and other means that they were not happy about being included in this project.) However, there were instances where the Ute students' answers to my questions appeared to have very little connection to the information presented in the narrative. For example, I gave the students this paragraph:

> Slim had been asleep when Rowdy frightened him—sound asleep. But he did not look as if he were asleep. His eyes were wide open. This did not seem strange to Slim. He had never closed his eyes in his whole life. He couldn't, because snakes have no eyelids. Slim's eyes stayed wide open all the time much like a Teddy Bear's glass eyes.
>
> (Harris and Harris 1955: 5)

I then asked each student, *If you looked at Slim Green, could you tell if he was sleeping?* I expected students to say that, because snakes have no eyelids, they could not tell if Slim Green was awake or asleep. And this was the response that the non-Indian students gave to the question. Ute students, in contrast, addressed any number of issues in their replies (see example 9.1), very few of which were connected to the text content.

In some cases, I decided to probe beyond the student's initial comments, to see what else the student could tell me about Slim Green's sleeping habits. Three of the Ute students made greater use of the story-line when they replied to these questions, and one Ute student (see example 9.2) concluded by giving me a "correct" answer to my original question.

The other nine Ute students used my follow-up questions as additional opportunities for creative response-making. And I had to introduce additional clues, or allow the student to reread relevant sections of the story, before a text-related response could be obtained (see example 9.3).

QUESTION-ANSWERING AS A NARRATIVE DISCOURSE

To understand why these Ute students overlooked text-content when answering text-related content-questions, we need to examine the assumptions about appropriate discourse that guided the Ute students' use of English in such settings.

As was the case when teachers ask students to reply to content-questions in classroom settings, I intended my questions to elicit statements that would show me what the Ute students had learned from their reading of the *Slim Green* text. I am not convinced, however, that Ute students were reacting to my questions in similar terms. The "content" in this discussion was a narrative, a

EXAMPLE 9.1
Sample Ute Student Replies to the Eyelids Question

Student 1

Interviewer: If you looked at Slim Green, could you tell if he was sleeping?

Ute student 1: He never close his eyes.

Interviewer: How come?

Ute student 1: Cause other things might get him.

Student 2

Interviewer: If you looked at Slim Green, could you tell if he was sleeping?

Ute student 2: His eyes were wide open.

Interviewer: How come?

Ute student 2: Maybe he couldn't sleep.

Student 3

Interviewer: If you looked at Slim Green, could you tell if he was sleeping?

Ute student 3: Yeah, because I could see his eyes.

Interviewer: What about his eyes?

Ute student 3: They're green.

Student 4

Interviewer: If you looked at Slim Green, could you tell if he was sleeping?

Ute student 4: Yeah. He was wide awake.

Interviewer: How come?

Ute student 4: Snakes never sleep.

EXAMPLE 9.2
Follow-up Discussion of the Eyelids Question
(Student 5)

Interviewer: If you looked at Slim Green, could you tell if he was sleeping?

Ute student 5: No. Because he looks like, to me it always looks like they are dead when I see snakes.

Interviewer: How come they look like they are dead?

Ute student 5: Cause they lay all still.

Interviewer: What about if you looked at his eyes? Could you tell if he was sleeping by looking at his eyes?

Ute student 5: (Shakes head.)

Interviewer: No? How come?

Ute student 5: Because he looks like he is awake and, um, he is, um . . .

Interviewer: He looks like he is awake? Is there something about him that looks like he is awake?

Ute student 5: He has his eyes open.

Interviewer: Yeah, and how come he has his eyes open?

Ute student 5: Cause he don't got no eyelids.

EXAMPLE 9.3
Follow-up Discussion of the Eyelids Question
(Student 6)

Interviewer: If you looked at Slim Green, could you tell if he was sleeping?

Ute student 6: No. You couldn't see his face that good. His head.

Interviewer: How come? Where is his face?

Ute student 6: Face could have been in a hole or something. Like scared. Could have been hiding in the tree with his face in the . . .

Interviewer: What if you found his face and you looked him in the face. Could you tell if he were asleep?

Ute student 6: No. I don't know.

Interviewer: Let's see what the story said about that.

Ute student 6: (Reads the appropriate passage silently.)

Interviewer: OK. When you looked at Slim Green, could you tell if he was asleep?

Ute student 6: Cause he has no eyelids.

---

time-sequenced description of characters and event; this made the discussion of the narrative a kind of story-telling and required the participants in that discussion to act like story-tellers.

Story-telling in all language traditions is a heavily rule-governed form of verbal behavior. At Northern Ute, whether the language of choice is Ute English or the ancestral tongue, speakers are expected to comply with certain principles of narrative discourse each time they tell, or *re*tell, a story. During my work at the schools, visits in homes, and participation in community events, I have listened to Ute people tell stories for various purposes and on various occasions. Table 9.1 summarizes the principles that guide their use of language in such settings, as I understand them.

The key element here is the idea of ***narrative ownership***. The ownership at issue here does not involve notions of language-as-property of the sort found in other American Indian settings. No one actually "owns" a narrative in Northern Ute culture. Traditional stories are resources that belong to the tribe

TABLE 9.1
Ute English Principles of Story-Telling

---

1. Establish narrative ownership;
2. Center the narrative around the concerns of the speaking situation;
3. Get to the point of the narrative;
4. Identify agency for the events described;
5. Involve the audience in the construction of narrative detail;
6. Maintain the original focus of the narrative.

---

as a whole; people tell these stories in public settings and discuss the details of the story-line and character development with their listeners, to make certain that the focus of the narration is clear to all participants.

Stories that describe contemporary events may not carry the voice of traditional authority, but they are also presented in public settings; people can tell these stories and discuss their meaning, even if they do not know about events through firsthand experience.

Because narratives are a form of shared knowledge, it is quite likely that listeners will already know something about the story-line that a Ute (or Ute English) speaker decides to tell and also likely that some of the listeners have told that story to others on some earlier occasion and will be telling it to others at a later time. Hence, effective story-tellers must do more than recount the details of a narrative; they also must attract the interest of an audience already familiar with the story-line and must maintain that interest throughout the presentation.

In most cases, story-tellers address this goal by focusing narrative content around issues of particular interest to the listener. Means to this end include modifying the setting or time-frame, rearranging the story-line, reorganizing details of particular events, and embellishing (or deleting from) the roster of characters. Importantly, certain elements in the story are never affected by these alterations; this ensures that the basic integrity of the text is maintained across speaking domains. Those similarities make the story-teller's adaptations in other areas of story content all the more evident to listeners, guaranteeing that each rendition of a narrative becomes a highly personalized, context-specific speech event.

Story-tellers begin to construct such situated ownership over a narrative as soon as their story-telling begins, because the opening remarks should focus the listener's attention on the central theme of the story *as it will be told in that setting.* Since the particulars here are influenced by listener interests and other contextual concerns, opening lines and introductory remarks vary considerably from story-teller to story-teller and speech event to speech event, even when "the same" story is being told in all cases. Understandably, then, Ute and Ute English narratives rarely begin with the elaborate scene-setting statements common to introductions in other story-telling traditions; nor do their opening comments offer preliminary assessments of character attitude or motivation or otherwise foreshadow actions occurring later in the narrative sequence. This information comes after the opening remarks, and some of it may not be presented until the narration is well under way.

Once the opening remarks establish a focus for the narrative, story-tellers focus the remainder of their narrative around the segments of the story-line relevant to that focus. They may, for example, discuss a single episode from the story-line in considerable detail, after briefly acknowledging events that are connected to it. Or they may describe two such episodes, with or without establishing any connections between them. It is very unusual for Ute/Ute English story-tellers to present "the whole story" in a single setting and equally unusual for story-tellers to organize their presentations in chronological terms. Neither of those strategies enhances the selective, nonexhaustive presentation of detail on which effective Ute/Ute English narrative performance so greatly depends.

Of course, if story-tellers present their narratives in terms of individual episodes rather than the narrative as a whole, there is always the chance that important features of the story-line will not show up in a particular presentation and that listeners' appreciation for narrative detail will be adversely affected by those deletions. Ute/Ute English narrative practice anticipates this outcome and addresses it in several ways.

For example, narratives must always acknowledge the relationships between events and the individuals responsible for them. Things never happen "on their own" in Ute/Ute English narration. Events occur because people (or other living things) make those events occur. Story-tellers are obligated to refer to those persons, and to their actions, each time they describe the event(s) with which they are associated. Accordingly, while they may find it appropriate to downplay references to setting or background events, they are much less likely to alter references to *agency*—that is, specific, unambiguous indication of those persons responsible for the events being explored in the text. Agency helps story-tellers maintain continuity in the story-line as they tell the same story to different audiences in different social settings. In addition, combined with clues to narrative focus presented in the opening lines of the text, agency offers listeners an entry-point for assessing and interpreting the story-teller's intentions regarding narrative meaning.

This information is critical in the Ute/Ute English approach to story-telling. Since story-tellers are likely to present only a portion of a narrative in any one setting, it is the listeners' responsibility to reconstruct the larger narrative framework out of which the specific events have been selected. Listeners draw on a range of clues, from inside and outside of the text, when addressing this goal. And what they reconstruct is not always identical to the story-line guiding the story-teller's performance. Such divergence is expected from a narrative process that stresses flexibility and situational adaptation in narrative settings. The required references to agency guarantee that the listener's recreation of the narrative will not move too far from the target-text, even under conditions of narrative ownership.

EXAMPLES: THE SPILLED MILK STORY

I developed this description of Ute English story-telling principles from my observations of adult Ute and Ute English narrative discourse. But I found considerable support for these claims in my studies of the English skills of elementary school Ute students. An important source of data in that regard was the Ute students' performance on structured story-retelling tasks, like the ones included in a spring 1988 assessment of third, fourth, and fifth grade Ute student English skills.[1]

Story retelling is a language assessment strategy that yields insights into several areas of respondent language skill. In such a task, the respondent listens closely as the investigator reads a story out loud, then the respondent tells the story (more accurately, what the respondent remembers of it) back to the investigator. The investigator tape-records the respondent's retelling, transcribes it, and analyzes it in terms of content omissions, revisions in grammatical forms, pronunciation patterns, and other points of contrast with the "target" version of the text. To make certain that the retelling is manageable, the text contains no more than 75–100 words. And to help respondents focus their retelling effort, the investigator usually makes available a set of pictures illustrating the key events from the story. Otherwise, respondents rely on their own resources to help them reconstruct the text.

The following is the "target narrative" for one of the stories used for retelling purposes during the spring 1988 English language assessment:

Target Version: The Lady and Her Cat
A lady was sitting in a chair watching t.v. and drinking a glass of milk. A kitty was sleeping behind her chair. Then the glass of milk fell down. The lady saw the mess and went to the kitchen to get a mop. While she was gone, the kitty drank the milk off the floor. When she got back, the milk was all cleaned up.

This text begins by weaving together certains facts about the lady, the kitty, and the glass of milk then identifies the central event of the narrative: *the glass of milk fell down*. The remainder of the text focuses on the consequences of this event for the two characters introduced in the opening lines (the lady, the kitty).

Of the 65 Ute third, fourth, and fifth graders participating in this activity, 18 retold the story in a form that closely approximated the target narrative. But 47 Ute students gave versions of that story which departed in various ways from the target text's content and form.

Example 9.4 presents a selection of these responses. Reading through them carefully shows a consistency with the target narrative in certain areas, but

EXAMPLE 9.4
THE SPILLED MILK STORY RETOLD BY UTE STUDENTS

R1 (third grade, female): One day . . . (pause) . . . [I: What happened in this picture ?] . . . she spilled the milk. Spilled on the floor (pause). Went to get a mop. And the cat licked it up. It was gone.

R2 (third grade, female): Once upon a time that lady was watching TV and drinking milk. And she spilled it. And she turn and saw the mess. And she went . . . she went go get a mop and then while she was gone, the cat licked it up. And when she got back, it was all gone.

R3 (third grade, male): Now this girl and she got a glass of milk. And she spilled it. Was a new glass of milk and she spilled it. And there was a cat sleeping behind her chair. Then she seen it spilled. And the cat looked at it. Then the cat licked it up. And she went to get her mop and a wash rag. And when she came back, it was all gone.

R4 (fourth grade, male): Mmmm. The lady was sittin' in the chair and she spilt her milk. And, mmmm, I forgot what that was. [I: You're doing fine. And then?] Milk . . . and then . . . the kitty was sleeping. [I: right.] Mmmmm . . . Kitty was sleeping, the . . . the milk was on the floor and . . . [I: right] and she went go get a mop and the kitty licked up the milk. When she got back, it was all gone.

R5 (fourth grade, male): This girl was watching TV. She spilled her milk. She looked down and it was all spilled all over the ground. She went to get a mop. Then kitty drinked it up, licked it up. Then she came back and it was all licked up from the floor.

R6 (fourth grade, female): One day . . . this lady was sittin' on de couch. She spilled her milk. (pause) [I: Mmmh.] She went to go get her mop. The cat licked it up. And it was gone.

R7 (fourth grade, female): A lady sitting in a chair. She spilled her milk. There was a kitty sleeping behind her. She looked back and saw the mess. The kitty drank the milk. She got back, the mess was all gone.

R8 (fifth grade, male): The . . . lady was sitting down watching TV. . . . she . . . drinking a glass of . . . water . . . she . . . I mean glass a' milk . . . she spilled the milk . . . the . . . I forgot. (pause) There was a lady sitting down watching TV. She was drinking a glass of milk. She spilled the milk. There was a cat sleeping behind her. Then she went to . . . she went . . . she saw the mess . . . she went to the kitchen to . . . so she could clean the mess . . . mmm . . . she got back, the mess was gone.

R9 (fifth grade male): This lady was sitting on a chair and then drinking a glass of milk and then she tipped the glass over and she looked at it. The kitty looked at it. And then she went to get a mop and she got back, it was all cleaned up.

also shows changes in references to characters and in other details in the story line.

These changes are evident in the opening lines of each student's text. The target narrative, consistent with standard English usage, goes to some length to introduce the relevant characters and set the scene for the event under discussion before moving on to the description of individual events. But the Ute students, in contrast, offered the listener a much more abbreviated version of those details: a lady is watching TV, drinks a glass of milk, spills the milk, and reacts to the mess she has made.

It is at this point in these narratives, considerably later than in the story-line of the target version, that the Ute students made their first reference to the kitty. Three of the students noted that the kitty was asleep on the floor; the remainder did not provide background comment about the kitty, noting only that *the* (otherwise unspecified) *kitty drank the milk.*

Once they mentioned the spilled milk, comments about the kitty aside, Ute students uniformly brought the retelling to a close. Some did this by focusing on the lady's intention to clean up the milk and her surprise when finding that it had disappeared. Others merely restated the fact that the milk was gone, leaving any follow-up action by the lady (or the kitty) without further comment.

Narrative ownership was a primary theme in the Ute students' presentation of these texts. While all students retained the basic elements of the target narrative—the lady, the kitty, and the spilled milk—none of them reproduced the target narrative in its entirety, and each of them constructed individualized alternatives to that text.

Particular points of contrast in that regard include:

o *Length of narrative*: Some students gave narratives that were brief and to the point (R1, R5), while others included one or more sets of supplementary details within their narratives (R4, R8).

o *Organization of events*: Some students recast the target narrative into a series of discrete events (R1, R6). Others centered the target narrative around one or more key events and highlighted the connections binding them into a larger narrative sequence (R3, R5). Still others presented the key events in self-contained terms, leaving the listener to establish connections between them as he or she feels appropriate (R8, R9).

o *Use of central characters*: Some students considered the lady to be the central character in the whole story and treated the actions of the kitty as secondary to the lady's experiences (R3, R6, R8, R9). Others considered the lady and the kitty to be central characters and gave their actions equal status in their narratives (R4, R7).

o *Cooperation with the task*: As expected, none of the Ute students appeared to be reluctant to participate in the retelling activity. However, some students were much less hesitant in responding than were others (compare R7 with R4 and R6), though not all forms of hesitation were expressed in similar means (compare R4 vs. R1 and R8). Some relied heavily on the guidance of the cue-cards (R8), while others required feedback from the investigator after presenting each segment of their story (R4).

But even though there were these differences in the individual students' presentations, there were also some areas of similarity. For one thing, their introductory statements provided only a minimum amount of detail. Usually there was just enough information to move the narration to the first major event in the story-line—the accident with the glass of milk.

Getting to the point is a particularly appropriate retelling strategy in this case, given the ambiguity in the description of that event in the target narrative: the text's statement—*The glass of milk fell down*—describes the action, but it says nothing about agency or cause. These are necessary elements for text construction in Ute language tradition and, accordingly, eight of the nine Ute students in the sample (almost 90%) restructured their versions of the target narrative to take causality into account: the lady not only drank the milk, she caused the milk to spill. In contrast, only 30% of the non-Indian students made similar adjustments in this segment of the text.

Of course, the lady is not the only actor in this narrative: the kitty's actions are also important, particularly in relation to the story's conclusions. The target narrative anticipated this point by introducing the kitty in the second sentence of the text. Almost all of the Ute students' texts postponed references to the kitty until after the accident was described. At that point, most Ute students established the kitty's "place" in the narrative by citing some particular action, such as the kitty saw the milk, the kitty licked it up. Beyond those statements, the Ute students' texts do not explain why the kitty happened to be near the milk when it fell, leaving the listener to determine those details on their own—exactly in the sense required by the Ute English rules of audience engagement.

Students R8 and R9 used a different reference strategy. Here, after describing the accident, the Ute students noted that the kitty was sleeping behind the chair, but they said nothing about the kitty's role in cleaning up the mess on the floor. Once again, listeners are expected to draw their own conclusions on this theme.

Note, however, that even with this appeal to listener inference, the Ute students have not eliminated the kitty's presence from the story-line. In fact, three of the Ute students (R3, R4, and R7) used a pronoun-reference (or *anaphoric*) strategy from Ute English grammar to maintain the kitty's connection to the narrative and the kitty's relationship to the actions assigned to the lady when they reconstructed the story.

To understand how this strategy works, let's look more carefully at student R3's narrative (example 9.5).

EXAMPLE 9.5
R3's Story, Reorganized

1	Now this girl and she got a glass of milk.
2	And she spilled it.
3	Was a new glass of milk and she spilled it.
4	And there was a cat sleeping behind her chair.
5	Then she seen it spilled.
6	And the cat looked at it.
7	Then the cat licked it up.
8	And she went to get her mop and a wash rag.
9	And when she came back, it was all gone.

Line 5—*Then she seen it spilled*—is a confusing statement, judged in terms of the rules of standard English anaphora, and its presence in this text could suggest to persons unfamiliar with Ute English grammar that the student (re)telling the story might not have understood this segment of the narrative. Here is the problem: standard English anaphora specifies that the antecedent of *she* in that sentence should be the preceding noun that is closest to the pronoun and agrees with the pronoun's gender, number, and (in most instances) case. This makes the subject of the sentence in line 4 (*a cat*) the subject of the sentence in line 5, even though that interpretation of line 5 contradicts the information presented in the following sentence (line 6).

The rules of Ute English anaphora described above make the interpretation of line 5 much less problematic and show that the student has a clear understanding of the kitty's involvement in the story-line. Under a Ute English interpretation, the first occurrence of the pronoun in the text establishes a connection between a pronoun (*she*) and a referent (*this girl*) that extends throughout the text as a whole. Additional occurrences of that pronoun cue the listener's attention back to the original referent and not to other nouns in the pronoun's immediate environment. And if references to other nouns of similar gender, number, and case are required, the speaker uses other conventions to identify them—usually, given the limited inventory of anaphoric markers in English surface structures, by repeating the noun-word.

Under this (Ute English-based reading), this girl is the only possible referent for the subject pronoun (she) in sentence 5. In fact, the pronoun in that sentence is part of a larger anaphoric chain that runs throughout the text and binds events described throughout the story-line to that actor (see example 9.6). Importantly, under this rule, text references to the kitty constitute a second anaphoric chain, binding a different set of actions to that character (see example 9.7).

EXAMPLE 9.6
ANAPHORIC CHAIN I IN TEXT R3 (HEADWORD: *THIS GIRL*)

1 Now *this girl* and *she* got a glass of milk.
2 And *she* spilled it.
3 Was a new glass of milk and *she* spilled it.
4 And there was a cat sleeping behind *her* chair.
5 Then *she* seen it spilled.
6 And the cat looked at it.
7 Then the cat licked it up.
8 And *she* went to get *her* mop and a wash rag.
9 And when *she* came back, it was all gone.

EXAMPLE 9.7
ANAPHORIC CHAIN II IN TEXT R3 (HEADWORD: *A KITTY*)

1 Now this girl and she got a glass of milk.
2 And she spilled it.
3 Was a new glass of milk and she spilled it.
4 And there was *a cat* sleeping behind her chair.
5 Then she seen it spilled.
6 And *the cat* looked at it.
7 Then *the cat* licked it up.
8 And she went to get her mop and a wash rag.
9 And when she came back, it was all gone.

EXAMPLE 9.8
R9'S STORY, REORGANIZED

1 This lady was sitting on a chair
2 and then drinking a glass of milk
3 and then she tipped the glass over
4 and she looked at it.
5 The kitty looked at it.
6 Then she went to get a mop
7 and she got back,
8 it was all cleaned up.

Under this arrangement, and in a manner quite unlike that in the target narrative, references to *the girl* and *a kitty* are introduced separately, but begin to intertwine as the narrative progresses—and the references indicated by the anaphoric chains begin to overlap accordingly. Hence the use of Ute English grammar in this case actually helps the listener keep track of each party's "place" within text meaning; certainly it makes it easier for the speaker to express those details in the reconstructed narrative.

To conclude this discussion of Ute English approaches to story-telling, let's consider one more version of the *Spilled Milk* story (R9's narrative: see example 9.8) and see how another Ute student used rules of Ute English narrative discourse described in this section to organize his presentation of this text.

The student gets to the point of the narrative by focusing listener's attention exclusively on the lady (*this lady was sitting on a chair*, line 1) and establishing the lady's role as agent and cause for the accident under discussion (*she tipped the glass over*, line 3). References to the kitty are postponed until line 5, after this focus is established.

Once again, Ute English anaphora plays an important role in text construction. All of the comments in the text are part of the anaphoric chain headed by the reference to *this lady* (line 1)—except for the single comment in line 5, where *the kitty* is the specified subject. This suggests that there is more to be said regarding the kitty's role in the story-line and that the story-teller wants the listeners to supply their commentary to that end.

Listener cooperation is especially important if the listener is to understand the point of the passive construction—*it was all cleaned up* (line 8). The student's wording of this comment appears to disguise agency, but he has included plenty of clues within the text to specify actor and cause here—for those listeners willing to interpret the text, not just accept it at face value.

The pronoun in this sentence (*it*) occurs two other times (lines 4 and 5) in this text. Under standard English anaphora, the referent of *it* in lines 4 and 5 is *the glass* (line 3), because of the close proximity between the pronoun and preceding nominal of similar gender, number, and case. That reading is not appropriate for line 8, however, because the verb (*cleaned up*) applies more readily to liquids than to solids. And since the lady *went to get a mop* (another clue that *it* refers to a liquid, not a solid object) and was out of the room when the cleaning occurred, the kitty becomes the only source of agency in line 8.

"SNAKES NEVER SLEEP" RECONSIDERED

I began this analysis suggesting that Ute students were doing much more than *responding* to the investigator's questions in situations like the *Slim Green* interview. They were adding events to the story-line, embellishing existing events in unexpected ways, and incorporating their own opinions and perspectives into the information supplied in the target narrative. They were, in other words, acting like good Ute-English story-tellers—adapting the terms of the target narrative to the particular interests of the story-telling situation and the interests of the co-participants in that setting.

In table 9.1, I presented a summary of the principles that guide the Ute English speakers as they adapt (or reconstruct) target narratives in story-telling settings. I have demonstrated the significance of these principles for Ute English story-telling in my analysis of the *Spilled Milk* narratives, and I want to use them to interpret the Ute students' responses to my question about Slim Green's sleeping habits.

o *Establish narrative ownership.* There was great diversity in the ways in which the Ute students responded to the target question (*If you looked at Slim Green, could you tell if he was sleeping?*). Responses ranged from text-literal answers (student 5's *Cause he don't got no eyelids*) through combinations of text-material and additional detail (student 1's *He never close his eyes . . . cause other things might get him*) to comments based completely in student-centered reference domains (student 4's *He was wide awake . . . Snakes never sleep.*)

The point is that none of the Ute students responded to this question merely by reproducing relevant segments from the *Slim Green* narrative. Their statements reworked the details of the target narrative into something much more creative, imaginative, and personalized—exactly in the sense suggested by the Ute English principle of narrative ownership.

o *Center the narrative around the concerns of the speaking situation.* The immediate situation concern in this instance was not the content of the question, but the fact of question-asking itself. Questions carry certain obligations in Ute English discourse: someone asks a question only if he or she has reason to believe the respondent can answer it. Far from being merely a request for information, a Ute English question conveys the speaker's endorsement of the intended respondent's knowledge and expertise and expresses confidence that the respondent can apply that information to the given task. To avoid responding to a question undermines that endorsement and betrays the confidence that underlies it.

The Ute students' willingness to respond, like the absence of dodges and hedges once the question was presented, reflected all of these themes. Even in instances where Ute students were unable to maintain a reconstruction of the narrative throughout the discussion (see comments leading up to the infrequently used *I don't know* in student 6's interview), other statements in the interview showed that the students are willing to participate in the task, all the same.

o *Get to the point of the narrative.* While Ute students used one of two strategies to deal with this requirement, the end product was largely the same: students cast aside extraneous details in the target narrative in favor of comments that centered listener attention directly on what they judged to be the central theme.

Some of the students used single words and phrases or one or two sentences to establish their response, briefly and succinctly, then terminated the discussion and signaled for the researcher to ask the next question. The responses of students 1, 2, 3, and 4 provide examples. Other students commented in detail on a single theme, without providing the larger contexts of setting, character reference, or action that would ground the commentary more securely within the target narrative (see the responses of students 5 and 6).

The personalized detail of each student's comments—student 5's elaboration on *the snake is dead*, student 6's shift of setting from *the ground* to *in a hole, in the tree*—was consistent with narrative ownership, as were the more tersely constructed statements of students 1, 2, 3, and 4. And it is important to note how often get-to-the-point strategies helped these students personalize their texts.

o *Identify agency for the events described.* All of the Ute students' comments (other than those of student 3—see below) were oriented around actions rather than attributes. In other words, the respondents talked about things Slim Green did or was able to do. This emphasis on action occurred throughout the larger corpus of Ute student responses to this question. It showed up in their choice of syntactic features (particularly, their use of anaphora), as well as in their decisions about text content.

Student 3's comment *I could see his eyes . . . They're green* is also agency-oriented. Here, however, the student is the agent, not Slim Green—a reasonable response, given the wording of my question (*If you looked at Slim Green, could you tell if he was sleeping?*) and the rules of Ute English anaphora that apply to its interpretation.

o *Involve the audience in the construction of narrative detail.* All of the responses are thought-provoking, both for persons familiar with the target narrative and for those who are not. And it is difficult for a listener to be presented with these comments and resist embellishing their themes. For example, student 1 said: *He never close his eyes . . . Cause other things might get him.* Well, *what other things*? Was the student referring to Marsh(a) Hawk, to the bullfrog, or to other dangers in the swamp mentioned in the story? Was the student alluding to other unnamed dangers or merely making a general observation about the condition surrounding any snake's existence? Whatever the intent, the respondent simply hinted at the larger picture through word choice and left it to the listener to construct that picture in whatever terms he or she found appropriate.

o *Maintain the original focus of the narrative.* According to this principle, certain details of the target narrative always need to be retained, in order for there to be continuity between the target narrative and the narrative-ownership-based, recreated texts.

Continuity with the target narrative is vividly displayed in the students' comments on the *Slim Green* text, their use of narrative ownership, get-to-the-point organization, and the like notwithstanding. Comments like *snakes never sleep* may appear to violate this constraint, but, as my analysis in this chapter has shown, such comments result from assumptions about question-answering and narrative form that Ute students have applied regularly and systematically to the terms of this task, and persons who understand these assumptions can always reconstruct the primary elements of the target narrative out of the student comments—which is all that the rules of Ute English discourse intend for the listener to do.

CONCLUSIONS

I suggested at the beginning of this chapter that Ute students considered discussions of narratives to be a kind of story-telling, and therefore used rules of narrative discourse to guide their answers to the content-questions in the *Slim Green* exercise. Given what I now know about those rules, I think it is likely that there are more substantial connections between question-answering and narration in Ute English grammar and that story-telling models may govern Ute student responses to a variety of requests for information and commentary in school settings. Teachers are not expecting students to answer their questions in such terms, and their reactions to the students' use of such discourse strategies could influence their assessment of classroom performance in any number of ways.

CHAPTER 10

WRITING UTE ENGLISH

Writing is an important element in the educational process at Todd School.[1] Writing assignments figure prominently in the seat-work activities and other forms of instruction in the teachers' daily lesson plans, and written work helps teachers monitor students' academic progress and identify their learning needs. Unavoidably, Todd School students must be proficient in classroom-related written as well as spoken English. Proficiency in this case includes several skills—recognizing the type of written text (narrative, opinion, comparison/contrast) required in an assignment, selecting a topic appropriate to each assignment, organizing ideas that will develop that topic effectively, and presenting this material coherently on the written page. Proficiency also includes appropriate use of punctuation, capitalization, spelling, and other features of written English mechanics.

According to teachers and parents, Northern Ute students have few problems choosing an appropriate topic, once they are given a writing assignment; and if asked to do so, they often suggest different ways to develop that topic. Converting those insights into effectively written English texts is another matter entirely. Some Ute students construct written compositions that explore a wide terrain of ideas. Sometimes the texts contain carefully stated connections between sentences and paragraphs; more frequently, they do not. Other Ute students package their written work quite succinctly, clustering their comments around a single idea, or around several ideas that, as before, may or may not be explicitly tied together within the text.

They may include a "topic sentence" at the beginning of their text or bypass any formal statement of topic and let the text-content stand on its own. They may capitalize the first word of the opening sentence and place a period after the final word in the concluding sentence. Otherwise, capitalization and punctuation are less than systematic, and their spelling (as comments in chapter 7 have already shown) shows the influences of any numbers of conventions in addition to those of the written English standard.

In my earliest studies of Ute student written English, I focused on similarities between features of written text construction and features in the students' spoken English. There are many such similarities, as I will show in the analysis of individual compositions later in this chapter. I have found, however, that "error analysis" alone cannot account for all of the characteristics found within these texts. More recently, following the approach used in my studies of inferencing, question-answering, and story-telling, I have focused on the assumptions that Ute students bring to the process of written text construction. Some of these assumptions build on principles of text construction found in spoken Ute English (and spoken Ute) discourse. Others touch on notions of causality, action, agency, and other principles of argumentation and rhetoric that also have a basis in language/culture traditions of this tribe. But all of these assumptions influence the ways Ute students organize their ideas in written compositions and present those ideas on the written page—and all of them are reflected in the details of Ute student English text construction, and are issues that Ute students address when I talk with them about their writing and the messages they want their written work to convey.

THE CLASSROOM CONTEXT

My primary database for this analysis has been a corpus of writing samples collected from fourth, fifth, and sixth grade Ute and non-Indian students during the period September 1983 through December 1984. I have continued to collect written materials from elementary school Ute students since that time and to refine my claims about Ute student written English skills derived from the original data-set. I focus the discussion in this chapter on writing samples from a single classroom setting, and, where possible, on materials submitted in response to the same assignments.

The classroom in question contained thirty-six students: twenty Ute students and sixteen non-Indians, sixteen males (nine Ute, seven non-Indians), and twenty females (eleven Ute, nine non-Indians). The teacher was Ute; she had been a member of the faculty of this school and had taught at several grade-levels since completing her undergraduate training in elementary education. She was a fluent speaker of her ancestral language and actively supported efforts using Ute language instruction to strengthen Ute students' language arts development; she did not talk the language in her classroom, though she generously made class time available to the Wykoopah program staff for this purpose each week.

There was no teacher aide assigned to the class, and students who required one-on-one instruction in reading, language arts, or mathematics met with one of the school's academic tutors/counselors. Students (Ute and non-Indian) told me during one-on-one interviews (see chapter 9) that they did not like being sent out of the classroom for these tutorial sessions because, each time they went, they missed out on some interesting activity. (Some of the non-Indians felt the same way about their interviews with me, as I have already noted.)

This teacher, like other members of the faculty, recognized that her students needed to be fluent, effective writers and that they needed as much hands-on experience with writing as they could get. So writing instruction in her class took a very practical bent: several times each week, she asked students to prepare written compositions on a given theme, usually a topic she and the students decided upon together, and she gave them as much time as they needed to carry out the assignment.

Sometimes she reviewed the compositions to check on the students' use of grammar, content, and style; more frequently she simply noted that the assignment was completed, assuming—as did many of her colleagues—that the more the students wrote, the more their written language skills would improve. In effect, in this classroom and elsewhere at Todd School, writing assignments became seat-work activities under this arrangement, and writing itself became part of the classroom management process.

APPROACHES TO TEXT CONSTRUCTION:
AUTUMN IN THE MOUNTAINS

Example 10.1 contains four Ute student compositions, part of a larger set of essays prepared on the topic *Autumn in the Mountains.*[2] The students decided to write on this topic after a twenty-minute discussion of alternative themes. The teacher led that discussion and elicited suggestions and comments from as many of the students as she could because (as she explained to me) she wanted to build interest in the task before the writing began. The strategy worked; all of the students turned in essays in response to this assignment, though four of her students (interestingly, all were Ute and all were male) modified the topic slightly and wrote compositions on the topic *Smurphs in the Mountains.*

The students who wrote about *Autumn in the Mountains* organized their ideas around one of several themes. A common tactic here was to focus on autumn color, an understandable reference choice given the visual brilliance of the autumn season at Northern Ute. The mountain range that dominates the

EXAMPLE 10.1
Four Ute Student Compositions

Passage A	Fourth grade, female

Autumn in the Mountains

Autumn is like a million of colors
floating in the air

Passage B	Fourth grade, female

Autumn in the Mountains

Once you look at the mountains
you will see the color of it. You'll
see The blue in the mountains, the brown,
The yellow and orange on the trees. Soon
You will see white on the top of the
mountains.

Passage C	Fourth grade, female

The Mountains in Autumn

In the mountains the deer is roaming By the Pond and
drinking from it, as he sees a butterfly on a Autumn leaf,
suddenly a Big Autumn wind rushes by and
all the animal take to their homes and Winter
begins,

Passage D	Fourth grade, male

Smurphs in the Mountains

Papa smurph was in the forest.
He came to a cliff he didnt know what was
in front of him then he fell in a cave in the ground
It became dark then he herd the smurphs they were hoping
through the trees they were singing they were singing
lalalalala – lalalalala

---

northern boundary of the reservation (the High Uintahs) is particularly important in this regard. Piñons, other conifers, cottonwoods, aspens, Russian olives, and other varieties of trees grow in abundance throughout these mountains. During the fall, the leaves on these trees blend into bands of red, yellow, gold, and brown weaving back and forth across the landscape—exactly as the writer in passage A said: *a million of colors floating in the air.*

Passage B also acknowledges the variety of colors found in the mountains during the autumn season. Here, however, the writer is more specific in her use of color references. She cites

o   the blue in the mountains;
o   the brown;
o   the yellow and orange on the trees.

These are already present *once you look at the mountains* and contrast those colors with *white on the top of the mountains,* which, the writer notes, will soon appear.

Read carefully, with a sense of the context under discussion, the writer's text becomes a guide to Utah mountain scenery in autumn and to the changes in that scenery that will unfold as autumn makes its transition into winter. The *blue in the mountains* suggests the rocks and boulders of the mountains, which become increasingly visible through the trees, now that the leaves have started to fall. *Blue* also reminds the reader of the Utah sky, which takes on exceptionally vivid shadings during the autumn and winter months.

Brown describes the mountain soil, also visible from a distance as the leaves disappear, as well as the common color of the autumn foliage once the initial round of brilliant colors (the *yellow and orange on the trees* cited in the next line) has faded. The *white* on the top of the mountains suggests the High Uintahs' snowcap, which disappears during the summer months but returns in early autumn to mark the impending arrival of the winter cold.

The Ute student who wrote passage C did not use a color-oriented scenario as above; instead, this student focused her text on a particular mountain location, *the Pond,* and a set of events that occurred there one day in late autumn. Again, the comments are brief, but the reader does not need additional information to appreciate the stillness of the pond (suggested by the references to *the deer* and *a butterfly on a Autumn leaf*), the abrupt appearance of the Big Autumn wind, and the disruption it creates (*all the animal take to their homes*).

These images suggest contrasts in meaning, directing the reader's attention beyond the text's description to its comments on transition and change. Unlike the case in passage B, the reader is not expected to infer the details of transition/change from text-wording; the final phrase of the text, *and Winter begins,* states the matter quite explicitly. This is not the reference suggested by the title of this passage—*The Mountains in Autumn,* but the contrast between "opening" and "closing" statements is another reflection of the text's underlying message.

For some readers—especially those who see nonstandard English usage as a barrier to Indian student school success—the imagery and description in these passages are overshadowed by their technical and mechanical flaws. Particularly noticeable in that regard is brevity. The teacher asked the students to prepare a one-page composition; submitting a single paragraph does not meet the basic expectations of this assignment, especially if the paragraph contains only two lines. (Had this been their submission in some classrooms at Todd School, teachers would not have given students full credit for the assignment.)

Brevity of statement does not necessarily indicate poorly developed writing skills, however. In fact, on closer inspection, the compact construction of these texts actually enhances the writer's presentation of the message.

A closer look at the brevity of passage A will illustrate this point. This writer of this passage has not prepared an extensive, exhaustive inventory of the features that the reader will find by traveling into the mountains in the fall. Instead, she has constructed an open-ended, image-rich scenario on the assigned theme, leaving ample room to fill in the outline with details and images of the reader's own choosing. Note that in order for the reading process to be successful in this case, the reader has to supply that information and, thereby, become an active participant—in effect, a co-author—in the creation of text-meaning. The reader willing to work with the writer in such cooperative terms will be quite pleased with the composition, whatever mechanical faults he or she may otherwise find in it. But if the reader expects the writer to have sole responsibility for message-making and intends only to respond after the fact to the terms of an established text-message, the reader is likely to be disappointed with the student's performance here.

Important in this regard are the number of clues these writers build into their text to guide the readers' participation in message-making. Many of these clues come from the writer's organization of information within a given composition—location of the "topic sentence" or "central theme" within the composition, arrangement of supporting data to develop the topic or theme, and choice of initial and final comment—or from the display of that information on the printed page—use of brief paragraphs or lengthy paragraphs or no paragraph indentation at all; use of capital letters, punctuation, and other visual markers to distinguish sequences of ideas within the text; and placement of the title, if appropriate to text design. These features of *text-form* may reflect assumptions about written English usage that the writer shares with other Ute students or they may be entirely writer-specific; either way, they are a valuable source of insight into text-meaning.

In the case of passage C (as in much of written Ute student English), the information displayed through text-form is considerable. To gain access to that information, I have found it helpful to divide the text into segments, as suggested by the writer's use of punctuation, placement of conjunctions and adverbs, and

EXAMPLE 10.2
PASSAGE C IN TEXT-SEGMENTS

1.	The Mountains in Autumn
2.	In the mountains
3.	The deer is roaming By the Pond
4.	and drinking from it,
5.	as he sees a butterfly on a Autumn leaf,
6.	suddenly a Big Autumn wind rushes by
7.	and all the animal take to their homes
8.	and Winter begins.

other features of surface-level syntax and to use that segmentation as the basis for text analysis.

Here is what I learned about the writer's approach to text construction and message-making when I recast passage C in these terms (see example 10.2). Passage C begins (the title, line 1) with a general statement identifying the setting of this passage (*The Mountains in Autumn*). Line 2 restates the reference to setting (*In the mountains*) and line 3 makes the reference even more precisely by specifying the particular context (*the Pond*).

A comparison of segments in this display confirms that line 3 is the only syntactically self-contained statement in the text. Line 4 is directly dependent for its grammatical status on the details of line 3: note line 4's dependent verb construction (participle, with AUX-marker deleted in surface structure) and the absence of a surface-level subject pronoun reference. The remaining lines are somewhat more independent, as far as syntax is concerned: each statement contains a verb action and assigns a subject (or "actor") to that action. The subject-verb reference in each case elaborates on the context established in the opening lines, connections displayed in text-form by the writer's choice of words—*as* (line 5), *suddenly* (line 6), *and* (line 7), *and* (line 8)—in initial position within each construction.

While the writer titled this composition *The Mountains in Autumn*, both of these terms appear to be secondary elements within the text-form, according to this display. *Mountain* occurs twice in the text—in the title (line 1) and in the following line. And *autumn* occurs only in the title, in line 5 (to describe the butterfly's point of rest), and in 6 (as one of the characteristics of the rushing wind).

The segmentation in example 10.2 shows that these are not arbitrary placements. Line 5, for example, is the only segment in this display that is bounded on both sides by punctuation. Importantly, the same markers are found at the beginning and conclusion of this statement—commas, not periods. This suggests a close connection between line 5 (and its reference to autumn) and the comments that immediately precede it in text construction (line 4, itself syntactically dependent on line 3 as already explained), as well as between line 5 and the comments that follow.

The placement of the *and* conjunctions before and after line 7 suggests that the comments following line 5 need to be read as a single statement. *Suddenly*, the initial word in line 6, is the item that connects this package of meaning to the preceding segments of the text. Lines 7 and 8 expand on the reference in line 6, by showing what happens once the *Autumn wind* goes rushing by; together these three lines suggest a scenario quite different from that earlier in the text—and earlier in the fall.

In effect, passage C presents a glimpse of traditional Ute life during autumn, things that define the priorities of this season among many families on the reservation to this day. Autumn is a time for concluding the social and personal business conducted at leisure during the summer months; it is a time to intensify the preparations necessary for shelter and subsistence during the winter. The natural environment during this period is filled with clues and reminders, prompting the Ute people to meet these responsibilities before the coming of winter, which begins as abruptly as the succinct statement in line 8 implies.

There is no reference, as such, to traditional life in the content of this text. But the details of text-form—particularly the ordered relationships between individual statements and the special status assigned to line 5 and line 6 within those relationships—draw attention to a packaging of references that makes such an interpretation difficult to avoid. This is particularly the case if the reader comes to the text already prepared to find a text-message constructed in Ute-centered terms.

APPROACHES TO TEXT CONSTRUCTION: *THE SMURPHS IN THE MOUNTAINS*

Passage D also contains examples of the importance of text form for Ute student written English. Unlikes passages A, B, and C, passage D is an event-oriented text. It does not construct a visual scenario; it tells a story. Narrative though it may be, however, the detail of the story-line extends only to a certain point then stops abruptly, without bringing events to an expected closure: Papa Smurph falls into a cave, it becomes dark, other Smurphs are nearby, Papa Smurph hears the other Smurphs—that much is clear. But is he rescued and does he get home safely? The wording of the text makes no comment on these questions.

I was able to discuss the ambiguous features of this text with the writer and with several of his Ute classmates during my student interviews. I was interested to determine if they saw any gaps in the content of the narrative. Their responses were almost identical: "This is a story about the Smurphs," they said, giving me curious and often impatient looks as they did so. It did not take much follow-up discussion to show me that, in my haste to assess the story content, I had looked only at the words and word-choices and had ignored the assumptions about the narrative that lay beneath them. Anyone who is familiar with the value system of Smurphdom knows that Papa Smurph has to be rescued: tragedy is simply not permitted within this domain.

EXAMPLE 10.3

PASSAGE D IN TEXT-SEGMENTS

1.	Smurphs in the Mountains
2.	Papa smurph was in the forest.
3.	He came to a cliff
4.	he didnt know what was in front of him
5.	then he fell into a cave in the ground
6.	it became dark
7.	then he herd the smurphs
8.	they were hoping through the trees
9.	they were singing
10.	they were singing lalalalala – lalalalala

What interests me are the ways in which the *form* of this text *anticipated* the likelihood of a happy ending, even though the wording of the text appeared to have little to say on the matter.

Once again, in order to highlight this dimension of text design, I found it helpful to segment the text as shown in example 10.3.

The title (*Smurphs in the Mountains*, line 1) sets the stage for the narrative as a whole, and it is important in other ways to the presentation of meaning in this text. The title identifies the general category of characters (*Smurphs*) of which the writer of this text selected his actors. These include *Papa Smurph*, whom we meet in the opening lines of the story, and an additional group, identified in line 7 as *the Smurphs* but otherwise unspecified. The writer uses modifiers—***Papa Smurph**, **the** Smurphs*—to indicate the relationship of these actors to the more inclusive, general category of which they are a part as well as their relationships to each other. Note, in contrast, the absence of modifiers in the title.

At first reading, actors and events coincide quite neatly in this narrative. Lines 2–5 (the first segment of events) introduce Papa Smurph and tell how he fell into danger. Lines 8–10 (the second event segment) point out that other Smurphs are frolicking in the area. Line 6 completes the description of Papa Smurph's predicament. Line 7 provides the transition between the segments, by linking references to both sets of actors in a single statement.

The significance of this linkage needs to be carefully assessed, however. Even though there are two sets of actors in this text, the writer presents the narrative from Papa Smurph's point of view. Papa Smurph is the first character we meet (line 2). He gets lost; he falls in the cave. The second set of actors (*the Smurphs*) are not even introduced until line 7 of this ten-line narrative. The wording shows that they are busy with their own activities (*hoping, singing*) yet the reader knows about those activities only because Papa Smurph himself became aware of them; the subject-verb construction in line 7—*then he [Papa Smurph] herd the Smurphs*—states this fact explicitly for the reader, with the remainder of the text (lines 8–10) extending the meaning of this statement by explaining what Papa Smurph actually heard. And that makes the second segment of the narrative just as much Papa Smurph–oriented—and Papa Smurph–dependent—as is the first segment.

It is very unlikely, given the central role that the text-form assigns to Papa Smurph throughout this story, that other actors would avoid coming to his aid. He is in difficulty, as lines 5 and 6 suggest, and that makes discovery by the other actors and an eventual return to safety the only reasonable conclusion for the reader to draw from this narrative, even if the writer did not give a formal statement of that conclusion within the text-content.

WRITING AS A READER-CENTERED DISCOURSE: *THE BOLD EAGLE*

My analysis of the *Autumn/Smurph in the Mountains* essays suggests how three principles of written English discourse guide Ute students as they construct written texts in classroom settings:

o *Non-exhaustive presentation of meaning:* Ute students are selective in their use of written description and narration; they suggest the complete scenario or the complete narrative, without being obligated to present all of the details within their written compositions.

o *Active reader engagement:* A nonexhaustive presentation of meaning involves the reader as well as the writer in the message-making process. The writer outlines the message, leaving the reader to fill in the gaps, construct necessary relationships between the isolated details, and formalize other connections between segments of the narrative. Both parties become co-participants in text-making, under such an arrangement.

EXAMPLE 10.4

> The bold eagle
> Is pourt of the
> indian nation. It is
> an indian spirit. in Inain.
> ways it brings messages
> to all kinds like
> a fire in the wood
> and if. One of ther
> people were in danger
> our if someone ways
> on. there secret mound.

○ *Communicative value of the text form:* How the writer organizes information within the narrative and arranges it on the page is as important a text-resource for the reader as are the details of the text-content.

My final example in this chapter shows how another fourth grade Ute student worked with these assumptions to construct a composition on the topic *My Favorite Animal* (passage E, example 10.4). This assignment was different from that leading to the essays discussed above. There the concerns were narrative and descriptive. Here the assignment asks the students to take a position on the indicated topic and then to explain and defend their position. The teacher assigned this topic without preliminary discussion. She gave the students the topic, explained her expectations about text length ("write one page, please"), and text design ("tell me about your favorite animal and why you like it") and gave them thirty minutes to organize their thoughts and express them on paper.

Read strictly from the point of view of standard English composition, this essay is not effective writing. The text contains no title. There is no topic sentence identifying the intended focus of the discussion or use of supporting evidence to elaborate on that topic. Instead, the text supplies individual comments on some unstated central theme, forcing the reader to infer the purpose of the composition from the whole of the text, not from the meaning of any single segment. Spelling errors and mistakes in punctuation distract the reader's attention from the text-content, and further weaken the effectiveness of the statement.

At the same time, this text *does* address the expectation of the assignment: the essay is about the writer's favorite animal and why she values that animal so highly. To grasp this message, the reader has to become an active participant in the creation of text-meaning, not just an at-distance evaluator. The writer never says in any direct sense "the eagle is my favorite animal." That fact has to be inferred from the information provided in the text, a difficult task because the text reveals very little about the student's personal opinions on this (or any other) theme. And what she says about the eagle—the movement between the worlds of nature and spirit, and the benefits that come to Indian people as a result of this movement—could be said by many members of the Northern Ute Tribe and by members of many other tribes, as well.

Withholding personal opinion from the essay is an appropriate action, given the issues under discussion here. Ute verbal etiquette deems it inappropriate for speakers to assert individual opinions on some issues, especially when other participants in the discussion hold different opinions on that theme. A much more successful approach to communication (and a much more valued one, from the point of view of Ute tradition) focuses the discussion on the assumptions that all parties have in common, with individual opinions introduced only as subsets to one or more of those assumptions.

This is the approach this writer used when constructing the text in passage E. The eagle is the writer's favorite animal because eagles are a favorite animal of Indian people as a whole. She values the eagle because its actions benefit all Indian people, not because of any outcomes that favor her individually. She expresses these "personal opinions," as required by this assignment, but does so with comments that affirm her membership within the Northern Ute Tribe and her "place" within its traditions and teachings. This composition is more than a casual, pro forma response to a classroom assignment and the written discourse it contains cannot be evaluated simply in classroom-centered, textbook terms.

Once again, text segmentation provides an alternative approach to such an evaluation (see example 10.5). The segmentation suggests that the text is constructed in two segments, lines 1–3 and lines 4–6. From the point of view of text meaning, the relationship between the two segments is different from that found in passage C (example 10.2); lines 4–6 in passage E do not introduce new information so much as they elaborate on information already presented in the preceding segment.

Importantly, the fact of repetition and elaboration is marked directly in the syntactic form of these statements. Lines 4, 5, and 6 are composed of

EXAMPLE 10.5
EXAMPLE E IN TEXT-SEGMENTS

1.	The bold eagle is pourt of the indian nation
2.	It is an indian spirit
3.	in Inaian. ways it brings messages to all kinds
4.	like a fire in the woods
5.	and if. One of ther people were in danger
6.	our if someone ways on. there secret mound.

TABLE 10.1
INTERNAL ORGANIZATION OF PASSAGE E

Line by line sequence	Idea by idea sequence
1	1
2	1a
3	1b
4	1b(1)
5	1b(2)
6	1b(3)

grammatically incomplete, therefore dependent, clause constructions, in contrast to the complete, and therefore independent, clauses found in lines 1, 2, and 3. Lines 4, 5, and 6 begin with conjunctions (*like, and if, our if*), each of which links the statement it governs to the other statements that surround it. Similarly, the references of lines 4, 5, and 6 are equally dependent on the references presented in the preceding lines.

Line 3—*In Inaian. ways it brings messages to all kinds*—plays a pivotal role in this text under this arrangement. Here lies the "main clause" governing the subordinate, dependent grammatical constructions in segment 2; and the kernel of meaning—*message bearing*—upon which the content of lines 4, 5, and 6 expands. Importantly, however, line 3 is not a completely independent element within the design of this text. The subject of line 3 is stated in pronoun form (*it*) and that pronoun ties this sentence (and its meaning) to the sentence (line 1) that contains the pronoun's referent (*bold eagle*). Line 2 is also connected, through a similar pronoun-referent chain, to line 1, yielding an overall organization for this essay as displayed in table 10.1.

The relationship between ideas depicted in that display bears little resemblance to the ways in which standard English writers are supposed to organize meanings on the printed page. Rather than moving the reader through a series of linked ideas, each with its own set of supporting documentation, the organization of passage E reiterates a basic kernel of information, further refining and enriching the commentary each time the point is represented.

According to this display, the central theme of the essay is stated in line 1; this kernel of information is restated and refined in each of the following statements. Note, however, that the meaning of line 1 (and its significance for the text meaning as a whole) can only be determined by reading the rest of the text: considered by itself, *The bold eagle is pourt of the indian nation* foreshadows very little of the commentary yet to come. This is why, central as it may be to the meaning of the text, line 1 can in no sense be considered the topic sentence of this composition.

If any sentence is to be singled out in that regard, it is line 3, which, as just noted, occupies a key position in the presentation of the message of this text. Line 3 links together the ideas of section 1, with which the line is directly bound, and section 2, over which the line is dominant. The pivotal, transitional status of this line explains, among other things, its irregular punctuation—the use of the mid-sentence period, also found in lines 5 and 6 but not in lines 1 or 2. Here is another instance where the form of a Ute English composition literally represents the message of that composition and, for that reason, does much to facilitate the reader's co-participation in the text-making process.

IMPLICATIONS

The goal of this section of this chapter was to explore what is commonly referred to as "the writing needs" of Ute Indian students. Consistent with the point of view on Indian English discourse used throughout this volume, I did not approach this analysis assuming that these students had writing problems, but rather focused on the students' assumptions about written English and assumptions about appropriate use of language in written contexts, to trace the effects of these assumptions on particular writing tasks and then to see what this showed me about these students' writing *skills*.

I have only discussed a small part of the written Ute English text material I collected during my work at Todd School, but I can nonetheless draw several generalizations about Ute student writing skills from this analysis.

1. Written Ute English compositions are coherent, organized, and rule-governed. The rules include the following principles:

o nonexhaustive presentation of meaning;
o active engagement of the reader; and
o communicative value of the text- form.

Each of these has its own effects on the writer's use of language during text-making and on the reader's interpretation of that text and the language it contains.

Using such rules in classroom settings yields compositions that are not always consistent with the expectations of standard English literacy and that violate expectations of non-Indian, nonstandard English as well. But the distinctivenes of the writing does not weaken its expressive power, particularly for those who understand the rules of language grammar and discourse associated with this usage.

2. There are features of Ute students' written classroom English that resemble their use of oral English within the classroom. The consistency in these

students' "knowledge of language" across situation and task is an important observation, since it places Northern Ute students at variance with Indian English speakers from the Rio Grande pueblos (Wolfram et al. 1979) or from Tohono O'odham (Goodman et al. 1984), for whom relationships between oral and written English seem to be less closely aligned. Perhaps at those sites Indian student writing needs can be handled as a separate, independent issue within the school's language arts curriculum. At Northern Ute, classroom strategies that hope to move Ute students' written English in the direction of standard English models have to pay attention to oral as well as written language development; and attempts to deal with these students' writing needs strictly as writing-centered problems will have only a limited level of effectiveness, according to these findings.

3. Written Ute English not only resembles oral Ute English usage, it also parallels in many ways the patterns of oral discourse found within the students' ancestral language tradition. Few of these students are fluent speakers of Ute and even fewer are fluent writers of that language. Yet there is a sense in which writing in Ute English—and using rules of grammar and discourse drawn from Ute language tradition when doing so—contributes to the retention of ancestral language skills within this speech community and gives a stronger foundation for the tribe's efforts at ancestral language renewal.

4. Improvement of written English skills needs to be a priority in the education of Ute Indian students; on this point, tribal government, parents, and school authorities agree. Whether eliminating fluency in Ute English needs to be part of this process is not nearly so self-evident. There is the danger, for reasons discussed in point 3, that an outright revision of community-based English skills could weaken the (already limited) extent of Ute fluency currently being maintained within this speech community and reduce even further the prospects for effective Indian language renewal in this context. Moreover, as the example essays reviewed here have so powerfully shown, there is a "new" tradition of written English taking shape at Northern Ute, the first steps toward a Ute-oriented style of English literature, similar to that now fully viable among Tohono O'odham, Hualapai, Navajo, and elsewhere. Just as they will want to do nothing to undermine continuity in Ute language fluency on this reservation, responsible educators will want to do all they can do to see this literary tradition continue to take root. Making certain that classroom-based language instruction does not undo tribal efforts toward language self-determination, in English as well as in Ute, is an appropriate goal for educators to address under these circumstances.

CONCLUSIONS

I remember my first encounter with American Indian English. It was early June, 1967. I was standing with some friends in the plaza at Taos Pueblo, watching as people browsed their way through the Indian pottery, blankets, silver jewelry, and other items that pueblo and Navajo craftspeople were offering for sale that afternoon. The occasion was a corn dance, though the dancing itself would not begin until late in the day. The crowd in the plaza included members of Taos pueblo, Indians from other pueblo communities and from other tribes, residents from nearby non-Indian towns, and plenty of tourists. There were a lot of people to watch. That's what we were doing—we were students in George Trager's summer field school in linguistics, and we were eager to study Indian languages and cultures firsthand. Trager said to us: "They're having a corn dance at the pueblo. Go and see what you can learn." So we did.

Several of us started talking with a Taos Indian man who seemed eager to tell us all about life at the pueblo. He patiently replied to our questions about architecture, economy, and the BIA. We were starting to ask questions about the afternoon's upcoming events when he said, somewhat abruptly: "See those people over there? They're from Montana. They're Crow."

"Oh," I said, "they're friends of yours?"

"No. I have not seen them before."

"So how do you know they are Crow?"

"Easy, listen to the way they talk."

I listened. They were talking English but it was not like the English that our Taos friend was using in this discussion—and it was *very* different from anything I had heard during my childhood in north Florida. Then I realized there was something distinctive about the way our Taos friend was speaking English. I could not quite identify the reason for distinctiveness, and I had not noticed it before he made his observation about the visitors from Montana. But now everything he said had a "special" quality, and I found myself paying as much attention to the way he talked as to what he was telling us about pueblo life.

I realize now, as I try to reconstruct what happened that afternoon, that my "discovery" of Indian English "orientalized" the remainder of the conversation. I fear, sometimes, that by emphasizing the uniqueness of these codes, I am also creating examples of "otherness" and strengthening the boundaries that already separate Indian and non-Indian people in U.S. society. This is why, throughout this book, I have tried to focus the discussion on the *speakers* of Indian English, on their knowledge of language, and on the consequences that fluency in these codes holds for them. This is also why I have treated the technical analysis of grammar and discourse as a means of getting at those details, rather than a subject matter in its own right.

At times it has been difficult to maintain this larger, speaker-centered vision—particularly when presenting the inventory of grammatical features (chapter 2) or exploring the syntactic basis of Indian English diversity and contrast (chapters 3 and 4). But my discussion of the functions assigned to these codes by members of Indian speech communities (and by other parties—chapter 6) reminds us that sentence form is an important part of the speaker's presentation of message in Indian English discourse and that a thorough analysis of technical details is as important to Indian English research in any setting as is content analysis of conversation or other text. The review of data in chapter 5 shows that both perspectives are essential to the study of Indian English histories. And the issues raised in chapters 6–10 suggest that they are equally important to effective research when assessing English language issues in American Indian education.

WHAT WE KNOW ABOUT INDIAN ENGLISH

My intention throughout this volume has been to summarize and synthesize what researchers have already learned about American Indian English. The following statements sketch out the parameters of this knowledge base, as I now see it.

1. American Indian English is an aggregate of English varieties, which differ, as a group and individually, from standard English (as expressed through the language of the metropolis) and from the varieties of English spoken by non-Indians in American society.
2. The distinctive characteristics of these codes derive, in large part, from their close association with their speakers' ancestral language tradi-

tions. In many cases, rules of grammar and discourse from that tradition provide the basis for grammar and discourse in these English codes—even in instances where the speakers are not fluent in their ancestral language.

3. Other components of Indian English grammar and discourse resemble features of nonstandard English; usually, however, these features express meanings not attested in other nonstandard codes. The similarities in form should not overshadow the significance that these features hold in each case.

4. While English has a lengthy history in Indian country, and individual members of Indian speech communities may have been speaking English for some time, communitywide English fluency is a relatively recent phenomenon for many of the tribes.

5. Indian English is the first language learned by two-thirds of today's American Indian youth. For more than two-thirds of them, Indian English is the only Indian-related language that they know.

6. Other functions of these codes—such as its role in child socialization, its recasting of contemporary ideas in traditional terms, its representation of tribal loyalty and Indian "identity," its ties to the language of the metropolis—make Indian English a valuable resource for other segments of the tribal speech community.

7. Indian English fluency becomes problematic for speakers in classrooms, the workplace, and other settings where the language of the metropolis (or other, non-Indian English codes) sets the "standards" against which fluency and proficiency are to be judged.

My work at Northern Ute has given me opportunities to explore each of these issues as they apply to Indian English fluency on that reservation. As was the case during my studies of Isleta English, I began by identifying ancestral language-related features of pronunciation, word structure, and sentence form in Ute English. I found many features of Ute language grammar in Ute English, as I have already explained here, and my data-gathering in classrooms and in community settings gave me many examples showing how these features feed into situationally specific Indian English discourse on this reservation.

In the process of that research, I began to see aspects of Indian English fluency that I had not recognized before. For example, I learned during the math avoidance study (Leap et al. 1982) that third, fourth, and fifth grade Ute students define themselves—as Utes and as individuals—in terms of a small set of descriptors, central to which was the idea that they should "follow their own initiatives inside and outside of the classroom, take responsibility for the consequences of their own actions," and expect that others will do the same (Leap 1987: 183). This definition of *self*, as I explained in chapter 7, parallels the wide variability that Ute students give to the target-words on their weekly spelling tests: each Ute student's test becomes a personalized linguistic product under this system, in the same way that their retelling of stories, constructions of inferences, design of written English compositions, and solutions to mathematics word problems become personalized statements, speaker by speaker and task by task. I think it is important to note that there is *consistency* in Ute student approaches to classroom English discourse in all of these cases; but it is more important to note how spoken and written English discourse, designed in these terms, explicitly encodes features of personal identity. This helps explain why Ute students value fluency in Ute English and why—classroom instruction notwithstanding—they actively seek to retain it.

IMPLICATIONS FOR RESEARCHERS

I hope what I have said in this volume will lead some readers to begin their own studies of American Indian English—either to expand on my comments or to find ways to refute and recast them. I particularly hope this will happen for readers who are speakers of these codes, because native speaker perspectives are as important here as they are in any other area of American Indian linguistics.

Chapters in this book have identified research questions that need attention—starting with assembling basic data on the Indian English codes that have yet to be described (and there are *plenty* of those), and moving into deeper levels of description and higher levels of theory. Equally important is the need to study situations where Indian English discourse takes on particularly powerful significance. These include classrooms and other school settings, hospitals and medical facilities, the supermarket, and the offices of the BIA. The connections between Indian English fluency and economic development should not be understated. We can predict that Indian English fluency affects speaker prospects for employment, job security, and job mobility. But we need confirmation and documentation of these themes—if only to help Indian-oriented vocational education and job counseling programs provide more effective training and direction to their clients.

I need to repeat two notes of caution already introduced in this section. First, whatever the topic, speech situation, or speaking task, studies of Indian English codes *must* explore grammar as well as discourse. Researchers cannot afford to isolate knowledge of language from language use, since speakers live their lives in terms of those connections.

Second, researchers cannot be distracted by appearances of similarity. Indian English sentences may resemble constructions found in other nonstandard English, but the ancestral language base underlying the Indian English code makes it unlikely that the surface-level similarities derive from similar causes. Data-gathering and analysis tasks have to be able to document differences and contrasts when they occur and they must generate the data that will refute the short-sightedness of those who see nothing unique in Indian English fluency.

IMPLICATIONS FOR TEACHERS

If Indian English fluency can have the effects on school experience and classroom performance suggested in part III of this book, then Indian English fluency becomes a matter of concern for all areas of the school curriculum, not just language arts and reading.[1] Acting on such concerns requires considerable revisions in instructional materials, classroom practice, testing procedures, and evaluation activities and, given how frequently Indian students change schools during their academic careers, it requires coordination of efforts across grade levels and across school district/administrative boundaries.

Whether researchers can join with tribal educators, parents, teachers, and school officials to create such conditions of change depends on any number of factors. In the meantime, while working toward those larger goals, there are things that teachers and other school authorities can do to make sure that day-to-day activities do not overlook the English language needs of the Indian students in their classrooms.

As a first step, all persons associated with the school need to recognize that Indian English is not a marker of language deficiency and that being fluent in these codes does not prevent speakers from acquiring fluency in other varieties of English. It may be true that Indian students need knowledge of a more standardized English to function effectively within school settings and other domains controlled by the metropolis, but they need proficiency in the Indian English code(s) of their home community—even if they are also fluent speakers of their ancestral language—in order to function effectively in those domains.

To be avoided, then, are classroom activities that require Indian students to renounce Indian English-related proficiency before they can develop standard English skills. Indian people within every tribal community have found ways to master the requirements of standard English proficiency without sacrificing control over Indian English tradition. Let these persons (and their language skills) serve as models for classroom-based language arts instruction and as goals for the school's language arts curriculum. Then keep the following suggestions in mind while preparing lesson plans and carrying out specific language development tasks.

o *Be realistic*: There is no language learning activity that, by itself, will transform nonstandard English-speaking students into proficient users of standard English. Do not spend time looking for "guaranteed" remedies or "teacher-proof" instructional packages that promise to "do it all." Instead, try to target instruction toward particular areas of student language need, making sure that instruction shows students how to combine new areas of language knowledge with the skills in English communication they already have acquired.

o *Broaden your own perspectives on local language use*: Do not let yourself be held captive by the expectations of standard English discourse. Be aware that the language tradition ancestral to the student's home community structures the flow of communication and the presentation of meaning in terms quite different from those familiar in non-Indian contexts. Spend some time listening to Indian students as they talk with each other, then look for similarities in the ways they participate in discussion within more formal teaching and learning settings. Spend some time exploring these themes with parents, community language authorities, tribal educators, or the many resource persons from the students' home community who may work at the school; some of them will be intrigued by the ideas you are exploring and may want to work with you in this area or in other ways. And think about using nontraditional approaches to classroom discourse to carry out traditional classroom tasks. For example, building on suggestions in Egan (1986), think about repackaging lesson plans so that teaching can become a kind of story-telling; this strategy seems especially appropriate for sites like Northern Ute, where elementary school Indian students are already actively using story-telling strategies to guide their approach to discourse in classroom settings.

o *Encourage diversity:* Assume that every response given in Indian English is in some sense or at some level a meaningful statement. Then try to (re)construct the meaning. If the signals are unclear, invite the student to recast the response, without making him or her feel as if the initial statement was poorly designed. For example, ask the student, or another classmate, to provide an alternative form for the statement. This question encourages students to think about language options and allows them to experiment with constructions of various types, without worrying about their statement containing content-errors.

o *Promote eloquence:* Classroom-based Indian English discourse is characterized by brevity, imagery, and frequent invitations to active listener engagement—features of communication that are often devalued and over-looked entirely in the tightly scheduled, businesslike environment of the standard English classroom. Make certain that the students have ample opportunities to express their ideas according to their own sense of completed, well-formed commentary.

IMPLICATIONS FOR INDIAN STUDENTS

None of these suggestions will work unless the students in the classroom are willing to recast their knowledge of English to include classroom- as well as community-centered English skills. Here again, the most eloquent arguments to this end will come from members of the students' own community and not from outsiders. So I close this volume with an essay prepared by a young man from Northern Ute. He is responding to one of my workshops on Indian English research and uses those issues to outline his own feelings about Indian English, standard English, and Ute language skills. (Note: the line numbering is in the original.)

Utelish

    In the opinion(s) of most Educated Indians there
is "no such thing as Indian English." The basic lifestyle of
most Native Americans dictates a simplification of all
things, bring it down to black and white if you will. So
5 in this narrowed view of the world there is only one
way of speaking Ute and only one way of speaking English.
The two languages are separate and distinct, no
crossing lines "no mixing of nothing."
    Looking back at this first paragraph I'm sure the
10 influence of "Indian English" can be seen in my writing.
First and foremost is the tendency toward redundancy
I put forth in all unedited or non-written papers. In
reading my father's notes (or my grand father's) I find this same
way of communicating.
15   I wasn't raised on the reservation. I grew up in [urban area].
But my spoken English differs little from that found on the reservation
the words are (usually) bigger and some I pronounce a little
different, but it is (close enough to be called) the same.
I guess it is because my father spoke the way he did and
20 hated to be corrected. I like him am sometime redundant.
(See lines 3–4, 7–9, 11 + 20, 15).
    Though I learned proper English through much reading
and association with people who spoke goo' (glottal stop) English, the

acquired English of my youth stills rears it ugly head through out most of my efforts to communicate. In writing I can usually cover my syntactic errors by the liberal application of quotation marks and calling it style. In speaking I've found that few people mind the lower forms of English (on paper that last sentence sounds like junk . . . spoken out loud it sounds all right.)

I hope you forgive the brevity of this paper. It is hard to "lookit" my English and realize that in a lot of ways I conform to the fourteen points I have listed as being peculiar to Ute English i.e. devoicing vowels and consonants, pronoun addition and/or "equi-deletion" (I cringe when I do that) reading whole words (+ being wrong).

Oh well, with luck, my understand of Ute English will improve as I learn more Ute. When I learned [another tribal language] I found my understanding of their version of English improved because I could follow the thought process. Now if I can only quit thinking [the other tribe's] English while talking Ute, I'll have it made.

NOTES

INTRODUCTION

1. Also of interest here is the English of the Native peoples of Alaska. My discussion of these codes will be limited, however, for reasons explained in the final section of this chapter.

2. Representative studies in this regard include Bartelt (1986), Basso (1979), Darnell (1985), Goodman et al. (1984), Kwachka (1988), Leap (1973, 1978, 1987, 1989), Manuel-Dupont (1985, 1990), McLaughlin (1989, 1991, 1992), Miller (1977), Penfield-Jasper (1980), Phillips (1972, 1983), Scollen and Scollen (1981), Stout (1979), Wolfram (1984), Wolfram et al. (1979), as well as the papers in such collections as Bartelt, Penfield-Jasper, and Hoffer (1982), Leap (1978), Reyhner (1992), and St. Clair and Leap (1982).

1. SPEAKERS AND SPEECH COMMUNITIES

1. I am not able to say anything in this chapter regarding the persons who *write* Indian English since systematic assessments of American Indian/Alaska Native written English skills have yet to appear.

2. Comments in this section are adapted from chapter 2 of Leap (1981a).

3. Given that the project was funded under a BIA contract, this study did not consider the English language needs of American Indian/Alaska Native students who are members of federally recognized tribes but live at some distance from their tribal land base or Indian/Alaska Native students who are not members of federally recognized tribes. It is unlikely that students in these categories are more proficient in ancestral languages than their reservation-based age-mates; even so, their English skills may still show the influence of Indian language traditions. Their absence from the research population restricts the broader validity of the study's claims.

4. Bear in mind that Roberts et al. defined their research population more restrictively than did Brod and McQuiston. Adding Indian/Alaska students not eligible for BIA educational services to the Roberts sample, to make the two samples more comparable

in background, is likely to increase the percentage of monolingual English speakers in table 1.1 and to increase the contrast between generations.

5. The Cherokee data come from the Berdan et al. (1982) study of language use within Oklahoma Cherokee communities. Remaining data come from an analysis (Leap 1985) of grant applications and reports submitted to the U.S. Office of Bilingual Education and Minority Language Affairs by American Indian and Alaska Native bilingual education programs in operation during 1981–1982.

6. Weibel-Orlando's richly detailed *Indian Country, L.A.* (1991) is a significant step forward in this regard. But even that volume pays little attention to urban interests in ancestral language maintenance and overlooks English language needs facing members of the Los Angeles Indian community almost entirely.

7. Even though I will not be using Ponca English data in the following chapters, I have included Ponca in this discussion because (1) it is a good example of a nonreservation, rural Indian speech community; and (2) I worked on ancestral language retention/renewal issues with members of the tribe and am familiar with social and linguistic settings there. My source materials for this profile include Howard (1965), Ponca Tribe (1978), U.S. Department of Commerce (1980), and field notes from my work at this site (1976–1978) and my follow-up visits.

8. In order to attend school in Ponca City, Ponca children had to travel considerable distances by school bus. This, plus questions about quality of instructional services and other concerns, prompted Ponca parents to take legal action to make the county schools more accessible to their children's needs.

9. Source materials for this profile include U.S. Department of Commerce (1980), Conetah (1982), Stewart (1983), and unpublished reports on language/education needs that I prepared for the Tribal Division of Education and its Indian and English language education programs (1978–1989).

10. Importantly, federal courts determined in 1984 that the transfer of on-reservation land to non-Indian owners did not compromise the original boundaries of the reservation, as established by Executive Order in 1861: under this ruling, the Northern Ute Tribe still retains sovereignty over all of the land within those boundaries, regardless of ownership.

11. My source materials for this profile include Ellis (1979), and field notes from my work at the pueblo(1967–1974) and from return visits since that time.

12. My source materials for this profile include Stewart (1983) and data from informal interviews with persons from the Parker, Arizona, area.

2. SOUND PATTERNS, SENTENCE FORMS, AND MEANINGS

1. A fundamental question throughout this section is whether the English language distinction between noun and verb is relevant to Indian language description and, by extension, to description of Indian English grammar. Constructing an analysis of Indian English syntax that is not dependent on these Western-based descriptive categories is intriguing, but it is not something I am able to explore at this time.

2. This does not mean, however, that culturally defined gender distinctions are irrelevant to Cheyenne experience, but only that the criteria that establish those distinctions are not necessarily based in Cheyenne syntax or even maintained by it. As Greville Corbett notes (1991: 23, citing the findings from Straus and Brightman [1982]),

not only can bilingual Cheyennes "assign gender to English words, but they can do so without problem if an item for which they cannot recall the Cheyenne word is merely pointed out. . . . The referent is sufficient to enable gender to be assigned—the linguistic form is not required."

3. AUX (an abbreviation for *auxiliary*) designates the grammatical category often labeled "helping verbs" in language arts texts. I discuss AUX properties in Indian English grammars elsewhere in this chapter.

4. Bartelt(1986) uses *Apachean English* to refer to Navajo English as well as English associated with different Apache language traditions. He argues that this code provides an intermediate identity for its speakers and that the appeal of that identity has prompted convergence in what may once have been distinctive Indian English traditions.

5. Miller assumes that the students' silence mean that they did not know what to say. It is possible that they knew how to respond, but simply chose not to reply. However, given that the students cooperated actively with her other research tasks, it seems unlikely that they would choose to be disinterested in this task alone.

6. I am grateful to AnCita Benally for bringing this example, and her interpretation of its meaning, to my attention.

7. I adapted the interview plan from one developed by M. F. Heiser (1975) during one of his studies of Navajo student English skills.

3. THE ANCESTRAL LANGUAGE BASE

1. Portions of this analysis originally appeared in Leap (1977b: 67–72).

2. Some—particularly older—speakers of Isletan Tiwa may use pairs of alternating consonants (*ch* vs. *sh* in this case) as well as affixes to indicate the shift of bases between word-types.

3. Portions of this analysis originally appeared in Leap (1977b: 72–77).

4. DIVERSITY AND CONTRASTS

1. The comparison of Isleta and Northern Cheyenne data here and in the following section builds on comments in Leap (1977a).

2. Comments in this section build on several studies of Ute student and Ute adult English I prepared for the Wykoopah bilingual education program during the period 1981–1986.

3. Penfield-Jasper used a reading passage as the basis for her comparisons so that she would be able to assess the students' treatments of final-position consonant clusters in identical word and sentence environments.

4. Examples like this one help us understand how American Indian and Alaska Native students could learn English in school settings—from the same teachers, the same classroom/dormitory monitors, and from each other—but still end up with tribally specific Indian English fluencies. This issue becomes particularly important when exploring how the boarding schools contributed to the formation of these codes, as I explain in chapter 5.

5. The Ute data included in table 4.3 come from a study of Ute student English phonology I conducted at an on-reservation elementary school in the fall of 1984. I

modeled one of the data-gathering tasks after Penfield-Jasper's work with text phonology, so that I could construct the comparisons I am describing here.

6. Both Tewa and Keresan grammars maintain such contrasts, though the tense systems of these languages are, on the whole, quite dissimilar.

7. Miller's database includes observations of student English use and student responses to task-specific questions about nonsense verbs (e.g.,"What is the past tense of *spo*?"). She did not include many examples in her discussion of findings (1977: 990–92), so I cannot provide Pima English illustrations for her claims in this summary.

8. Penfield-Jasper reports no instances of *have* or *had* among the helping verbs in her corpus; I explore reasons for this finding elsewhere in this chapter.

9. The analysis in this section differs somewhat from Penfield-Jasper's (1980: 116–27) interpretation of Mohave English uninflected tense; the concluding point of both discussions—the influence of ancestral language grammar—is the same.

10. The patterning in table 4.7 also suggests that Mohave English negative verb constructions (pattern 4) are a structural variant of the verb constructions containing inflected AUX and uninflected base (pattern 2)—provided that, as in Northern Ute and other Indian English varieties, negative reference is assigned the status of "tense" in Mohave English grammar.

5. THOUGHTS ON THE HISTORY OF INDIAN ENGLISH

1. Sherzer's (1991) description of tribal speech communities and Indian language discourse at the beginning of the colonial period offers an alternative, and somewhat more conservative, discussion of these themes.

2. Taylor (1982) reports that the "women's" variety of Gros Ventres was also the "appropriate" variety for communication with outsiders. His comments—compared to, for example, Bell's description (1990) of the rules restricting Creek women's participation in public discourse—make it worthwhile to wonder how greatly tribal assumptions about language and gender may have influenced language choice-making in these multilingual settings.

3. Reyhner and Eder (1989: 38–61) provide examples of teacher comments and language-related policy statements from this period; the absence of Indian student English skills—and hence, the absence of a base for effective Indian education—is a constant theme in these documents.

4. This section expands on ideas originally presented in Leap (1978).

5. Recent historical analysis by Noriega (1992: 378) shows that many of Pratt's ideas about Indian education—including the infamous "Outing" system—were modeled after " 'the chain gang' concept utilized in the prison systems of the Southern states" and pursued vigorously by mission schools in Kentucky, Kansas, Oklahoma, and other southern states before the Civil War.

6. Both stories come from interviews I conducted with older Indian language educators and community activists, during which I asked them to reflect on life in boarding school settings as they remember it and as their parents described it to them.

7. In traditional Navajo architecture, structures are round or multisided; walls do not come together at 90-degree angles in a building of Navajo design. To find a location suitable for Navajo discourse, the elder explained, the students had to find a location

without 90-degree angles. The oval-shaped layout of the track was ideal in that regard. Moreover, without keeping pace with these teenagers as they ran their laps each day, non-Indian faculty and Navajo speaking monitors had no way of judging which language the students were using on the field.

8. Page (1990) reviews the literature that explains the creation of student-centered, school-based cultures; Fordham's (1987) study of African American inner-city high school students' resistance to the school's pressures to "act white" illustrates the complexity of such cultural constructions—and their consequences for minority- student educational experience.

9. These essays were written in the spring semester of 1915 and later shipped from Haskell to the National Archives (Washington, D.C.), where they have remained undisturbed until this time. It is likely that the other examples of Indian student written English texts are housed in the archives, though there has been no attempt to review and catalog their collections with this question in mind.

6. FUNCTIONS OF INDIAN ENGLISH

1. Everything I say in this section applies to metropolis-satellite relationships affecting Native peoples of Alaska, as well as to the tribes in the 48 contiguous states. I focus the discussion around urban-to-reservation/rural community ties in the "lower 48" because my work in these settings has let me observe the impact of the metropolis on Indian life firsthand.

2. Examples in the case studies in chapter 1 include Ponca City for the Ponca, Las Lunas and other nearby Hispanic towns for Isleta pueblo, Roosevelt and Vernal for Northern Ute, and Parker for the Colorado River Tribes.

3. English-centered linguistic conventions that cue listeners to the speaker's point of view are not unique to the Northern Ute speech community. Bunte and Kendall (1981: 4) note that adult members of the Kaibab Paiute Tribe (northern Arizona) indicate that they are reporting rumor or inference by adding *aik*—a Paiute marker with the same function—to the final position of English sentences, when talking English to other members of their tribe. Similarly, Valley Verde Yavapai adults (northern Arizona) use sentence final -*'ikm* to distinguish statements of supposition from statements of established fact. And both groups of speakers replace these markers with *they say*, when talking English to non-Indians. I have heard Indian people from elsewhere in Utah, as well as Nevada, California, Oregon, and Idaho, commonly use sentence-final -*ne'* to elicit validation of an English statement from another Indian. And "Tonto"-style English is widely used—and widely enjoyed as political commentary—throughout Indian country.

4. This use of *Seminole* may be misleading to some outsiders, since the term can also refer to Indian tribes in Florida and in Oklahoma and to the ancestral language(s) of those tribes as well. The Brackettville Seminole are historically related to these tribes and their language traditions. However, there are no speakers of "ancestral language Seminole" in Brackettville or Del Rio. The language variety at issue in this section is an entirely different linguistic formation; I refer to it as *Seminole* because that is how its speakers refer to it.

5. I first heard this anecdote from a member of the Mississippi Choctaw delegation and have paraphrased his narrative here. Subsequently I heard the same story, applied to

the same meeting, from an Oklahoma Choctaw source: in this version, the person asking the question was from Oklahoma. The event itself may be apocryphal; what the story reveals about intertribal perceptions of Indian English differences is what matters.

6. This inventory does not identify the English spoken by the young people of full-blood background who have lived on the reservation all their lives or by the older members of the mixed-blood population.

7. Goldfrank herself actually came up with the idea for this project, while she and I were discussing my plans to continue Indian English research at Isleta pueblo. Wayne got in touch with Goldfrank when he began his analysis; she remained supportive and enthusiastic throughout the project, since she saw how this research enhanced appreciation for Joe Lente and his "place" in Isleta society.

8. Goldfrank includes in her collection the letter that Lente wrote to H. W. Dorsey, at the Bureau of American Ethnology, outlining the initial draft of his proposal. This is the letter that initiated contact with Parsons, as Goldfrank explains (1967: 4–5). This letter is different enough in its presentation of argument and use of syntax to suggest that someone else—the B. G. Young to whom he refers, perhaps—must have helped with its construction; consequently Wayne did not refer to it in his analysis, and I have not included it here.

9. Wayne selected this feature because it is especially prominent in Isletan English spoken discourse, and because of its close connections to ancestral language syntactic and semantic rules. He assumed, in other words, that Lente's treatment of subject-verb agreement would predict the overall use of Isleta vs. metropolitan models in these letters.

7. CONTEXTS OF SCHOOLING ON THE NORTHERN UTE RESERVATION

1. My thanks to Laura Laylin, my research assistant during the Northern Ute math avoidance study, for tape-recording this material.

2. I examine relationships between Ute English classroom discourse and Ute student strategies for solving mathematics word problems in Leap (1987).

3. At this stage of the analysis, I was not analyzing non-Indian student spelling tests, because I wanted to concentrate exclusively on the Ute students' spelling skills. When I classified non-Indian students' spelling errors according to the same typology, I found a much greater concentration of errors in the Open Court-related categories and almost no examples of syllable structure adjustments, further evidence that something specific to the Ute students' knowledge of English was influencing their performance on these tasks.

4. A total of thirty students—eighteen Utes and twelve non-Indians—participated in this spelling test. Other Ute students' spellings of particular words may differ from the spellings presented here, but the overall patterning of spelling errors is consistent with the theme of this discussion. As before, non-Indian student errors were almost entirely Open Court related, with little alteration of syllable structure.

9. QUESTION-ANSWERING AS STORY-TELLING

1. The Wykoopah Community Literacy Program in the Northern Ute Tribe's Division of Education was the home-base and local sponsor. Sonia Manuel-Dupont (Department

of English and Speech Pathology, Utah State University) was project coordinator. I served as the project's Ute English consultant, assisted in the training of the fieldworkers, and supervised the analysis of the discourse materials. Data-gatherers included participants in the tribe's on-reservation teacher training program as well as Judy Lewis and Ellen Berner, students at the American University's Department of Anthropology at that time. Lewis, Berner, Donna Donaldson, and other students in that department worked with me in carrying out segments of the analysis. Lewis has recently published (1991) a summary of her research findings; her analysis confirms many of the observations about Ute student English narrative skills outlined in this chapter.

10. WRITING UTE ENGLISH

1. Portions of this chapter originally appeared as Leap (1989).
2. Except when otherwise noted, I present the Ute students' essays with the spelling, capitalization, punctuation, and line-by-line arrangement of words found in the original texts.

CONCLUSIONS

1. An earlier version of this section appeared in Leap (1992: 150–52).

BIBLIOGRAPHY

Alford, Dan
    1974   *The Cheyenne Dialect of English and Its Educational Implication*s. Box Elder, Mont.: Northern Cheyenne Bilingual Program.

Bartelt, H. G.
    1982a   Apachean English Metaphors. In *Essays in Native American English*, ed. H. Guillermo Bartelt, Susan Penfield-Jasper, and Bates Hoffer, pp. 85–94. San Antonio: Trinity University Press.
    1982b   Tense, Aspect and Mood in Apachean English. In *Essays in Native American English*, ed. H. Guillermo Bartelt, Susan Penfield-Jasper, and Bates Hoffer, pp. 67–85. San Antonio: Trinity University Press.
    1986   Language Contact in Arizona: The Case of Apachean English. *Anthropos* 81: 4–6.

Bartelt, H. Guillermo, Susan Penfield-Jasper, and Bates Hoffer, eds.
    1982   *Essays in Native American English*. San Antonio: Trinity University Press.

Basso, Keith
    1970   "To give up on words": Silence in Apache Culture. *Southwest Journal of Anthropology*, 26(3): 213–38.
    1979   Portrait of the Whiteman. Cambridge: Cambridge University Press.

Baugh, John
    1983   *Black Street Speech: Its History, Structure and Survival*. Austin: University of Texas Press.

Bayles, Kathryn A., and Gail A. Harris
    1982   Evaluating Speech-Language Skills in Papago Indian Children. *Journal of American Indian Education* 21 (2): 11–19.

Bell, Amelia Rector
    1990   Separate People: Speaking of Creek Men and Women. *American Anthropologist* 92: 332–45.

Berdan, Robert, Alvin So, and Angel Sanchez
    1982   *Language Use among the Cherokee: Patterns of Language Use in Northeastern Oklahoma*. Los Alamitos: National Center for Bilingual Research.

Bickerton, Derek
1975   *Dynamics of a Creole System*. Cambridge: Cambridge University Press.

Bloomfield, Leonard
1964   Literate and Illiterate Speech. In *Language, Culture and Society: A Reader in Linguistics and Anthropology*, ed. Dell Hymes, pp. 391–96. New York City: Harper and Row.

Blu, Karen I.
1980   *The Lumbee Problem: The Making of an American Indian People.* Cambridge: Cambridge University Press.

Brandt, Elizabeth A., and Christopher MacCrate
n.d.   Multilingual Variation, or Contact Vernacular in the Southwest: "Make like seem heap Injin." Unpublished manuscript.

Brewer, Jeutonne P., and R. W. Reising
1982   Tokens in the Pocosin: Lumbee English in North Carolina. In *Essays in Native American English*, ed. H. Guillermo Bartelt, Susan Penfield-Jasper, and Bates Hoffer, pp. 33–54. San Antonio: Trinity University Press.

Brod, Rodney, and John M. McQuiston
1983   American Indian Adult Education and Literacy: The First National Survey. *Journal of American Indian Education* 22(2): 1–16.

Brophy, William A., and Sophie D. Aberle
1966   *The Indian: America's Unfinished Business*. Norman: University of Oklahoma Press.

Browne, John Ross
1868   *Adventures in the Apache Country*. New York: Harper.

Bunte, Pamela A., and Martha B. Kendall
1981   When Is an Error Not an Error? Notes on Language Contact and the Question of Interference. *Anthropological Linguistics* 23(1): 1–7.

Burt, Marina, Heidi Dulay, and Eduardo Hernandez-Chavez
1975   *Bilingual Syntax Measure*. New York City: Harcourt, Brace, Jovanovich.

Callaway, Donald G., Joel Janetski, and Omer C. Stewart
1986   Ute. In *Handbook of North American Indians*, vol. 11: *Great Basin*, ed. Warren L. D'Azevedo, pp. 336–67. Washington, D.C.: Smithsonian Press.

Carus, Marianne, Thomas G. Anderson, and Howard Webber
1982   *The Headway Program: Teacher's Guide, Level E*. La Salle, Ill.: Open Court.

Chessen, Linda, and Emily Auerbach
1982   Teaching Composition to Northwest American Indians. In *Essays in Native American English*. ed. H. Guillermo Bartelt, Susan Penfield-Jasper, and Bates Hoffer, pp. 173–86. San Antonio: Trinity University Press.

Chu, Daniel, and Samuel Chu
1967   *Passage to the Golden Gate: A History of the Chinese in America to 1910*. Garden City: Doubleday.

Conetah, Fred
1982   *A History of the Northern Ute Tribe*. Salt Lake City: University of Utah Printing Service.

Cook, Mary Jane, and Margaret Amy Sharp
  1966   Problems of Navajo Speakers in Learning English. *Language Learning* 16: 21–29.
Corbett, Greville
  1991   *Gender.* Cambridge: Cambridge University Press.
Crawford, James M.
  1978   *The Mobilian Trade Languages.* Knoxville: University of Tennessee Press.
Cuch, Forrest
  1987   Cultural Perspectives on Indian Education: A Comparative Analysis of the Ute and Anglo Cultures. *Equity and Excellence* 23(1,2): 65–76.
Damico, Jack
  1983   Functional Language Proficiency. Unpublished ms. Albuquerque: American Indian Bilingual Education Center.
Darnell, Regna
  1985   The Language of Power in Cree Interethnic Communication. In *Language of Inequality,* ed. Nessa Wolfson and Joan Manes, pp. 61–72. Berlin: Mouton.
Davis, Irvine
  1964   *The Language of Santa Ana Pueblo.* Bureau of American Ethnology Bulletin 191, Anthropological Papers no. 69. Washington D.C.: U.S. Government Printing Office.
Dillard, J. L.
  1972   Pidgin English in the United States: Black, Red and Yellow. In *Black English,* pp. 139–85. New York City: Random House.
Dozier, Edward
  1956   Two Examples of Linguistic Acculturation: The Yaqui of Sonora and the Tewa of New Mexico. *Language* 32: 146–57.
Dreschel, Emmanuel
  1977   Historical Problems and Issues in the Study of North American Indian *Marginal* Languages. In *Studies in Southwestern Indian English,* ed. William Leap, pp. 131–40. San Antonio, Tex.: Trinity University Press.
Dubois, Betty Lou
  1977a   Early Day Communicative Relations of the Mescalero Apache with English Speakers (1846–1880). In *SWALLOW V,* ed. Betty Lou Dubois and Bates Hoffer, pp. 105–13. San Antonio: Trinity University Press.
  1977b   Spanish, English and the Mescalero Apache. In *Studies in Southwestern Indian English.* ed. William L. Leap, pp. 175–96. San Antonio: Trinity University Press.
Dubois, Betty Lou, and Guadalupe Valdés-Fallis
  1976   Problems in Historical Sociolinguistics: The Mescalero Apache. Paper presented at the annual meetings, Southwest Anthropological Association, April 15–17, San Francisco.
Egan, Kieran
  1986   *Teaching as Story-telling: An Alternative Approach to Teaching and Curriculum in the Elementary School.* Chicago: University of Chicago Press.
Ellis, Florence Hawley
  1979   Isleta Pueblo. In *Handbook of North American Indians: The Southwest,* ed. Alfonso Ortiz, ed. pp. 351–65. Washington, D.C.: Smithsonian Press.

Fasold, Ralph
    1969   Tense and the Verb BE in Black English. *Language* 45: 763–76.

Fillmore, Charles J.
    1966   The Case for Case. In *Universals in Linguistic Theory*, ed. Emmon Bach and Robert T. Harms, pp. 1–90. New York: Holt, Rinehart and Winston.

Fishman, Joshua
    1970   *Sociolinguistics: A Brief Introduction*. Rowley: Newbury House.

Flanigan, Beverley Olson
    1982   Language Variation among Native Americans: Observations on Lakota English. Paper presented at the 11th Annual Conference on New Ways of Analyzing Variation in English, Georgetown University, October 21–23, 1982.
    1984a   Bilingual Education for Native Americans: The Argument from Studies of Variational English. In *On TESOL '83*, ed. John Handscombe, pp. 81–93. Washington, D.C.: TESOL.
    1984b   Language Variation among Native Americans: Reflections on Lakota English. Unpublished ms.
    n.d.   American Indian English and Error Analysis: The Case of Lakota English. Unpublished manuscript.

Fletcher, J. D.
    1983   What Problems Do American Indians Have with English? *Journal of American Indian Education* 23(1): 1–14.

Fordham, Signithia
    1987   Black Students' School Success as Related to Fictive Kinship: An Ethnographic Study in the District of Columbia Public School System. 2 vols. Ph.D. diss., Dept. of Anthropology, American University, Washington D.C.

Garborino, Merwyn
    1971   Life in the City: Chicago. In *The American Indian in Urban Society*, ed. Jack O. Waddell and O. Michael Watson, pp. 168–205. Boston: Little, Brown.

Goldfrank, Esther S.
    1967   *The Artist of "Isleta Paintings" in Pueblo Society*. Washington, D.C.: Smithsonian Press.

Goodman, Yetta, et al.
    1984   *A Two Year Case Study Observing the Development of Third and Fourth Grade Native American Children's Writing Processes*. Final Report on NIE Grant NIE-G-81-0127. Tucson: Program in Language and Literacy, College of Education, University of Arizona.

Grobsmith, Elizabeth S.
    1979   Styles of Speaking: An Analysis of Lakota Communication Alternatives. *Anthropological Linguistics* 21: 355–61.

Gundlach, James H., and Ruth C. Busch
    1981   Reservation Residence and the Survival of Native American Languages. *Current Anthropology* 22: 96–97.

Guyette, Susan
  1981   An Examination of Cherokee Language Vitality. *Anthropological Linguistics*
         23: 215–25.
Hall, Edwin S., Jr.
  1975   The Eskimo Storyteller: Folktales from Noatak, Alaska. Knoxville: Univer-
         sity of Tennessee Press.
Hancock, Ian
  1977   *Further Observations on Afro-Seminole Creole*. Society for Caribbean
         Linguistics Occasional Paper. Dept. of Linguistics, University of Texas,
         Austin, Tex.
Harris, Louise Dyer, and Norman Dyer Harris
  1955   *Slim Green*. Boston: Little, Brown.
Harvey, Byron, III
  1963   Masks in a Maskless Pueblo. *Ethnology* 2(4): 478–89.
Haynes, Lillith M.
  1977   Candid Chimaera: Texas Seminole. In *SWALLOW V*, ed. Bates Hoffer and
         Betty Lou Dubois, pp. 280–99. San Antonio: Trinity University Press.
Heiser, M. F.
  1975   Amerindian Language Loyalty, Acculturation and Language Competence. In
         Southwest Languages and Linguistics in Educational Perspective, ed. M. F.
         Heiser, and Gina C. Harvey, pp. 379–86. San Diego: Institute for Cultural
         Pluralism.
Hodge, William H.
  1965   *The Albuquerque Navajos*. Anthropological Papers of the University of
         Arizona, no. 11. Tucson: University of Arizona Press.
Howard, James H.
  1965   *The Ponca Tribe*. Bureau of American Ethnology, Bulletin 195. Washington,
         D.C.: U.S. Government Printing Office.
Hymes, Dell
  1974   *Foundations of Sociolinguistics*. Philadelphia: University of Pennsylvania
         Press.
Jorgensen, Joseph G.
  1964   Ute Education. In The Ethnohistory and Acculturation of the Northern Ute,
         pp. 304–19. Doctoral dissertation. Bloomington: Indiana University.
  1970   Indians and the Metropolis. In *The American Indian in Urban Society*, ed.
         Jack O. Waddell and O. Michael Watson, pp. 66–113. Boston: Little, Brown.
Kuhlman, Natalie A., and Milo Kalactaca
  1982   Assessing Indian English. In *Essays in Native American English*, ed.
         H. Guillermo Bartelt, Susan Penfield-Jasper, and Bates Hoffer, pp. 195–217.
         San Antonio: Trinity University Press.
Kwachka, Patricia
  1988   *Oral and Written English of the Koyukon Athabaskan Area: A Preliminary
         Analysis*. APEL Research Report vol. 4. Nenana, Alaska: Yukon-Koyukon
         School District.
Labov, William
  1969   Contraction, Deletion and Inherent Variability of the English Copula.
         Language 45(4): 715–62.

1972   Negative Attraction and Negative Concord. In *Language in the Inner City*, pp. 130–99. Philadelphia: University of Pennsylvania Press.

Leap, William L.
1973   Language Pluralism in a Southwestern Pueblo: Some Comments on Isletan English. In *Bilingualism in the Southwest*, ed. Paul Turner, pp. 275–94. Tucson: University of Arizona Press.
1977a   On Consonant Simplification in Isletan English and Elsewhere. In *Studies in Southwestern Indian English*, ed. William L. Leap, pp. 45–54. San Antonio: Trinity University Press.
1977b   Two Examples of Isletan English Syntax. In *Studies in Southwestern Indian English*, ed. William L. Leap, pp. 65–78. San Antonio: Trinity University Press.
1978   American Indian English and Its Implications for Bilingual Education. In *International Dimensions of Bilingual Education*, ed. James Alatis, pp. 657–69. Washington, D.C.: Georgetown University Press.
1981a   *American Indian Language Education*. Los Alamitos: National Center for Bilingual Research.
1981b   American Indian Language Maintenance. In *Annual Review of Anthropology* 10: 209–36.
1981c   American Indian Languages. In *Language in the U.S.A.*, ed. Charles A. Ferguson and Shirley Brice Heath, pp. 116–44. Cambridge: Cambridge University Press.
1985   Linguistic and Academic Characteristics of American Indian and Alaska Native Students. In *A Study of American Indian and Alaska Native Bilingual Education Programs Funded by Title VII*. Reston, Va.: MESA Corporation.
1987   Assumptions and Strategies Guiding Mathematics Problem-solving by Ute Indian Students. In *Language Perspectives on Mathematics Learning*, ed. Rodney Cocking and José Mestre, pp. 161–86. New York: Erlbaum and Associates.
1988   Applied Linguistics and American Indian Language Renewal: Introductory Comments. *Human Organization* 47: 283–91.
1989   Written Ute English: Texture, Construction and Point of View. *Journal of Navajo Education* 7(1): 3–9.
1992   American Indian English. In *Teaching American Indian Students*, ed. Jon Reyhner, pp. 143–53. Norman: University of Oklahoma Press.

Leap, William L., ed.
1978   *Studies in Southwestern Indian English*. San Antonio: Trinity University Press.

Leap, William L., Joel Cantor, Robert Baker, Laura Laylin, and Ann Renker
1982   *Dimensions of Math Avoidance among American Indian Elementary School Students*. Final Report on NIE Grant NIE-G-79-0086. Washington, D.C.: American University.

Leechman, Douglas, and Robert A. Hall
1955   American Indian Pidgin English: Attestations and Grammatical Peculiarities. *American Speech* 30: 163–71.

Levinson, Stephen C.
1983 *Pragmatics*. Cambridge: Cambridge University Press.
Lewis, Judy M.
1991 The Story-telling Strategies of Northern Ute Elementary Students. *Journal of Navajo Education* 9(1): 24–33.
Liebe-Harkort, M. L.
1883 A Note on the English Spoken by Apaches. *International Journal of American Linguistics* 49: 207–8.
Malancon, Richard, and Mary Jo Malancon
1977 Indian English at Haskell Institute, 1915. In *Studies in Southwestern Indian English*, ed. William L. Leap, pp. 141–54. San Antonio: Trinity University Press.
Manuel-Dupont, Sonia
1985 Analysis of the English Language Usage of Hualapai Children in an Academic Setting. Doctoral dissertation. Lawrence: Department of Linguistics, University of Kansas.
1990 Narrative Literacy Patterns of Northern Ute Adolescent Students. In *Effective Language Education Practices and Native Language Survival*, ed. Jon Reyhner, pp. 53–94. Choctaw, Okla.: Native American Language Issues, Inc.
McLaughlin, Dan
1989 The Sociolinguistics of Navajo Literacy. *Anthropology and Education Quarterly* 20: 275–90.
1991 Curriculum for Cultural Politics: Literacy Program Development in a Navajo School Setting. In *Case Studies in Computer Aided Learning*, ed. Robert L. Blomeyer, Jr., and C. Dianne Martin, pp. 151–64. London: Falmer Press.
1992 *When Literacy Empowers: Navajo Language in Print*. Albuquerque: University of New Mexico Press.
Medicine, Bea
1987 Learning to Be an Anthropologist and Remaining Native. In *Applied Anthropology in America*, ed. Elizabeth Eddy and William Partridge, pp. 282–96. New York: Columbia University Press.
Mehan, Hugh
1985 The Structure of Classroom Discourse. In *The Handbook of Discourse Analysis*, vol. 3, ed. Reun A. van Dijk, pp. 119–29. London: Academic Press.
Meriam, Lewis
1928 *The Problem of Indian Administration*. Washington, D.C.: Brookings Institute.
Miller, Mary Rita
1977 *Children of the Salt River: First and Second Language Acquisition among Pima Children*. Language Science Monographs, no. 16. Bloomington: Indiana University Press.
Miller, Wick
1965 *Acoma Grammar and Texts*. University of California Publications in Linguistics, no. 40. Berkeley: University of California Press.
Mulder, Jean
1982 The Tsimshian English Dialect: The Result of Language Interference. In *Essays in Native American English*, ed. H. Guillermo Bartelt, Susan

Penfield-Jasper, and Bates Hoffer, pp. 95–112. San Antonio: Trinity University Press.

Munro, Pamela
1974   Topics in Mohave Syntax. Doctoral dissertation. San Diego: University of California at San Diego, Department of Linguistics.

Noriega, Jorge
1992   American Indian Education in the United States: Indoctrination for Subordination to Colonialism. In *The State of Native America: Genocide, Colonization, and Resistance*, ed. M. Annette Jaimes, pp. 371–402. Boston: South End Press.

O'Malley, Michael
1981   CESS Survey 6:4.

Page, Reba
1990   Cultures and Curricula: Differences between and within Schools. *Educational Foundations*, 4: 49–75.

Parsons, Elsie Clews
1919   Folk-lore of the Cherokee of Robeson County, North Carolina. *Journal of American Folklore* 32: 384–93.
1932   Isleta, New Mexico. In *Bureau of American Ethnology, 47th Annual Report*, pp. 193–466. Washington, D.C.: Government Printing Office.
1962   *Isleta Paintings*, ed. Esther S. Goldfrank, Bureau of American Ethnology Bulletin 181. Washington, D.C.: Smithsonian Institution.

Penfield-Jasper, Susan
1977   Some Examples of Southwestern Indian English Compared. In *Studies in Southwestern Indian English*, ed. William L. Leap, pp. 23–44. San Antonio: Trinity University Press.
1980   Selected Grammatical Characteristics of Mohave English. Doctoral dissertation. Tucson: Committee on Linguistics, University of Arizona.
1982   Mohave English and Tribal Identity. In *Essays in Native American English*, ed. H. Guillermo Bartelt, Susan Penfield-Jasper, and Bates Hoffer, pp. 23–32. San Antonio: Trinity University Press.

Phillips, Susan U.
1972   Participant Structures and Communicative Competence: Warm Springs Children in Community and Classroom. In *Functions of Language in the Classroom*, ed. Dell Hymes, Courtney Cazden, and Vera John, pp. 370–94. New York: Teachers College Press.
1983   *The Invisible Culture: Communication in Classroom and Community on the Warm Springs Indian Reservation*. New York: Longman.

Ponca Tribe
1978   *The Ponca World*. Oklahoma City: Oklahoma Indian Affairs Commission.

Powers, William K.
1986   *Sacred Language: The Nature of Supernatural Discourse in Lakota*. Norman: University of Oklahoma Press.

Pye, Clifton
1985   Language Loss in the Chilcotin. Paper presented at the 84th annual meeting of the American Anthropological Association, November 18, Washington, D.C.

Renker, Ann, and Greig W. Arnold
    1988   Exploring the Role of Education in Cultural Resource Management: The Makah Culture and Research Center Example. *Human Organization* 47: 302–7.

Reyhner, Jon, ed.
    1992   *Teaching American Indian Students.* Norman: University of Oklahoma Press.

Reyhner, Jon, and Jeanne Eder
    1989   *A History of Indian Education.* Billings: Eastern Montana College.

Roberts, William T., et al.
    1981   *Comprehensive Indian Bilingual-Bicultural Education Needs Assessment.* Washington, D.C.: U.S. Department of the Interior, Bureau of Indian Affairs.

Rosier, Paul, and Mary Ellen Farella
    1976   Bilingual Education at Rock Point: Some Early Results. *TESOL Quarterly* 10: 379–88.

St. Clair, Robert, and William Leap, eds.
    1982   *Language Renewal among American Indian Tribes.* Rosslyn: National Clearinghouse for Bilingual Education.

Schuchardt, Hugo
1980, original, 1889
    Notes on the English of American Indians: Cheyenne, Kiowa, Pawnee, Pueblo, Sioux and Wyandot. In *Pidgin and Creole Languages: Selected Essays by Hugo Schuchardt,* ed. Glenn G. Gilbert, pp. 30–37. Cambridge: Cambridge University Press.

Scollon, Ron, and Suzanne B. Scollon
    1981   *Narrative, Literacy and Face in Interethnic Communication.* Norwood, N.J.: Ablex Publishing Company.

Sherzer, Joel
    1991   A Richness of Voices. In *America in 1492: The World of the Indian Peoples before the Arrival of Columbus,* ed. Alvin M. Josephy, Jr., pp. 251–76. New York: Alfred Knopf.

Silverstein, Michael
    1972   Chinook Jargon: Language Contact and the Problem of Multilevel Generative Systems. *Language* 48: 378–406, 596–625.

Smitherman, Geneva
    1977   *Talkin and Testifyin: The Language of Black America.* Detroit: Wayne State University Press.

Spicer, Edward
    1962   *Cycles of Conquest: The Impact of Spain, Mexico, and the United States on the Indians of the Southwest, 1553–1960.* Tucson: University of Arizona Press.

Stefansson, V.
    1909   The Eskimo Trade Jargon of Herschel Island. *American Anthropologist* 11: 217–32.

Stewart, Kenneth M.
    1983   Mohave. In *Handbook of North American Indians,* vol. 10: *The Southwest,* ed. Alfonso Ortiz, pp. 55–70. Washington, D.C.: Smithsonian Press.

Stout, Steven O.
   1977   A Comment on Selective Control in English Expression at Santa Ana
           Pueblo. In *Studies in Southwestern Indian English*, ed. William L. Leap,
           pp. 55–64. San Antonio: Trinity University Press.
   1979   Sociolinguistic Aspects of English Diversity among Elementary-Aged
           Students from Laguna Pueblo. Doctoral dissertation. Washington, D.C.:
           Department of Anthropology, American University.
Straus, A. T., and R. Brightman
   1982   The Implacable Raspberry. *Papers in Linguistics* 15: 97–137.
Swisher, Karen, and Michelle Hoisch
   1992   Dropping Out among American Indians and Alaska Natives: A Review of
           Studies. *Journal of American Indian Education* 31(2): 3–23.
Szasz, Margaret
   1974   *Education and the American Indian: The Road to Self-Determination
           1928–1973*. Albuquerque: University of New Mexico Press.
Tarpent, Marie-Lucie
   1982   A Tsimshian English Expression: "Them Fred." In *Essays in Native
           American English*, ed. H. Guillermo Bartelt, Susan Penfield-Jasper, and
           Bates Hoffer, pp. 113–21. San Antonio: Trinity University Press.
Taylor, Allan
   1981   Indian Lingua Francas. In *Language in the U.S.A.*, ed. Charles Ferguson
           and Shirley Brice Heath, pp. 175–95. Cambridge: Cambridge University
           Press.
   1982   "Male" and "Female" Speech in Gros Ventres. *Anthropological Linguistics*
           24: 301–7.
Thomason, Sandra Grey, and Terrence Kaufman
   1988   *Language Contact, Creolization and Genetic Linguistics*. Berkeley:
           University of California Press.
Tindall, Allan
   1975   Ethnography and the Hidden Curriculum in Sport. *Behavioral and Social
           Science Teacher* 2(2): 5–28.
U.S. Department of Commerce
   1980   *Federal and State Indian Reservations and Indian Trust Areas*. Washing-
           ton, D.C.: U.S. Government Printing Office.
Valdés-Fallis, Guadalupe
   1977   Early Day Communicative Relations of the Mescalero Apache with
           Spanish Speakers 1540–1846. In *SWALLOW V*, ed. Bates Hoffer and Betty
           Lou Dubois, pp. 83–101. San Antonio: Trinity University Press.
Vandergriff, Jim
   1982   Kotzebue English: Some Notes on Inupiaq English. In *Essays in Native
           American English*, ed. H. Guillermo Bartelt, Susan Penfield-Jasper, and
           Bates Hoffer, pp. 121–56. San Antonio: Trinity University Press.
Watahomigie, Lucille J., and Akira Y. Yamamoto
   1987   Linguistics in Action: The Hualapai Bilingual/Bicultural Education Pro-
           gram. In *Collaborative Research and Social Change: Applied Anthropol-
           ogy in Action*, ed. Donald D. Stull and Jean J. Schansul, pp. 77–98. Boulder:
           Westview Press.

Wayne, Jr., John R.
   1977   Isletan English in the Letters of Joe B. Lente. In *Studies in Southwestern Indian English*, ed. William L. Leap, pp. 175–96. San Antonio: Trinity University Press.
Weibel-Orlando, Joan
   1991   *Indian Country, L.A.: Maintaining Ethnic Community in Complex Society.* Urbana: University of Illinois Press.
Witherspoon, Y. L.
   1961   Cultural Influences on Ute Learning. Doctoral dissertation. Salt Lake City: University of Utah.
Wolfram, Walt
   1984   Unmarked Tense in American Indian English. *American Speech* 59(1): 31–50.
Wolfram, Walt, and Donna Christian
   1979a   A Description of Selective Structures in a Variety of Indian English: The case of San Juan English. In *Variability in the English of Two Indian Communities and Its Effect on Reading and Writing*, ed. Walt Wolfram, Donna Christian, Lance Potter, and William Leap, pp. 25–231. Final Report on NIE Grant NIE-G-77-0006. Arlington, Va: Center for Applied Linguistics.
   1979b   The Intercommunity Comparison of Varieties of Indian English: San Juan and Laguna English. In *Variability in the English of Two Indian Communities and Its Effect on Reading and Writing,* ed. Walt Wolfram, Donna Christian, Lance Potter, and William Leap. pp. 231–330. Final Report on NIE Grant NIE-G-77-0006. Arlington, Va: Center for Applied Linguistics.
Wolfram, Walt, Donna Christian, Lance Potter, and William Leap
   1979   *Variability in the English of Two Indian Communities and Its Effect on Reading and Writing.* Final Report on NIE Grant NIE-G-77-0006. Arlington, Va.: Center for Applied Linguistics.
Wolfram, Walt, and Ralph Fasold
   1974   *The Study of Social Dialects in American English.* Englewood Cliffs: Prentice-Hall.
Young, R. W.
   1968   *English as a Second Language for Navajos: An Overview of Certain Cultural and Linguistic Factors.* Albuquerque and Window Rock: Bureau of Indian Affairs, Albuquerque and Navajo Area Offices.

INDEX

adverbs as tense/aspect markers, 67–69, 130

American Indian/Alaska Native defined, 14–17

American Indian languages
current language diversity, 3
Indian English fluency. *See* Indian English, ancestral language base; Indian English, ancestral language fluency
precontact language diversity, 148–51

Apachean English. *See also* Navajo English; White Mountain Apache English
pidgin/creole base, 66
tense/aspect marking, 65–66

articles and demonstratives, 55–58

auxiliary (AUX) constructions, 61–62, 69–70, 135–37. *See also* copula/AUX deletion

auxiliary (AUX) defined, 291n.3

bilingual education, 36, 40–41, 212

Black English vernacular (BEV). *See* Indian English, Black English vernacular

boarding schools, 157–65

Brackettville/Del Rio (Seminole) English
ancestral language
functions, 186–88

Chilcotin English
acquisition/language socialization, 176–78

Cherokee English
variability, 204–6

Choctaw English, 192–93

choice-making, 8, 175

Cheyenne English
consonants, 49–50, 115–16
gender marking, 59–60, 290–91n.2
prepositional phrases, 76
semantics (verbal imagery), 79
tense/aspect marking, 63–64

cloze testing, 237–43. *See also* Indian English, testing

Colorado River Tribes
community profile, 41–43, 189
schooling for, 42–43, 189, 190–91

consonants
glottal stops, 49–50
nasals, 49
position restrictions, 113–26
pronunciation, 45–47, 116–18
segments, 47–50

copula/AUX deletion, 70–71, 134–38

dialect diffusion. *See* Indian English, Black English vernacular; Indian English, pidgins and creoles

discourse defined, 7

gender marking, 58–60, 290–91n.2

grammar defined, 7

Indian English
acquisition/language socialization, 176–84
alternative to ancestral language fluency, 183–84; 184–88, 189–90
ancestral language base, 3, 48–49, 53–